6/04

The Heart of Reality

The Heart of Reality

Essays on Beauty, Love, and Ethics

by

V. S. SOLOVIEV

Edited and translated by

VLADIMIR WOZNIUK

UNIVERSITY OF NOTRE DAME PRESS
NOTRE DAME, INDIANA

Manufactured in the United States of America

Library of Congress Cataloging-in-Publication Data
Solovyov, Vladimir Sergeyevich, 1853–1900.
[Essays. English. Selections]
The heart of reality : essays on beauty, love, and ethics / by V. S.
Soloviev ; edited and translated by Vladimir Wozniuk.
p.   cm.
Includes bibliographical references (p.   ) and indexes.
ISBN 0-268-03061-8 (cloth : alk. paper)
1. Aesthetics.   2. Ethics.   3. Aesthetics—Religious aspects—Orthodox
Eastern Church.   4. Christian ethics—Orthodox Eastern authors.
5. Literature—Philosophy.   I. Wozniuk, Vladimir.   II. Title.
B4262.A5 W69   2003
197—dc21

2002155287

∞ *This book is printed on acid-free paper.*

Contents

Acknowledgments

My thanks to Robert L. Jackson for key words of advice and encouragement at an early stage of this project's development, and to Jeff Gainey, Denise Thompson-Slaughter, and various reviewers, all of whose many helpful comments substantially improved the final product. Thanks are also due to Western New England College for course-related time to complete the project, and to Sandy for providing patience and moral support, something that all writers need. This book is dedicated to her.

Introduction:
"Beauty will save the world"

How can Dostoevsky's enigmatic declaration concerning beauty as the agent of salvation be best understood? A significant portion of the work of Vladimir S. Soloviev, Dostoevsky's disciple and the bearer of his mantle in Russian fin de siècle intellectual circles, would be dedicated to answering this question. Soloviev approached Christian soteriology from a traditional credal perspective, subscribing to the decisions of Nicea and other church councils, but he modified and reinterpreted biblical wisdom and the experience of the Universal Church in order to make them more relevant for modernity in light of scientific discovery and historical understanding. The significance of his contributions to ecumenical discourse, long recognized among Orthodox theologians, has been officially noted more recently by the Vatican.[1]

Soloviev's unyielding Christian ethos often irritated one social group or another in the Russia of his day, just as his mentor Dostoevsky's had done.[2] He too endured attacks that centered on the charge of trying to introduce a "new" teaching not consistent with Orthodox Christianity. In answer to accusations of heretical teaching, Soloviev wrote: "I can answer this briefly and definitively: I do not have my own teaching; but in view of the dissemination of harmful counterfeits of Christianity, I consider it my duty to explain the basic idea of Christianity from various aspects, in various forms . . . the idea of the Kingdom of God as the plenitude of human life, not only individual, but also social and political, united through Christ with the fullness of Divinity."[3] And in response to regular attempts to dismiss him as a mystic, Soloviev confounded his critics by asserting: "I not only believe in all that is supernatural, but properly speaking, *it is only in this that I believe*."[4] These comments provide a reliable frame of reference in which the entire corpus of Soloviev's work may be interpreted.

Soloviev's return to Christian faith might be understood as a conversion experience not unlike that of St. Augustine some fifteen hundred years earlier, one that likewise dramatically energized him with an evangelical fervor regarding his new life's work to explain the message of Christ to a much loved but unbelieving and decadent European civilization. After a brief flirtation with the prevalent ideologies of his day—materialism, atheism, and the political ideas of anarchy and social revolution—Soloviev became an insightful critic of the political movements and social activism that surrounded him in the Russia of his day, and which were linked with names such as Bakunin, Kropotkin, Chernyshevsky, and Herzen, among others.[5] Soloviev showed little concern for reputation, or how he was perceived by others, but instead embarked on a mission to help along what he considered to be the universal process of reconciliation toward the eventual *telos* of what he called *vseedinstvo*—"all-unity" or "unity-of-everything"—which represented an overarching and all-encompassing grand unifying theory of spiritual and material forces in the universe, based, however, on traditional Judeo-Christian teachings.

Attempts were made at that time (and sometimes still are) to pigeonhole Soloviev's diverse intellectual pursuits in the areas of social commentary, theology, moral philosophy, history, poetry, and literary criticism; but his message remained at root Christian and, as he tirelessly sought to explain in myriad ways, squarely set in the tradition of ecclesial apologetics based on the Gospels and the Nicene Creed.[6] His ecumenical, Bible- and Christ-centered writing was permeated with an integrity of vision and humility that no doubt astounded some of those around him; his willingness to endure poverty and champion causes that in one way or another related to human rights added credibility to his words.[7]

Although almost all of Soloviev's writing was accomplished under the scrutiny of what he once termed the "censorship's terror," which was part and parcel of a Russian writer's life at the time, his essays on aesthetics, ethics, and sexual love seem to have passed by the censor's desk with few, if any, changes.[8] Despite the philosophical language and mode of argument that Soloviev employs, his writing often veers away from the rules of strict philosophical discourse, and this contributes to the problem of categorizing Soloviev, or trying to limit the characterization of his work to "religious philosophy." The highly erudite Soloviev could shift from the classics to political philosophy, from religion and history to scientific principles, quite easily. And so one categorizes Soloviev's writing at one's own risk; it defies such attempts due to its exegetical purpose—to provide a single, indivisible integration point for all of human knowledge and experience. For Soloviev, this was the Resurrected Christ, who embodied in his person the underlying principles of reconciliation of all individual differences and oppositions, and the redemption of reality in its entirety. Soloviev understood Christ as the predecessor of a new, redeemed, perfected and immortalized humanity, epitomizing "spiritual corporeality."[9]

Nicholas Berdyaev's acknowledgment of Soloviev as "the most outstanding Russian philosopher of the nineteenth century" might be interpreted as containing irony in light of the fact that Russia has produced no universally acclaimed "great" philosophers of the status, say, of a Hobbes, Hume, Rousseau, or Kant. To Soloviev himself, this did not seem to be an important matter. Yet the sheer breadth and scope of his undertakings make this characterization, in fact, indisputable. And it is important to note that this status held by Soloviev in Russian thought derives directly from his work in moral philosophy, and that this work itself was a function of his own Christian faith, with specific reference to the justification of Christian morality and ethics.

All these considerations have led to assessments of Soloviev's work as rather unoriginal, as primarily derivative from Platonic and German idealism, and somewhat obscurantist in its religious mysticism. While Soloviev was indeed broadly influenced both by Plato and the German idealists, the essays in this volume also appear to be more directly informed by the work of Aristotle, Aquinas, and Dostoevsky. Soloviev the philosopher has been given many labels, ranging from idealist to pantheist to transcendental mystic, but evaluations of Soloviev that fail to recognize the centrality of incarnational Christianity in his thought, of the manifold implications of the appearance of the fully God-man (*bogochelovek*) Christ for the transformation of the world into a perfect and just reflection of the divine will, end up missing the point of his endeavors entirely. For Soloviev, all moral systems based on extra-biblical claims fell short of a comprehensive interpretation of reality and an adequate justification of the necessity of morality, whether they were based on a positivistic scientific or social-revolutionary worldview, or on mystical perspectives outside the realm of biblically revealed truth.

Evaluation of Soloviev's work as unoriginal or excessively derivative may seem to carry more weight in his formal philosophy than in his other pursuits. The indifference with which his work in this sphere was largely received is reflected, for example, in the novelist Lev N. Tolstoy's disquisition "What is Art?". Tolstoy (with whom Soloviev carried on a running debate about just what constituted Christianity) indirectly appraised Soloviev's contributions to aesthetics in philosophy as insignificant, for he failed to mention Soloviev at all in his review of the literature on aesthetics in this lengthy and somewhat cumbersome essay, while himself arriving only at an idiosyncratic and ultimately problematic definition of "true" art.[10] While Soloviev's writings on aesthetics may not have produced much enthusiasm in his day, a reappraisal is now in order, if not from a formal philosophical perspective, then from the points of view of both literary criticism and universal Christian thought—especially with regard to the sphere of incarnational theology in the latter.

The core essays on aesthetics and love in this book are sandwiched in between Soloviev's three addresses on Dostoevsky at the one end and essays on the poets Pushkin, Mickiewicz, and Lermontov at the other. The latter three essays feature the application of developed moral and aesthetic criteria to understand the poets and their works. Soloviev's inseparable trinitarian view of beauty, truth, and the good—a view that consistently expresses itself in all the essays of this book—can be seen as taking shape under the influence of Dostoevsky and Soloviev's own immersion in the Bible and the writings of the church fathers.

The "Three Addresses in Memory of Dostoevsky" represent not only a eulogy of Soloviev's mentor, but also an encapsulation of Soloviev's thinking on the essence of aesthetics and a new mission for art in the modern world. Soloviev predicts the arrival of a fundamentally "new religious art," one of whose first precursors was Dostoevsky himself, and into the service of which its future representatives will enter freely and enthusiastically. For both Dostoevsky and Soloviev, aesthetics, morality, and truth coexisted in eternal unity. In describing his mentor, Soloviev could proclaim in his second address that Dostoevsky in his convictions never separated truth from beauty and the good; in his artistic creativity he never placed beauty apart from the good and the true. And he was right, because these three live only in their unity.[11]

When the central essays in this volume—"Beauty in Nature" (1889), "The Universal Meaning of Art" (1890), and "The Meaning of Love" (1892–1894)—are read together, they may be seen as part of a wider nineteenth-century polemic concerning the shortcomings of positivism. The question of whether beauty was objective or subjective was of no real concern or consequence to medieval thinkers, but it had taken on more importance in modern thought.[12] Soloviev rejected "art for art's sake" as well as positivism; and he attempted to reconcile medieval and modern thought, reconsidering aspects of medieval, especially Thomistic, aesthetics—e.g., the centrality of the symbolic element in reality—in light of German idealism and the discoveries of science, where Darwin's genius had only recently pointed out new worlds for investigation. Soloviev innovatively appropriated Darwin in the critique of positivism, and his high regard for the English scientist can be seen in the lengths to which he goes to reproduce Darwin's scientific observations for a literate Russian audience at the end of the essay "Beauty in Nature," where he introduced Darwin in the following way:

At a time when many rectilinear minds attempted to reduce human aesthetics to utilitarian bases in the interests of a positivistic-scientific worldview, the greatest representative of this very worldview in our century showed the independence of aesthetic motive from utilitarian goals even in the animal kingdom, and upon this positively based an authentically ideal aesthetic for the first time.[13]

One of my initial purposes in embarking on this project of annotated translations was to place "The Meaning of Love"—perhaps Soloviev's best known and most popular achievement—in the context of the rest of his developing thought during this period, and thereby provide English reading audiences for the first time with a vivid background for understanding his evolving views on beauty, truth, and the good in the attempt to demonstrate "all-unity" in religion, philosophy, science, and art. Most of the essays in this volume are first translations into English, originally appearing in Russian journals such as *Vestnik Evropy* (Messenger of Europe), *Mir iskusstva* (World of Art), and *Voprosy filosofii i psikhologii* (Problems of Philosophy and Psychology).

"Beauty in Nature," "The Universal Meaning of Art," and "The Meaning of Love" all first appeared (the latter, serially) in *Voprosy filosofii i psikhologii*, one of the more heterodox "liberal" intellectual forums in the Russia of his day. It may be argued that Soloviev's inquiry into the meaning of love, more than any other of his philosophical endeavors, represents his most original, daring, and most valuable foray into the subjects of metaphysics, phenomenology, and ontology. But the context in which this and other of his works on aesthetics and love were conceived and produced also holds considerable importance for understanding it. By 1890 Soloviev had in great frustration abandoned his decade-long project of justifying theocratic rule in light of Holy Scripture, trying to construct a Christian political theory of the State—a "theocratic Leviathan"—based on what he called "free theocracy." It is at this point that his "erotic" interests, as they have sometimes been referred to, begin to evidence themselves in his prose.[14]

As suggested above, Soloviev's investigation into the meaning and relationship of beauty, sexual expression, and reproduction—and therefore life itself—can be understood as a synthetic attempt to reconcile the worlds of medieval aesthetics, Platonic and German idealism, and Darwinian evolutionary theory. Could the diversity of worldviews represented by thinkers such as Plato, Aristotle, the Apostle Paul, Thomas Aquinas, Kant, Hegel, and Darwin all ultimately be reconciled on these topics? Was there a *Ding an sich* with reference to sexual love? Soloviev's conclusion seemed to be that the sexual act and preparation for it are reflections of the fundamental nature of the universe as the all-unity idea—originating in the mind of God, but only imperfectly realized in corporeal reality.

Keys to understanding the mystery of cosmic all-unity, according to Soloviev, lay in two interdependent principles: the mystery of eternal divine femininity, an inherent characteristic of the Deity that appears as the source of potential regeneration for all humanity, and the closely associated idea of "syzygy," a term originating with the Greeks and referring to a kind of astral or cosmic alignment, conjunction, or combination of forces. Soloviev specifically used the latter with reference to the centrality of sexual union for an understanding of the divine purpose in its hitherto only feeble embodiments in corporeal reality and to perfected ideas that exist in another reality (akin to Plato's world of forms), mirroring the essence of the mind of God and visible in multifarious ways throughout the natural world.

The essay "Beauty in Nature," which praises Darwin, begins with direct references to Aristotle's "Poetics" and Plato's *Republic*, and more obliquely reflects aspects of medieval thought, especially that of Thomas Aquinas and his mentor Albertus Magnus on divine beauty producing order and harmony. Thomistic observations such as the following seem to have left a deep imprint on Soloviev's understanding of beauty, nature, and sex:

> It is always the case that whatever creatures may have in the way of communion and coming together, they have it due to the power of beauty.[15]

Soloviev adopts this as axiomatic and believes it to be revealed in the nature of the universe. The principle of proportionality, key to the medieval understanding of beauty in nature (and hence, all other forms) could be traced back to Plato; Soloviev also harvested, rejuvenated, and applied other medieval Christian principles—e.g., the importance of symbol and allegory—in order to critique the literary art of his own era.[16] In "A First Step toward a Positive Aesthetic," Soloviev both castigates what he calls the "aesthetic separatism" of modern literature—as visible in the "art for art's sake" movement—and, at the same time, foresees the implications of claims that "boots are more important than Shakespeare": regimentation of art in the service of the State (what was to become socialist realism).

Soloviev makes frequent and extensive reference to the poets F. I. Tiutchev and A. A. Fet, understanding their art as models of truth and beauty. His critical work on other key figures in the development of Slavic literature (apart from Tolstoy and Dostoevsky) has not received as much attention as it perhaps should. The essays on Pushkin, Mickiewicz, and Lermontov follow the form and approach of Soloviev's addresses on Dostoevsky in so far as they subject these writers to a consistent standard of ethical evaluation. I have chosen these three in particular from among Soloviev's critical pieces because they have much in common, reviewing the thought-worlds of the poets in question from a holistic perspective. All three essays serve as ethical as well as intellectual commentaries on the aesthetics of these writers in light of their temperaments and their literary and sexual predispositions. Each of these essays provides insight into the motivation and ultimate outcome of poetic genius in a way that perhaps only Soloviev could have achieved. The essay on Lermontov is the prime example: Soloviev appears as the first critic to link Nietzsche with

Lermontov. He specifically understood Lermontov's will-to-power, manifested most prominently in the exertion of sexual control and power that Lermontov's self-love required over women, as directly anticipating Nietzsche. Scholars of Nietzsche too might benefit from close attention to Soloviev's argument.

Two appendices reinforce the main thrust of the essays in the body of the book. The first appears as an addendum to the three addresses on Dostoevsky and reveals some of the key, recurrent biblical sources for both Soloviev's and Dostoevsky's perspectives on nineteenth-century Russian and European societies. The second demonstrates a lighter, but still serious, side of Soloviev in his critique of an emerging, and later influential, literary school—Russian symbolism. Soloviev's assessment and parody of early symbolist poetry in some ways anticipated problems of postmodern art, and could in fact be leveled at various aspects of it.

Soloviev the normative philosopher raised questions about the responsibility of the artist to society as well as the purposes art serves in community life. His views on the roles of art and aesthetics in the public sphere and the responsibility to society of those producing art were largely ignored and almost forgotten in Russia, and they are not well known in the West.[17] The essays on Pushkin, Mickiewicz, and Lermontov, and the addendum on the symbolists do not simply constitute literary criticism, but also seem to anticipate more contemporary questions: To what extent are aesthetics a public good in modern society? Should any civic responsibilities, educative or otherwise, be formally associated with artistic creativity; and if so, in what way? Is community intervention into the realm of creative art a bad thing? Are any limitations on artistic expression based on normative grounds doomed to failure in modern society? While these "contemporary" questions are at least as old as Plato, modern discourse on aesthetics and censorship continues to produce sharp disagreements over public policies intended in response to them.

Some final comments are in order regarding matters of language in the translation itself. Translations of Soloviev's works, few in number relative to the overall volume of his *oeuvre*, have sometimes tended to reflect a degree of incoherence in the final product. This has had the unfortunate effect of obscuring and/or distorting the meaning as it appears in the original Russian.[18] Soloviev's wide-ranging intellectual prowess makes translation of his work a consistently difficult and sometimes frustrating task. Moreover, Soloviev loved to play with language, and sometimes his prose even seems to suggest poetry; but unfortunately, these qualities of his language often defy any translation at all into English. With regard to poetry specifically, I have rendered the lines that Soloviev quotes from verse almost literally, with no attention at all to considerations of either meter or rhyme-scheme. (However, my transliterations in the notes are intended for Slavicists or linguists concerned with poetic cadence, rhyme, and sonority.)

Additionally, some of Soloviev's passing references to concepts, authors, and works that bear no citation of source require attention and explanation where possible, especially for audiences not familiar with Russian culture and history, nineteenth-century European intellectual debates, or theological principles and the finer points in biblical accounts. Not surprisingly, Soloviev's references are often intended to reinforce what he believed to be the unity of his thought across the spectrum of his political, theological-philosophical, historical, and literary endeavors. I have attempted to provide appropriate explanations wherever possible for these textual references in my notes, which are meant not only to give some of the rich flavor of Soloviev's language, but also to elaborate upon the many passing references to classical and contemporary sources and figures that would likely not have needed much explanation for his contemporaries.

Soloviev himself translated literature and philosophy in several languages, and in the last years of his life he grappled with an extensive translation project of the Platonic dialogues. Emphasizing the need to avoid both "inappropriate invention" and "dead literalism," he insisted that readers (and the original author) had a right not to be deceived by unfaithful translations.[19] Of course, realizing this goal is a particularly thorny problem with regard to the lofty abstractions of philosophy. In the process of making complex and subtle distinctions among abstract phenomena, philosophers sometimes lose clarity and precision, and the original meaning itself can be lost in translation. As a translator of Plato's *Republic* once astutely observed, "the subject of our study is not intentionally talking nonsense."[20]

Unique translation problems accompany the rendering of complex philosophical concepts and argument either into or out of the Russian language. Russian can become frustratingly convoluted in its syntax: attempts at fine distinctions of necessarily abstract philosophical concepts can sometimes end unsatisfactorily. The greatest difficulties appear to present themselves with the introduction of metaphysical and ontological ideas. One might (only half-jokingly) suggest that among the reasons for the glaring lack of any universally recognized "great" Russian philosophers may be the daunting difficulties that philosophical discourse presents in Russian, in some measure simply as a function of its grammar. Without any definite or indefinite articles, the highly inflected character of Russian nouns and adjectives threatens to become a tangled jungle of abstraction that subsequently may appear at times to border on complete nonsense.

Other less daunting problems associated not with translation but with transliteration from another alphabet also present themselves. (In fact, the Bolsheviks implemented a new Russian orthography after the revolution, one that Soloviev did not himself use.) Transliteration from cyrillic presents scholars with some annoying hindrances: one of the most irritating is how to deal most effectively with the Russian "soft sign" [ь] denoting the palatalization of a consonant, which is today often rendered in Latin script as an apostrophe ['], according to modern linguistic convention. This issue appears distinctly in the case of the author's name, which appears in Russian with a soft sign and, therefore, is sometimes rendered as Solov'ev. I have chosen the form that the author himself used in signing his English and French correspondence, instead of the former or more phonetic renditions (e.g., Solovyov), in hopes of making it less awkward for the heterogeneous audience to which these essays address themselves. I have tried to keep in mind reading utility; in some names and places less critical for smooth reading in the text, I have retained the apostrophe as soft sign, while in other places—particularly in names—I have replaced it with the letter *i*. I have utilized the Library of Congress system of transliteration (except for commonly used names such as Dostoevsky). I have also omitted diacritical marks throughout (including from some lines of Polish verse in my notes), and transliterated several Greek phrases for the reader's convenience. Lastly, for the sake of greater clarity, I have capitalized the noun "God" and other titles for Divinity (Providence, Creator, Author, etc.) as well as the word "Idea" whenever it implies divine perfection or can be understood as referring to Plato's perfected world of forms.

The author's notations appear mostly as they originally did, either parenthetically within the text or at the bottom of each page in footnote form, while the editor-translator's comments appear at the end of the book in notes consecutively and separately numbered for each essay. All emphases are from the original unless explicitly noted otherwise. Ellipses are likewise Soloviev's unless noted otherwise. In the few places where I have had to add a word or two to the text for clarity, I have done so with square brackets.

Three Addresses in Memory of Dostoevsky

FOREWORD

In these three addresses, I occupy myself neither with Dostoevsky's personal life nor with the literary criticism of his works. I have in view only one question: What was Dostoevsky devoted to, what idea inspired all his activity?

To dwell on this is all the more natural since neither the details of his private life nor the artistic virtues or deficiencies of his works in themselves explains the special influence which he had in the last years of his life, and the extraordinary impression left by his death. On the other hand, the bitter attacks to which the memory of Dostoevsky is still subjected are not directed at the aesthetic aspect of his works at all; for everyone alike acknowledges in it a first-order artistic talent, rising sometimes to the level

Sources: Novoe vremia, no. 2133, 1882 (Second Address). *Rus'* no. 6, 1883 (Third Address). All three addresses first appeared together under the title "Tri rechi v pamiat' Dostoevskago" (1881–1883), separately published in 1884. The first address was first published at this time. The second address was given on 1 February 1882, the third address on 19 February 1883. No date is available on the first. Reprinted together in *Sobranie sochinenii* 3: 186–218.

of genius, even if not completely free from serious shortcomings. But, rather, the idea to which this talent was devoted strikes some as true and salutary, and others as spurious and unhealthy.

A definitive appraisal of all Dostoevsky's activity depends on how we view the idea that inspired him, in what he believed and what he loved. "And he loved before all else the living human soul everywhere and in everything, and he believed that we all are *of divine origin;* he believed in the infinite power of the human soul, triumphant over any external coercion and over any internal depredation. Having taken into his soul all life's evil, all the burden and blackness of life, and having abolished all this by the infinite power of love, Dostoevsky proclaimed this victory in all his works. Having learned the meaning of the *divine* power in the soul piercing through every human frailty, Dostoevsky came to a knowledge of God and Godmanhood.[1] The *reality* of God and Christ was opened to him in the *inner* power of love and all-forgiveness, and he preached this all-forgiving, abundant power as the foundation also for the outward realization on earth of that kingdom of truth which he thirsted for and toward which he strived all his life."*

It seems to me that it is not possible to look upon Dostoevsky as a typical novelist, as upon a talented and intelligent literateur. There was something greater in him, and it is this "something greater" that constitutes his distinctive particularlity and explains his effect upon others. It would be possible to introduce very many pieces of evidence in corroboration of this. I will limit myself to one that is worthy of special attention. Here is what Count L. N. Tolstoy says in a letter to N. N. Strakhov: "How I would like to be able to articulate all that I feel about Dostoevsky. In describing your feeling, you have expressed a part of mine. I never knew this man and never had relations with him directly; and suddenly, when he died, I understood that he was to me the closest, most dear and indispensable person. And it never entered my head to compare myself with him, never. Everything that he did (the actual good that he did) was such that the more he did, the better for me. Art calls forth in me envy, intellect does the same, but a matter of the heart—calls forth only joy. I so much counted him as my friend, and did not think otherwise than that we would see each other; but it did not happen, and this was my loss. Suddenly I read that he died, and I for some reason lost my bearings. I lost my head, and then

---

* From words spoken at Dostoevsky's grave, 1 February 1881.

it became clear how dear he was to me, and I cried and I still cry. Some days before his death I read *The Insulted and the Injured* and I was moved." And in a previous letter, "A few days ago I read *House of the Dead*. I had forgotten much, reread it, and do not know a better book from all of modern literature, including Pushkin. It's not the tone, but the point of view that is remarkable: sincere, natural, and Christian. A good, edifying book. I enjoyed the entire day yesterday as I have not enjoyed a day for a long time. If you see Dostoevsky, tell him that I love him."*

Those heartfelt qualities and that point of view to which Count Tolstoy refers are closely tied to the principal idea that Dostoevsky carried in himself all his life, but which only toward the end began to exercise complete dominion over him. My three addresses are dedicated to the elucidation of this idea.

FIRST ADDRESS

In humanity's primitive days, poets were priests and prophets, the religious idea controlled poetry, and art served the gods. Then, when life became more complex, when civilization based on a division of labor appeared— art stood apart and was separated from religion, just as was the case with other human activities. If earlier artists were servants of the gods, then art itself now became a deity and an idol. There appeared priests of pure art, for whom perfection of the artistic form became the chief concern, apart from any religious content. The two-fold spring of this liberated art (in the classical world and in modern Europe) was sumptuous, but not everlasting. We have seen with our own eyes the end of the flowering of neo-European art. The blossoms have fallen off, but the fruits are yet only budding. It would be unjust to require from a seed the qualities of ripe fruit: one can only guess in advance what these future qualities will be. It is necessary to relate to the status of art and literature today precisely in this manner. Today's artists cannot and do not want to serve pure beauty, to create perfect forms; they search for content. But alien to the previous religious content of art, they turn wholeheartedly toward current reality and put themselves in a slavish relationship to it *doubly:* first, they attempt to copy phenomena of this reality slavishly; and second, they attempt just as slavishly to serve

---

* In volume I, "Collected Works of Dostoevsky," supplement, pp. 69 and 67.

the topic of the day, to satisfy the public mood of a given minute, to ad-vocate a popular ethics, thinking to make art useful through that.[2] Of course, neither the one nor the other of these goals is attainable. In the unsuccessful pursuit of only apparently real* details, the actual reality of the whole is lost; and the striving to join extrinsic instructiveness and utility with art, to the detriment of its intrinsic beauty, transforms art into the most useless and unnecessary thing in the world, for it is clear that poor artistic work with the best intention will teach nothing and can yield no utility.

It is very easy to articulate an absolute condemnation of the contem-porary status of art and its prevailing tendency. A general decline of cre-ative work and particular infringements on the idea of beauty are much too striking—and yet condemnation of all this would be unfair. In this coarse and debased contemporary art, beneath this dual image of a slave, tokens of divine greatness are hidden. The requirements that art serve contempo-rary reality and have direct utility, nonsensical in their crude and dark ap-plication of today, allude, however, to a lofty and profoundly true idea of art which neither the representatives nor the expounders of pure art have yet approached. Not satisfied by the beauty of form, contemporary artists want more or less consciously for art to be a *substantive force,* elucidating and regenerating the entire human world. Previously, art *distracted* man from the darkness and rage that rule the world; it carried him away to its serene heights and *entertained* him with its pure images; today's art, on the contrary, *attracts* man to the darkness and spite of the humdrum with a sometimes obscure desire to illuminate this darkness, to calm this rage.

But where will art take this enlightening and regenerative power from? If art must not be limited to the distraction of man from the evils of life, but must correct the evils themselves, then this great goal cannot be achieved by the simple reproduction of reality. To configure does not yet mean to transfigure, and unmasking still is not improvement. Pure art lifted man above the earth, carried him off to Olympic heights; new art returns to earth with love and compassion, and not in order to be plunged into the darkness of earthly life.[3] We do not need art for that, but rather for the healing and renewal of this life. For this it is necessary to be in communion and to be close to the earth, to have love and compassion; but something

* Every detail, taken separately, in itself is not real, for only *everything taken to-gether* is real; and therefore a realistic artist, for all that, looks at reality *out of himself,* understands it in his own way, and, consequently, this is not *objective* reality.

greater still is also necessary. To have a powerful effect upon the earth, to turn it around and to recreate it, it is necessary to attract and apply *unearthly forces* to it. Art, having separated itself and kept itself aloof from religion, should appear together with it now in a new and voluntary connection. Artists and poets should once again become priests and prophets, but now in another, yet more important and elevated sense: the religious idea will not just reign over them, but they themselves will direct it and consciously control its earthly incarnations. The art of the future, which after long suffering will *itself* return to religion, will not at all be that primitive art that earlier had not yet become detached from religion.

In spite of what is—to all appearances—the antireligious character of contemporary art, a keen scrutiny will be able to distinguish within it the indistinct features of the future of religious art, namely in a concurrent two-fold aspiration: first, in aspiring toward a full embodiment of the ideal in the most paltry material details, approaching fulfillment in a merger with present reality; and second, in the aspiration *to influence* real life, correcting and improving it in agreement with certain ideal requirements. True, these requirements themselves are still rather base and efforts suggested by them are rather unsuccessful. In not acknowledging the religious character of its mission, realistic art rejects the lone solid foundation and sturdy lever for its moral effect in the world.

But all this coarse realism of contemporary art is only that tough membrane behind which, for the time being, the winged poetry of the future is hidden. This is not only an idiosyncratic aspiration—positive facts lead to it. Artists are now appearing who achieve religious truth out of the reigning realism, connect the tasks of its work with religious truth, draw their social ideal from it and sanctify their social service by it, all the while remaining in significant measure on its base soil. If we see in contemporary realist art something like a prophecy of a new religious art, then this prophecy is now beginning to be realized. There are as yet no representatives of this new religious art, but already its precursors are appearing. And Dostoevsky was one such precursor.

According to the character of his activity, belonging as he does to the ranks of artists-novelists—and though inferior to some of them in one respect or another—Dostoevsky has a chief advantage over them all in that he sees not only around himself, but also far ahead of himself. . . .

Apart from Dostoevsky, all our best novelists take the life that surrounds them just as they find it, as it takes shape and expresses itself in its present concrete and apparent forms. Such are the novels of Goncharov and Count Lev Tolstoy in particular. Both of them reproduce a Russian society generated over centuries (landowners, bureaucrats, sometimes peasants) in the forms in which it existed long ago, now in part outmoded or becoming obsolete. The novels of these two writers, despite all the particularities of their separate talents, are decidedly similar to their artistic subject. The distinctive particularity of Goncharov is a power of artistic generalization, thanks to which he could create such an all-Russian type as Oblomov, an equal to which *in its breadth* we will not find in any other Russian writer.* And concerning L. Tolstoy, all his work is distinguished not so much by a breadth of types (not one of his heroes has become a common noun), as by a mastery of detailed painting, by the vivid portrayal of all kinds of details in the life of man and nature, his chief power being in the most subtle representation *of the mechanism of psychical phenomena.* But even this painting of extrinsic details and this psychological analysis are on the immutable background of a prepared life that has already taken shape, namely the life of the Russian gentry family, shaded still more by the fixed images of simple people. The soldier Karataev is too submissive by himself to put the gentry into the background, and even the universal-historical figure of Napoleon cannot draw back the curtain of this constricted horizon: the ruler of Europe shows himself to be such only to the extent that he has contact with the life of a Russian gentleman; and this contact may be very limited—for example, the famous bathing scene in which the Napoleon of Count Tolstoy worthily vies with Gogol's General Betrishchev. In this immobile world all is clear and defined, all has become fixed; if there is a desire for something else, a striving to exit from these frames, then this striving is turned not ahead, but back to an even more simple and changeless life—to the life of nature ("The Cossacks," "Three Deaths").

The artistic world of Dostoevsky presents a completely contrasting character. All is in ferment here, nothing has been fixed, all is still only coming to be. The subject of the novel here is not the *static life* of a society, but rather social *movement*. Of all our exquisite novelists, Dostoevsky alone took social movement for the chief subject of his creative work. Turgenev is usually compared with him in this respect, but without suffi-

---

* In comparison with Oblomov, the Famusovs and the Molchalins, Onegins and Pechorins, Monilovs and Sobakevichs—not to mention the heroes of Ostrovsky—all have only *particular* significance.

cient basis. In order to characterize the general significance of a writer, it is necessary to take his best, and not his worst, works. The best works of Turgenev, in particular "A Sportsman's Sketches" and "A Nest of Gentlefolk," represent marvelous pictures, but only of social *status*, of that same old gentry world that we find in Goncharov and L. Tolstoy—and in no way of social movement. While Turgenev then continually tracked our social movement and in part submitted to its influence, the significance of this movement was not forecast by him, and the novel dedicated especially to this subject (*Virgin Soil*) turned out to be totally unsuccessful.*

Dostoevsky did not submit to the influence of the reigning tendencies around him, he did not follow obediently the phases of societal movement—he guessed the turning-points of this movement and *passed judgment* on them in advance. And he could judge by right, for he himself had a standard of judgment in his faith, which placed him above the prevailing currents and allowed him to observe these currents much farther, and not be carried away by them.[4] By virtue of his faith, Dostoevsky correctly guessed in advance the higher, further goal of the entire movement, clearly saw its digressions from this goal, and by right judged and correctly censured them. This proper and justified censure related only to the false paths and poor methods of the social movement and not to the movement itself, which was both necessary and desired; this censure related to a base understanding of social truth, to a false social ideal, and not to a search for social truth, not to the aspiration to realize a social ideal. The latter lay ahead even for Dostoevsky: he believed not only in a past, but also in an approaching Kingdom of God, and he understood the necessity of labor and action for its realization. He who knows the true goal of a movement can and must judge deviations from it. And Dostoevsky had a right to this all the more because he himself originally experienced these deviations; he himself stood on that erroneous path. The positive religious ideal that had so loftily elevated Dostoevsky over the prevailing currents of social thought did not immediately come easily to him, but was endured by him in a long and difficult struggle. He passed judgment on what he knew and his judgment was true.[5] And the clearer the higher truth became for him, the more resolutely he had to censure the false paths of societal activity.

---

* Although the word "nihilism" belongs to Turgenev in the general application of its meaning, the practical meaning of the nihilistic movement was not foreseen by him; and its much later manifestations, deviating widely from the conversations of Bazarov, were a grave surprise for the author of *Fathers and Sons*.

The overall point of Dostoevsky's entire activity, or the significance of Dostoevsky as a public figure, consists in a solution of the two-fold problem concerning a higher societal ideal and an actual path to its attainment.

The legitimate rationale for a social movement consists in the contradiction between the moral requirements of individuality and the structure of the society that has taken shape. Dostoevsky began from here as well: as narrator, interpreter, and at the same time active participant of the new social movement. A profound sense of social falsehood was expressed in his first tale, "Poor People," in a most inoffensive form. The social meaning of this tale (to which the later novel, *The Insulted and the Injured* is also adjoined) is reduced to an old and eternally new truth that in the existing order of things *the best* (morally) people are at the same time for society *the worst*, that they are fated to be poor people, insulted and injured.*

If social falsehood had remained for Dostoevsky only the theme of tale or novel, then he himself would have remained only a man of letters and would not have attained his special significance in the life of Russian society. But for Dostoevsky the content of his tale was at the same time a life's mission. He imediately placed the question on moral and practical ground. Having seen and censured that which is occurring in the world, he asked: What should be done?

First of all, a simple and clear solution presented itself: having become united, the best people, seeing social falsehood in others and sensing it in themselves, should rise up against it and recreate society in their own way.

When the first naive attempt† to carry out this solution led Dostoevsky to the scaffold and to hard labor, he along with his comrades could at first see the outcome of their schemes only in terms of their own failure and the malevolent power of others. The sentence that befell him was severe. But the sense of insult did not prevent Dostoevsky from understanding that he was incorrect in his scheme of social revolution, which was imperative only to him and his comrades.

---

* This is the same theme as in Victor Hugo's *Les Misérables*—the contrast between the intrinsic moral virtue of a man and his particular situation. Dostoevsky valued this novel very highly, and he himself underwent a certain, although rather superficial, influence from Victor Hugo (a penchant for antitheses). Apart from Pushkin and Gogol, Dickens and George Sand exerted a more profound influence on Dostoevsky.

† Naive especially on the part of Dostoevsky, to whom the paths of social revolution appeared in completely indistinct characteristics.

Amid the horrors of the house of the dead, Dostoevsky for the first time consciously met up with the truth of people's sentiment and, in its light, clearly saw the error of his revolutionary aspirations.[6] Dostoevsky's comrades in jail were, in the vast majority, from among the common people and, with a few vivid exceptions, all of these were the "worst" people of the nation. But even the worst of the common people usually safeguard that which people of the intelligentsia lose: faith in God and consciousness of their sinfulness. Common criminals, separated from the masses of the people by their evil acts, do not distance themselves at all from them in their sentiments and perspectives, and in their religious worldview. In the house of the dead, Dostoevsky found real "poor (or, in the people's expression, unfortunate) people." Those whom he had left behind still took refuge from social resentment in a sense of special virtue, in their personal superiority. Convicts did not have *this*, but there was something greater. The worst people of the house of the dead returned to Dostoevsky that which the best people of the intelligentsia removed from him. If there, amid the representatives of enlightenment, a residue of religious sentiment made him pale from the blasphemies of a progressive man of letters, then here, in the house of the dead, this sentiment had to resurrect and renew itself under the impression of the humble and devout faith of convicts. Forgotten by the Church and oppressed by the State, these people believed in the Church and did not repudiate the State. And, in the most difficult moment, the stately and meek image of the peasant serf Marei, encouraging the frightened gentleman's son with love, stood in Dosteovsky's memory behind the wild and savage mob of convicts. And he felt and understood that, before this supreme truth of God, all his self-made truth was a lie and the attempt to foist this lie upon another was a crime.

In place of the rage of an unsuccessful revolutionary, Dostoevsky carried away from penal servitude the outlook of a morally regenerated man: "The more faith, the more unity, and if love is added, then all has been done," he wrote. This moral power, renewed by contact with the people, gave Dostoevsky the right to an exalted place at the head of our social movement, not as a servant of the topic of the day, but as a true catalyst of social thought.

Though a positive social ideal was not yet fully apparent to the mind of Dostoevsky upon his return from Siberia, three truths were absolutely clear: he understood first of all that individual persons, even if they are the best people, do not have a right to exert force upon society in the name of their personal superiority; he understood as well that social truth is not invented by individual minds, but is rooted in nationwide sentiment; and, finally, he understood that this truth has religious significance and is necessarily connected with Christian faith, with the ideal of Christ.

In his consciousness of these truths Dostoevsky was far ahead of the prevailing tendency of social thought at the time and, thanks to this, could *guess in advance* and indicate whither this tendency leads. We know that the novel *Crime and Punishment* was written just before the crime of Danilov* and Karakozov, and the novel *The Devils* before the trial of the Nechaevites. The meaning of the first of these novels, with all its profound details, is very simple and clear, although even it was not understood by many. The major character is a representative of the view that any powerful man is a master to himself, and everything is permitted to him.[7] In the name of his personal superiority, in the name of the fact that he is a *force*, he deems that he has the right to commit murder, and he actually does so. But suddenly a matter that he considered only a violation of a meaningless law and a daring challenge to social prejudice turns out to be for his personal conscience somehow much greater—a sin, a violation of intrinsic moral truth. A violation of the external law receives legitimate retribution outwardly in exile and hard labor; but the inner sin of pride, of self-deification, separating a powerful man from humanity and leading him to murder, can be atoned only by an inward moral act of self-abnegation. Boundless self-assurance must vanish before a faith in that which is greater than *self*; and self-made justification must become humble before God's supreme truth, living in those very simple and weak people upon whom the powerful man gazed as upon worthless insects.

The same theme—if not made more profound, then significantly broadened and made more complicated—appears in *The Devils*. An entire company of people, possessed by a dream of violent revolution to remake the world in their own way, commits bestial crimes and perishes in a shameful way; but a Russia made whole by faith kneels before its Savior.

The social significance of these novels is great; *foretold* in them are important social phenomena that did not then take long to come to light; at the same time these phenomena are censured in the name of supreme

---

* Danilov was a student of Moscow University, who, having killed and robbed a pawnbroker, also had some kind of special plans.

religious truth, and the best way out for the social movement is indicated in the acceptance of this very truth.

Censuring any pursuit of willful abstract truth that generates only crime, Dostoevsky contrasts to this the people's religious ideal based on Christian faith. Returning to this faith is a general way out both for Raskolnikov and for everyone possessed by the devils of society. The Christian faith alone, living within the people, contains in itself that positive social ideal in which an individual personality is in solidarity with all. From a person having lost this solidarity, first of all is required that he reject the pride of being set apart, in order that he might reunite spiritually with the entire people by a moral act of self-sacrifice. But in the name of what? Only in the name of the fact that it—the people—is sixty million more than one individual, or a thousand? There are probably those who understand it precisely in this way. But such an extremely narrow understanding was completely foreign to Dostoevsky. By requiring that a person who has set himself apart return to the people, he first of all had in view a return to the true faith which is still preserved in the people. In the social ideal of brotherhood or the universal solidarity in which Dostoevsky had faith, the chief thing was its religiously moral, and not national, significance. Already in *The Devils* there is harsh mockery of those who bow to the people only for the reason that they are the people, and who value Orthodoxy as an attribute of Russian nationality.

If we want to specify and designate the social idea at which Dostoevsky arrived with a single word, then this word will not be the nation, but the *Church*.

We believe in the Church, as in the mystical body of Christ; we know the Church also as the collection of believers of one or another confession. But what exactly is the Church as a social ideal? Dostoevsky did not have any theological pretensions, and thus we also do not have the right to look within him for any logical definitions of the Church in its essence. However, in preaching the Church as a social ideal, he expressed an absolutely clear and definite requirement, just as clear and definite as the requirement declared by European socialism—although in direct contrast to it. (Therefore, in his last diary, Dostoevsky also called people's faith in the Church our Russian socialism.) European socialists require a violent reduction of all to one purely material level of satiated and complacent workers; they require the reduction of the State and society to the level of a simple economic association. "Russian socialism," about which Dostoevsky spoke, on the contrary, *elevates* all to the moral level of the Church as a spiritual brotherhood, although with the preservation of an outward inequality in social circumstance; it requires the spiritedness of the entire State and social structure through the embodiment of Christian truth and life in it.

The Church as a positive social ideal was to appear as the central idea of a new novel or a new series of novels, of which only the first was written—*Brothers Karamazov.**

If this social ideal of Dostoevsky appears in direct contrast to the ideal of the contemporary agents that are depicted in *The Devils*, the paths to its attainment diverge for them in precisely the same way. There the path is violence and murder, here the path is *moral action*: the two-fold action of moral self-abnegation. In order that a person disavow his arbitrary opinion, what is first of all required is deliberate veracity for the sake of the common national faith and truth. A person should bow before the people's faith, not because it is the people's, but because it is true. This then means that in the name of this truth in which the people believe, the nation too should renounce and get rid of everything in itself that does not concur with religious truth.

The possession of truth cannot constitute the privilege of the nation just as it cannot be the privilege of an individual person. Truth can be only *universal*, and an act of service to this universal truth is required from the nation, even if (and *absolutely* as well), it means the sacrifice of national egoism. And the nation should justify itself before universal truth, and the nation should lay down its soul, if it wants to save it.

Universal truth is incarnated in the Church. The final ideal and goal is not in nationality, which in itself is only an auxiliary force, but in the Church, which is the supreme object of service, requiring moral action not only from the individual, but also from the entire nation.

So then, there is the Church—as the positive social ideal, as the basis and goal of all our thoughts and concerns—and there is national endeavor—as the direct path for realization of this ideal: this is the final word at which Dostoevsky arrived, and which illuminated all his activity with a prophetic light.

---

* Dostoevsky communicated to me in brief the main features, thought, and, in part, plan of his new work, as well, in the summer of 1878. It was then (and not in 1879 as told erroneously in the memoirs of N. N. Strakhov) that we journeyed to Optina Pustyn.

Second Address

I will speak only about what is most important and essential in Dostoevsky's activity. Embracing as it did such a rich and complex nature, such an unusual impressionability and responsiveness to all the phenomena of life, Dostoevsky's spiritual world represented too much of a great diversity of feelings, thoughts, and impulses to reconstruct it in a brief address. But while he responded to *everything* with heartfelt ardor, he always acknowledged only *one thing* as chiefly and absolutely necessary, and to which everything else *must attend.* This central idea, which Dostoevsky served in all his activity, was the Christian idea of a free all-human unity, a universal brotherhood in the name of Christ. Dostoevsky advocated this idea when he spoke about the true Church, about universal Orthodoxy; in her he saw a spiritual essence of the Russian people yet to be manifest, the universal-historical mission of Russia, the new word that Russia must speak to the world. And although eighteen centuries has already passed from the time that this word was first proclaimed by Christ, in truth it appears in our days as a completely new word, and a preacher of the Christian idea such as Dostoevsky can be justly called a "clairvoyant foreseer" of true Christianity.[8] Christ was for him not just an element of the past, a distant and inscrutable marvel. If one looks at Christ thus, then it is easy to make out of Him a dead image, bowed to in churches on holidays, but with no place in actual life. Then all Christianity shuts itself within the walls of a temple and becomes transformed into ritual and the words of a prayer, but life's activity remains wholly un-Christian. Such a superficial Church also contains in itself true faith, but this faith is so weak that it is attained only at festive moments. This is *temple* Christianity. And it must exist before all else, for on earth the extrinsic is prior to the intrinsic; but it is not enough. There is another view, or degree, of Christianity, where it is not satisfied by liturgy and wants to guide the active life of a human being; it comes out of the place of worship and takes up residence in human dwellings. Its domain is the individual's interior life. Here Christ appears as the supreme moral ideal, religion is concentrated in personal morality, and the whole point lies in the salvation of the individual human soul. There is true faith in such a Christianity as well, but even here it is still weak; it is attained only in the *personal* life and the *private* concerns of a person. This is *domestic* Christianity. It must exist, but it too is insufficient. For it forsakes and consigns all social, civic, and international concerns—the entire world common to humanity—to the power of evil, anti-Christian principles.

But if Christianity is the supreme absolute truth, then it must not be thus. True Christianity cannot be only a domestic faith, just as it cannot be only a temple faith: it should be *universal*, it should apply to all humanity and to all human concerns. And if Christ is really the incarnation of truth, then He should not be left only as a representation in the place of worship or only as a personal ideal; we should acknowledge Him as the universal-historical principle, as the living foundation and cornerstone of an all-human Church. All human concerns and relations should finally be directed by the same moral principle to which we bow in the place of worship and which we acknowledge in our domestic life, i.e., the principle of love, of unrestrained harmony and brotherly unity.

Dostoevsky confessed and proclaimed such a universal Christianity.

Temple and domestic Christianity exist in reality—they are a fact. There is still no universal Christianity in reality; it is only a *mission*—and what an enormous mission, to all appearances exceeding the power of humanity. In reality all common human concerns—politics, science, art, social economy—finding themselves outside the Christian principle, divide people and separate them instead of uniting them; for all these concerns are directed by egoism and private advantage, rivalry and struggle, and they beget oppression and force. Such is reality, such is fact.

But all of the merit and significance of people such as Dostoevsky exists in just this, that they do not bow before the power of fact and do not serve it. Against the vulgar power of that which is, they possess the spiritual power of faith in truth and the good—in that which should be. It is an act of faith not to be seduced by the visible dominion of evil and, for the sake of it, not to renounce the invisible good. The entire power of the human being exists in this. He who is not capable of this act will do nothing and will say nothing to humanity. It is not people of "fact" who create life; they live a life created by others. It is people of faith who *create life*. They are the ones who are called dreamers, utopians, God's fools—it is they who are the prophets, the truly "best" people and the leaders of humanity. Today, we remember such a man.

Perplexed neither by the anti-Christian character of all our life and activity nor by the lifelessness and inactivity of our Christianity, Dostoevsky believed and preached a living and active Christianity, a universal Church, a universal orthodox cause. He spoke not only about what is, but also about that which should be. He spoke about a universal orthodox Church not only as a divine institution abiding immutably, but also as the *mission* of an all-human unification in the name of Christ and in the spirit of Christ—in the spirit of love and mercy, of action and self-sacrifice. The true Church that Dostoevsky preached is all-human, first of all in the sense that, in her, the separation of humanity into rivalrous and hostile tribes and nations must in the end disappear. Not losing their national character, but only being emancipated from their national egoism, all of them can and must join in the one common cause of universal revival. Thus, in speaking about Russia, Dostoevsky could not have in mind national isolation. On the contrary, he considered the entire purpose of the Russian people to be in service to true Christianity; in it there is neither Hellene nor Jew.[9] True, he considered Russia the chosen nation of God, but chosen not for rivalry with other nations and not for dominion and precedence over them, but for unrestrained service to all nations and for the realization, in brotherly union with them, of true all-humanity or of the universal Church.

Dostoevsky never idealized the nation, bowing to it as to an idol. He believed in Russia and foretold a great future for her, but the chief presentiment of this future was, in his eyes, precisely the weakness of national egoism and exclusiveness in the Russian nation. Two features in it were especially dear to Dostoevsky. First, the extraordinary capacity to adapt the spirit and idea of foreign nations, to be reincarnated in the spiritual essence of all nations—a feature that especially expressed itself in the poetry of Pushkin. Second, an even more important characteristic that Dostoevsky pointed out regarding the Russian nation is the consciousness of its sinfulness, the incapability of elevating its imperfection to law and right and resting content upon it: from here comes the requirement of a better life, a thirst for purification and deed. Without this there is no true activity either for a person separately or for the nation as a whole. No matter how profound the fall of man or nation, no matter how full of foulness its life, it can come through this and elevate itself, if *it wants*, i.e., by acknowledging the bad reality only as a bad fact that need not exist; and it does not make out of this bad fact an immutable law and principle, elevating its sin to truth. But if man or nation does not reconcile with its bad reality and condemns it as sin—this now means that it has some kind of impression or idea, or even just a foreboding, of another better life, of that which *should* be. Here is why Dostoevsky maintained that the Russian nation, in spite of its visible bestial image, carries another image in the depths of its soul—the image of Christ—and when the time comes it will show Him openly to all nations and will attract them to Him, and together with them will fulfill the all-human mission.

And this mission, i.e., true Christianity, is all-human not only in the sense that it must unite all nations *by one faith,* but chiefly in that it must unite and reconcile all human *concerns* in one universal common cause, without which a common universal faith would be only an abstract formula and dead dogma. Dostoevsky not only preached, but, to a certain degree, also demonstrated in his own activity this reunification of concerns common to humanity—at least of the highest among these concerns—in one Christian idea. Being a *religious* person, he was at the same time a free *thinker* and a powerful *artist.* These three aspects, these three higher concerns were not differentiated in him and did not exclude one another, but entered indivisibly into all his activity. In his convictions he never separated truth from good and beauty; in his artistic creativity he never placed beauty apart from the good and the true. And he was right, because these three live only in their unity. The good, taken separately from truth and beauty, is only an indistinct feeling, a powerless upwelling; truth taken abstractly is an empty word; and beauty without truth and the good is an idol. For Dostoevsky, these were three inseparable forms of one absolute Idea. The infinity of the human soul—having been revealed in Christ and capable of fitting into itself all the boundlessness of divinity—is at one and the same time both the greatest good, the highest truth, and the most perfect beauty. Truth is good, perceived by the human mind; beauty is the same good and the same truth, corporeally embodied in solid living form. And its full embodiment—the end, the goal, and the perfection— already exists in everything, and this is why Dostoevsky said that beauty will save the world.

The world must not be saved by force. The mission is not in the simple joining of all parts of humanity and all human concerns into one common concern. Imagine people working together on some kind of great mission, bringing and subjecting to it all their particular activity; if this task is *foisted* upon them, if it is something fated and importunate for them, if they are joined together by blind instinct or by internal coercion, then even if such a unity be extended to all humanity this will not be true pan-humanity, but only a huge "anthill."[10] We know models of such anthills in eastern despotisms—in China and in Egypt—and they have now been realized recently in small dimensions by communists in North America.[11] Dostoevsky rose up with all his strength against such an anthill, seeing in it a direct contrast to his social ideal. His ideal requires not only the unity of all people and all human concerns, but primarily—a *humane* unity among them. The point is not in unity, but in the free *agreement* for unity. The main concern is not in the greatness and importance of a common mission, but in the voluntary acknowledgment of it.

The final condition of a true all-humanity is freedom. But where is the guarantee that people will freely arrive at unity and not go their separate ways in all directions, at odds with one another and exterminating one another just as we see at present? There is one guarantee: the infinity of the human soul, not allowing man to rest upon something partial, petty, and incomplete forever, but forcing him to strive for and search for a full all-human life, a common and universal concern.

A faith in this infinity of the human soul is given by Christianity. Christianity alone of all religions presents *perfect man*, in which the fullness of divinity resides corporeally, together with perfect God. And if the full reality of the infinite human soul was realized in Christ, then the possibility—a portion of this infinity and fullness—exists in every human soul, even in the most fallen; and Dostoevsky showed this to us in his favorite character-types.

The plenitude of Christianity is all-humanity, and the entire life of Dostoevsky was a fervent upsurge toward all-humanity.

But one does not want to believe that his life passed in vain. One wants to believe that it was not for nothing that our society so harmoniously mourned the death of Dostoevsky. He did not leave any theory, any system, any plan or project. But the guiding source and goal, the highest social mission and idea were set by him on an unprecedented height. It will be shameful if Russian society removes his social idea from this height and substitutes the great common concern with its petty professional and corporate interests under various fine-sounding names. Of course, even in acknowledging a great all-human concern, people still have their private concerns and pursuits, their professions and specialities. And if there is nothing contrary to moral law in them, then it is completely unnecessary to throw them away. The all-human concern is pan-human because it can accomodate everything and exclude nothing, apart from evil and sin. What is required from us is only that we do not set our little part in place of the great whole, that we not become isolated in our private affairs, but that we strive to connect them with humanity's business in order that we never lose sight of this great cause, that we set it higher and prior to everything, and then place all the rest afterwards. It is not in our power to resolve when and how the great cause of all-human unity will be perfected. But it is in our power to set it as one's own, as the supreme task, and to serve it in all one's affairs. It is in our power to say: here is what we want, here is our supreme goal and our banner—and we are not concordant with another one.

Third Address

The outward, organic formation of Russia—the formation of its *corpus*— was concluded during the reign of Aleksandr II, at which time the process of *its spiritual* birth pangs and disorders began. A period of *agitation* inevitably precedes each new birth and each creative process, introducing these existing elements in new forms and combinations. When the corpus of Russia was taking shape and the Russian state was being born, the Russian people—from princes with their armed retinues to the lowliest peasant farmer—wandered over the entire country. All Rus' ambled along separately. Outward state consolidation was evoked as well by means of such external disruption so that Russia would take shape as one great body. This process of the outward consolidation of Russia's organization by the State was begun by the princes in Muscovy and was concluded by the emperors in Petersburg.

It is thanks to this process that the formerly roving armies were transformed into landed gentry, the formerly free hosts became petty bourgeoisie, and the transient peasants at liberty became serfs. This consolidation presented a static national and social life and activity in a rigid, fixed framework. After the Petrine reform, and especially from the reign of Aleksandr I on, the framework remained inviolable even when diverse ideas and intellectual currents of Western Europe began to seize the educated stratum of Russian society. Neither the mystical belief of the Russian masses nor the humanitarian ideas of the agents of the forties, in spite of the morally practical direction they often took among us, had an important influence on the vitality of the social foundations or interfered with educated people, who discoursed in a new way but lived in the old way, in forms bequeathed by tradition.

Right up to the act of emancipation by the former regime, the life and activity of Russian people did not depend essentially on their thoughts and convictions, but were defined in advance by the prepared framework in which birth placed each man and each group of people. A special question about the tasks of life—*What do we live for, and what is to be done?*— could not arise in the society of that time, because its life and activity were not conditional upon the question *For what?* but on the foundation of *Why?*[12] The landowner lived and acted in a certain way not *for the purpose* of anything in particular, but first of all *because* he was a landowner; and precisely in the same way a peasant was obligated to live thus and not otherwise, because he was a peasant. And between these extreme forms, all the remaining groups in the prepared conditions of community life found sufficient basis by which the circle of their lives was defined, leaving no place for the question: What is to be done?

If Russia were only a nation-state *corpus*, as for example China, then it could have been satisfied by such an outward rigidity and definition of life and could have remained in its consolidated organization. But Russia—baptized into the Christian faith still in its very infancy—received the pledge of a higher spiritual life. And upon attaining maturity, having taken shape and become defined physically, Russia should have sought out a free moral definition for itself. But for this purpose, the forces of Russian society should have first of all received their liberty, the possibility and inducement to leave the outward immobility that was conditional upon the structure of serfdom. The entire significance of the past regime was in this (emancipatory, and not reformist) concern. The singular, great deed of this regime is the emancipation of Russian society from the former obligatory framework for the future creation of new spiritual forms; and in no way is the regime's great deed the very creation of the latter; this creation has still not begun even now. Before being educated to these forms, the emancipated society must undergo an inward spiritual *upheaval.* Just as, prior to the education of the State body, there was a period when everyone wandered, so it must also be prior to the spiritual birth of Russia. It is at this time of inward upheaval that the question appears with irresistible force: What do we live for and what is to be done?

This question appears at first in a false sense. There is something erroneous already in the very posing of such a question on the part of people recently torn from certain superficial grounds of existence, not yet having replaced them with any higher ones, not yet having taken control of self. To ask directly: What is to be done? means to propose that there is some *prepared* business to which it is necessary only to apply one's hands; it means skipping another question: Are those who will do the work themselves prepared?

Meanwhile, in any human occupation, great and small, physical and spiritual, two questions alike are important: *What* is to be done? and *Who* is doing it? A poor or unprepared worker can only spoil the very best occupation. The occupation's purpose and the qualities of the one who will do the work are indissolubly linked in every enterprise: and wherever these two aspects part company, a valid enterprise does not result. Then, first of all, the sought-for enterprise bifurcates. On the one hand, there appears the image of an ideal system of life, and a certain definite "social ideal" is established. But this idea is independent of any inner labor whatsoever on the part of man himself; it consists only in a certain economic and social system determined in advance and made compulsory from without. Thus, everything that man can do for the attainment of this *outward* ideal is reduced to the elimination of external *impediments* to it. In this way, the ideal itself appears exclusively only in the future; in the present, man has business only with that which contradicts this ideal, and all his concern apart from the inessential ideal is turned exclusively to the *destruction of that which exists*. And since the latter is maintained by people and society, then this whole *enterprise* turns to the exertion of force over people and the entirety of society. In an inconspicuous way the social ideal is substituted by antisocial activity. To the question: What is to be done?—a clear and definite answer is obtained: Kill all opponents of the future ideal order, i.e., all defenders of the present.

In the face of such a solution of the matter, the question: Are those who will do the work prepared? is really superfluous. Human nature in its contemporary condition and in its very worst aspects is fully prepared and suited for *this kind* of service to the social ideal. In attaining the social ideal by the path of destruction, all evil passions, all the evil and insane elements of humanity, will find themselves a place and purpose; such a social ideal stands wholly on the ground of the evil that reigns in the world. It does not present to its servants any moral conditions; it does not need spiritual power, but only physical force; it requires from humanity not an inward *conversion*, but an outward *revolution*.

Before the appearance of Christianity, the Jewish nation awaited the advent of the Kingdom of God, which the majority under this reign understood to be an outward, forcible revolution, which was to give dominion to the chosen people and destroy its enemies. People expecting such a reign—at least the most resolved and zealous of them—had a clear and definite answer to the question of "What is to be done": rise up against Rome and slaughter Roman soldiers. And they carried this out; they began to slaughter Romans and they themselves were slain. Their cause perished, and the Romans ravaged Jerusalem. Only a few in Israel understood, under the approaching kingdom, something more profound and more radical; they knew another enemy, a more frightening and more enigmatic enemy than the Romans, and searched for another, still more difficult, but for all that more fruitful victory. For these people there was only an enigmatic and indefinite answer to the question: What is to be done?, one which the teachers of Israel could not accommodate. "Truly, truly I say to you: he who is not born from above, cannot see the kingdom of God."[13] The few people who were not confused by this strange and obscure answer, who accepted the new birth and believed in the spiritual kingdom of God, vanquished the Romans and subdued the world.

And among us now, too, in this epoch of spiritual agitation, adherents of "the social ideal"—an ideal as superficial and perfunctory as the "kingdom" of the earlier Jewish materialists—rise up and kill, destroy others and themselves perish fruitlessly and infamously, while others are either lost in intellectual chaos or wallow in indifferent self-interest. There now appear only a few people, who, not satisfied by any outward goals and ideals, feel and proclaim the necessity of a profound *moral* revolution and indicate the conditions of a new spiritual birth of Russia and humanity. Of these few harbingers of the Russian and the universal future, the first was inarguably Dostoevsky, for he foresaw more profoundly than others the essence of the approaching kingdom and foretold it more powerfully and with greater animation. The basic advantage of Dostoevsky's views is precisely that for which he is sometimes reproached: the absence, or better to say, conscious repudiation, of any *outward* social ideal, that is, one that is not connected with the inward conversion of man or his birth from above. Such a birth is not necessary for the so-called social ideal; it is satisfied with human nature as it is. This is a crude and superficial ideal, and we know that attempts toward its realization only confirm and multiply the already prevailing evil and folly in the world. Dostoevsky did not have such a crude and superficial, godless, and inhuman ideal—and in this is his first merit. He knew too well the depths of the human fall; he knew that evil and madness constitute the basis of our perverted nature, and that if this perversion is accepted for the norm, then it is not possible to arrive at anything other than force and chaos.

As long as the dark basis of our nature—evil in its exclusive egoism and insane in its striving to realize this egoism, to relate everything to itself and to define everything by itself—is not converted, and this original sin is not smashed, then for us it is not possible to actually *do* anything; and the question *What is to be done?* has no rational meaning. Imagine a mob of people, blind, deaf, crippled, possessed, and suddenly out of this crowd the question resounds: What is to be done? The only rational answer here is: Search for healing, because until you recover, there is nothing for you to do; and while you pose as healthy, there is no healing for you.

According to his very essence, a man who is morally ailing, who bases his right to act and remake the world in his own way, upon his own evil and madness, no matter what his outward fate and concern, is a *murderer*.[14] Such a man will inevitably impose force on others and destroy them, and he himself will inevitably perish by force. He considers himself powerful, but he is in the power of alien forces; he is proud of his freedom, but he is a slave to appearance and chance. Such a man will not recover until he makes a first step toward salvation. The first step toward salvation for us is to sense our powerlessness and our bondage: he who senses this fully will not now be a murderer; but if he *rests* on this feeling of his powerlessness and bondage, he will then arrive at *suicide*.[15] Suicide—violence against the self—is already something more elevated and freer than violence against others. Acknowledging one's insolvency, man by the same token *rises above* his insolvency, and in pronouncing for himself a death sentence not only suffers as defendant, but also acts authoritatively as supreme judge. But his verdict is unjust here as well. There is internal contradiction in the resolution for suicide. This resolution proceeds from a consciousness of his powerlessness and bondage; meanwhile, suicide itself is already a certain act of power and liberty—Why not utilize this power and liberty for life?

But the point is that a suicide not only recognizes human insolvency in himself, but also elevates it to a universal law—which is now madness. He not only feels evil, but also *believes* in evil. Acknowledging his ailment, he does not believe in healing, and therefore can only use the power and the liberty acquired by this consciousness for self-destruction. Everyone who acknowledges all-human evil, but does not believe in the superhuman good, arrives at suicide. A man of reason and conscience is saved from suicide only by this faith. He should not remain on the first step—consciousness of his evil—but should take a second step—acknowledging an existing good above himself. And in order to end at a good that is independent of man, while sensing all the evil in man, a little common sense and a little exertion of good will are necessary in order to appeal to this good and to give it a place in oneself. For this existing good itself now searches for us and turns us to itself, and it is left to us just to yield to it, only not to oppose it.

With faith in a superhuman good, i.e., in God, faith too returns to man, who here now appears not in his solitude, feebleness, and bondage, but as a free participant of divinity and a bearer of the power of God. But now having actually believed in the superhuman good, we in no way can allow that its occurrence and activity had anything to do with our subjective condition exclusively, as if the Deity in its revelation depended only on the personal action of man. Certainly, beyond our religious attitude, we should acknowledge the positive revelation of the Deity also in the external world, and we should acknowledge objective religion. To limit the Divinity's action to man's moral consciousness alone means to negate His plenitude and infinity, and it means not to believe in God. In actually believing in God, as in a good knowing no boundaries, it is also necessary to acknowledge the objective incarnation of Deity. That is, His union with the very essence of our nature, not only in the spirit, but also in the flesh, and through it also with the elements of the external world.

And this means to acknowledge nature *as capable* of such an incarnation of the Deity in it. This means to believe in redemption, sanctification, and the deification of matter. Not only faith in man, but also faith in nature returns to us with a real and complete faith in the Deity. We *know* nature and matter separated from God and perverted in itself, but we *believe* in its redemption and its union with divinity, its transformation into *God-matter;* and as intermediary of this redemption and renewal we acknowledge a true, perfect man, i.e., a *God-man* in His free will and action. A true man, born from above by the moral deed of self-renunciation, guides the living power of God to the mortified body of nature and shapes the entire world in the universal Kingdom of God. To believe in the Kingdom of God means to combine faith in man and faith in nature with faith in God. All delusions of the mind, all false theories, and all practical one-sided attitudes and abuses have descended and continue to descend from the division of these three faiths. All truth and all good come out of their intrinsic combination. On the one hand, man and nature have meaning only in their connection with the Deity. For man, left to himself and confirmed in his godless foundation, wipes out his inner falsehood and arrives, as we know, at murder and suicide; and nature, divided from the Spirit of God, appears as a dead and senseless mechanism without reason and goal. And, on the other hand, God, divided from man and nature outside of his positive revelation, also appears for us as either empty abstraction or all-consuming indifference.

The entire free enlightenment of Europe passed through such a pernicious division of three principles and three faiths. Here *mystics* (quietists and pietists) appeared, who strove to drown themselves in the contemplation of Deity, having despised human freedom and precluded material nature. Further, *humanists* (rationalists and idealists) who worshiped the human principle appeared here, having declared the absolute self-legitimacy and leadership of human reason and ideas conceived by it, having seen in God only the embryo of man, and in nature—only his shadow. But even this shadow provided a powerful sense of its reality. And finally, with the destruction of idealism, there now come to the forefront of contemporary enlightenment *naturalists* (realists and materialists), who, banishing from their worldview all traces of spirit and Deity, bow down before the dead mechanism of nature.

All these one-sided tendencies confirmed one another's guilt in falsehood and displayed their insolvency abundantly; and our rudimentary enlightenment passed through these three abstract tendencies. But the spiritual future of Russia and humanity does not abide in them. False and fruitless in their disagreement, they find both truth and fruitful strength in their intrinsic combination—in the plenitude of the Christian idea. This idea claims the incarnation of the divine principle in natural life through the free act of man, combining faith in God-man and in God-matter (the Blessed Virgin) into faith in God. Adopted instinctively and semiconsciously by the Russian nation from the time of baptism, this triune Christian idea should become the foundation as well for a conscious spiritual development of Russia in connection with the fate of all of humanity. Dostoevsky understood this and announced it.

More than anyone among his contemporaries, Dostoevsky conceived the Christian idea *harmoniously* in its three-fold plenitude; he was at one and the same time mystic, humanist, and naturalist. Possessing a vital sense of the intrinsic connection with the superhuman, and being in this sense a mystic, he found the liberty and power of man in this feeling. Knowing all human evil, he believed in all human good and was by general acknowledgment a true humanist. But his faith in man was free of any unilateral idealism or spiritualism: he took man in all his fullness and reality. Such a man is closely tied to material nature, and Dostoevsky turned to nature with profound love and tenderness, understood and loved the earth and all that is earthly, believed in the purity, holiness, and beauty of matter. There is nothing false and sinful in *this kind* of materialism. Just as a true humanist does not bow before human evil only for the fact that it is human, so too true naturalism is not slavery to perverted nature because it is natural.

Humanism is *faith* in man, but there is no reason to believe in human evil and feebleness—they are present and obvious; and there is also no reason to believe in distorted nature—it is a visible and palpable fact. To believe in man means to recognize in him something *more* than what is present; it means to recognize in him that power and that freedom that connect him with the Deity. And to believe in nature means to recognize in it the innermost radiance and beauty that make it *God's body*. True humanism is faith in *God-man* and true naturalism is faith in *God-matter*. Justification of this faith, the positive revelation of these principles, the reality of God-man and God-matter are given to us in Christ and the Church, which is the living body of the God-man.

Here, in orthodox Christianity, in the universal Church, we find a firm basis and the essential rudiment for a new spiritual life, for the harmonious formation of true humanity and true nature. Here then is also the stipulation of a valid enterprise. Genuine work is possible only if there are positive and liberated powers of light and good both in man and in nature; but without God neither man nor nature has such powers. Separation from the Deity, i.e., from the plenitude of the good, is evil. And, acting on the basis of this evil, we can create only something bad. The final act of a godless man is murder or suicide. Man introduces evil into nature and takes from her death. Only by rejecting his false situation—his insane concentration on self, his evil solitude—only by connecting the self with God in Christ and with the world in the Church, can we actually do serious Godly work—that which Dostoevsky called the *Orthodox enterprise*.

If Christianity is a religion of salvation, if the Christian idea consists of healing—and an intrinsic union of principles, the discord of which means ruin—the essence of true Christian concern will be that which in the language of logic is called *synthesis*, and in the language of morality *reconciliation*.

In his Pushkin address, Dostoevsky marked the calling of Russia with this general outline. This was his last word and testament. And there was something much greater here than a simple calling to peaceful sentiments in the name of the breadth of the Russian spirit: here as well now was enclosed an indication of Russia's positive historical tasks—or better, responsibilities. It is not for nothing that it was felt and said at that time that the dispute between Slavophilism and Westernization was abolished. And abolition of this dispute means abolition *in theory* of the multi-century historical discord itself between East and West; this means finding for Russia a new moral posture, saving her from the necessity of continuing the contra-Christian struggle between East and West and placing on it the great responsiblity to serve morally both East and West, reconciling both in itself.

And this appointment and this responsibility were not invented for Russia but given to her by Christian faith and history.

Such a division between East and West, in the sense of discord and antagonism, mutual enmity and hatred, *should* not exist in Christianity; and if it appeared, then this is a great sin and a great pity. But at the precise time that this great sin was committed in Byzantium—Russia was born for its atonement. Having taken Orthodox Christianity from Byzantium, should Russia adopt for itself forever—together with the Sacred—the historical sins of the Byzantine kingdom, which prepared its own downfall, as well? If, contrary to the plenitude of the Christian idea, Byzantium incited anew the great universal dispute and took one side—the side of the East—then its fate is not a model for us, but a lesson.

From the beginning Providence placed Russia between the non-Christian East and the western form of Christianity—between the *Islamic infidels* and *Roman Catholics*.[16] At that time Byzantium was unilaterally at enmity with the West, was gradually being penetrated more and more exclusively by eastern principles and was being transformed into an Asiatic kingdom. Hence, it turned out to be powerless both against Latin crusaders and Islamic barbarians alike—and finally submitted to the latter. At the same time, Russia defended itself with resolute success against both East and West, triumphantly repelling Islamic infidels and Roman Catholics. This outward struggle with both adversaries was necessary for the outward gathering and consolidation of Russia, for the formation of its state *corpus*. But with this, the superficial task was fulfilled; the corpus of Russia was formed and developed. Alien forces cannot now devour it—and the ancient antagonism loses its significance.

Russia showed its physical powers sufficiently to both East and West in the struggle with them—now it will have to show them its spiritual power in reconciliation. I speak not about a superficial drawing together and a mechanistic transferral to us of alien forms (like the reform of Peter the Great), necessary only as preparation. The actual task is not in *copying* but in *understanding* foreign forms, identifying and adopting the positive essence of another's spirit and morally joining with it in the name of supreme universal truth. The essence of reconciliation is God. A reconciliation is necessary *in essence*; a true reconciliation in order to relate to the adversary not human-like, but "god-like." This is the more urgent for us because now both our chief adversaries are no longer outside, but in our midst. Roman Catholics, in the person of the Poles, and Islamic infidels, i.e., the non-Christian East in the person of the Jews, have entered into the composition of Russia; and if they are our enemies then they are now internal enemies, and if there should be a war with them, then this will now be an internecine war.[17] Not Christian conscience alone, but also human wisdom speaks of reconciliation here. And there are insufficiently amicable feelings here toward adversaries, both as people *in general* and as completely *unique* individuals with distinct qualities. And a profound understanding precisely of these, their particular qualities, is necessary for real reconciliation; it is necessary to turn to their very spiritual essence and relate to it in a god-like manner.*

The spiritual principle of the Poles is Catholicism, the spiritual principle of the Jews is the Judaic religion. To reconcile truly with Catholicism and Judaism means first of all to separate in them that which is from God and that which is from men. If within us ourselves there is a vital interest in the cause of God on earth, if the Sacred is dearer to us than all human relations, if we do not weigh the abiding power of God on the same scales with the transient affairs of people—then beneath the cruel exterior of sins and errors we will recognize the seal of divine selection, first upon Catholicism, and then also upon Judaism. Seeing as the Roman Church in ancient times stood alone on a solid cliff, against which crashed all the dark waves of anti-Christian movements (heresies and Islam); and seeing as in our time also Rome alone remains chaste and steadfast amidst a stream of anti-Christian civilization and from it alone resounds a calming, but cruel word of censure as well to the godless world, we will not ascribe this to some kind of incomprehensible human obstinacy alone, but will also recognize here the clandestine power of God. And if Rome, unshakable in its holy place, and striving moreover to bring to this holy place all humanity, moved forward and changed, fussed about, profoundly fell and arose anew, then it is not for us to judge it for these fussings and falls—because we did not support it and lift it up, but viewed contentedly the difficult and slippery path of our western confrere, while we ourselves sat in our place, and, sitting in our place, did not fall.

If all that is humanly bad and all that is petty and dirty is so striking to us, if we so manifestly and meticulously see all this dust of the earth;

---

* From what has been said, it seems clear to me that it is a matter *not of concessions and compromises* in an intrinsic conflict (ecclesial-political and national), but of an alienation of the intrinsic *cause* of this conflict through spiritual reconciliation on purely religious ground. Until the time that their religious internal unity is restored, the political and religious conflict remain within their rights.

and, on the contrary, all that is divine and holy for us is imperceptible, dark and unbelievable, then this means only that there is little of God within us ourselves. Let us give Him more of a place within ourselves and let us see Him more clearly in the other. Then we will see His power not only in the Catholic Church, but also in the Jewish synagogue. Then we will understand and accept the words of the Apostle about the Israelites: "Theirs is the adoption as sons, the divine glory and covenants, and the law, and temple worship and promises; theirs are the patriarchs, and from them Christ in the flesh, God over all. . . . Or has God rejected his people? By no means! God has not rejected his people, whom he foreknew. . . . But so that you may not be conceited, I do not want you to be ignorant of this mystery, brothers: Israel has been blinded in part until the full number of Gentiles has come in. And then all Israel will be saved . . . for God has bound all over to opposition so that he may have mercy on all."[18]

In truth, if the Word of God is more faithful than all human arrangements and the cause of the Kingdom of God is dearer than all earthly interests for us, then it is for us to open the path of reconciliation with our historical enemies. But won't it be said: Will our adversaries themselves go for peace; how will they relate to this and what will they answer us? Another's conscience is unknown to us and others' concerns are not within our power. It is not within our power that others will relate well to us, but it is in our power to be worthy of good relations. And it is not for us to think about what others will say to us, but about what we will say to the world.

In one discourse Dostoevsky applied to Russia the vision of John the Divine about a wife, clothed in the sun and in pangs wanting to give birth to a male son: the woman is Russia, and what is given birth to by her is that new Word, which Russia should speak to the world. Whether this interpretation of "a great sign" is accurate or not, Dostoevsky correctly divined the new Word of Russia. This is the word of reconciliation for East and West in a union of God's eternal truth and human freedom.[19]

Here is the supreme mission and obligation of Russia, and such is the "social ideal" of Dostoevsky. His foundation—the moral rebirth and spiritual effort now not of a solitary, individual person, but of an entire society and nation. As in days of old, such an idea is obscure for the teachers of Israel, but there is truth in it, and it can conquer the world.[20]

Beauty in Nature

Beauty will save the world.
                        —*Dostoevsky*

It seems frightening to place the salvation of the world upon beauty, when it is necessary to save beauty itself from artistic and critical attempts to replace the ideal of the beautiful with ugliness in reality. But if we are not perplexed by the crude—and sometimes also absolutely absurd—expressions of the latest aesthetic realism (and utilitarianism), and we investigate the essential meaning of its claims, then an involuntary and contradictory, but nonetheless an especially valuable, acknowledgment of beauty's universal significance will also be found within them: beauty's apparent persecutors attach to it precisely this same task of saving the world. Pure art, or art for art's sake, is rejected as a playful game; ideal beauty is held in contempt as an arbitrary and empty embellishment of reality. So, therefore, in order that actual art be a *matter of importance*, its capacity to act profoundly and powerfully upon the real world must be acknowledged as true beauty.

Source: "Krasota v prirode," *Voprosy filosofii i psikhologii* 1 (1889): 1–50. Reprinted in *Sobranie sochinenii* 6: 33–74.

Having liberated the claims of the new aesthetes (realists and utilitarians) from the logical contradictions they usually get tangled up in, and reducing these claims to one, we obtain the following formula: the aesthetically beautiful should lead to an *actual improvement of reality*. The claim is fully justified; and, generally speaking, even ideal art never rejected it, and ancient aesthetes also acknowledged it. So, for example, according to Aristotle's definition (in his "Poetics"), ancient tragedies should have created an actual betterment of the human soul through purification (*catharsis*). And Plato (in the *Republic*) similarly ascribes real-moral action to several kinds of music and lyric that fortify the courageous spirit.[1]

On the other hand, plastic art, apart from its aesthetic influence upon the soul, additionally produces a direct and abiding effect upon extrinsic, material nature. Although this effect is perhaps completely insignificant, superficial, and partial, it is nonetheless a real effect on the material from which this art creates its product. A beautiful statue in relation to a simple piece of marble is inarguably a new and real object, and what's more — better, more perfect (in an objective sense), more complex, and at the same time more detached and remote. If in this case the augmenting effect of art on a material object has a purely extrinsic character, not in the least changing the essential features of the thing itself, then, however, there are no grounds to hold that such a superficial type of effect should without fail belong to art in general, always and in all its forms. On the contrary, we have every right to think that the influence of art on the nature of things, as well as on the human soul, allows different degrees, can be more or less profound and powerful.

But, in any case, no matter how weak the ambiguous effect of the artist, he nevertheless creates certain new objects and conditions — a certain new beautiful reality — which would not exist at all without him. This beautiful reality, or this realized beauty, constitutes only a very insignificant and feeble part of all our far-from-beautiful reality. In human life artistic beauty is only a symbol of a better hope, a momentary rainbow against the dark background of our chaotic existence. It is against this insufficiency of artistic beauty — against this, its superficial character — that the opponents of pure art revolt. They reject it not because it is too elevated, but because it is not sufficiently real; i.e., it is not in a condition to command our entire reality, to transform it, to make it thoroughly beautiful. In not clearly acknowledging this themselves, perhaps they require from art much more than it has given and continues to give. In this they are correct, for the limitation of present artistic creativity — this illusoriness of ideal beauty —

expresses only an imperfect stage in the development of human art, and in no way flows from its very essence. It would be an obvious mistake to consider the methods and the range of today's extant artistic activity as definitive and absolutely obligatory. As it is with all that is human, art is a conventional phenomenon, and we have in our hands maybe only fragmentary rudiments of true art. Let us suppose that beauty itself is changeless; but the capacity and power of its realization, in the form of beautiful reality, have a multitude of stages. There is no basis for a reasoning soul to stop once and for all at the present historical moment, at a place where we did not succeed in achieving it, even if this moment would continue for millennia more.

Having in mind a philosophical theory of beauty and art, it is worthwhile recalling that all such theories, which explain their subject in its present form, should reveal as well the breadth of its future horizons. A theory that only notes and abstractly generalizes the virtual connection of phenomena is fruitless: this is simple empiricism, towering above folk-wisdom's observations by only one notch. A true philosophical theory, while comprehending the meaning of a fact—i.e., its relationship with everything that is cognate to it—by the same token ties this fact together with an indefinitely ascending series of new facts. No matter how bold such a theory might seem to us, there is nothing arbitrary and fantastic in it if only its broad foundation is constructed on the authentic essence of a subject, discovered by reason in a given phenomenon or aspectual phase of this subject. For the essence of a subject is necessarily greater and more profound than a given phenomenon; and consequently, according to necessity, the essence is the source of new phenomena that gradually express or realize it more and more.

But, in any case, the essence of beauty should first of all be understood in its authentic present phenomena. Of the two regions of beautiful phenomena—nature and art—we will begin with that which is more extensive according to capacity, more simple according to content, and naturally (in the order of existence) precedes the other. The aesthetics of nature will give us the necessary foundation for a philosophy of art.

I.

According to its chemical content, diamond—i.e., crystallized carbon—is the very same as ordinary coal. It is also undoubtedly the case that the song of a nightingale and the frenzied cries of a mating cat, according to their psycho-physiological basis, are one and the same, namely, an acoustic expression of intense sexual instinct. But a diamond is beautiful and is dearly valued for its beauty, whereas even the most unpretentious primitive would hardly want to utilize a piece of coal in the form of adornment. And while the nightingale's singing always and everywhere has been taken as one of the manifestations of the beautiful in nature, feline music, not any less vividly expressing the very same psychic-physical motive, has never, nowhere, and to nobody ever conveyed aesthetic pleasure.

From these elementary examples, it is now clear that beauty is something formal and specific, not directly dependent on or reducible to the material basis of a phenomenon. Independent of the material foundation of objects and phenomena, neither is beauty produced by a subjective evaluation of them according to everyday use and the feeling of pleasantness they can convey to us. The fact that the most beautiful objects can be completely useless in the sense of the satisfaction of daily needs—and that, likewise, the most useful things can be completely unsightly—does not, of course, require proof; but it is not possible to circumvent the theory that *obliquely* defines beauty by virtue of utility. This theory confirms that beauty is utility that has ceased to act, or is a recollection of former utility. That which was of utility for our ancestors becomes adornment for their descendents. In a bold application of Darwinism, it is possible to extend this understanding of *former* utility very far, and to count not only monkeys and seals, but very likely even oysters as our ancestors as well. The weight of factual truth is in this theory of the metamorphosis of the utile into the beautiful, and there is no need for us to reject it. The only thing that is doubtless is the fact that this theory is completely insufficient in the sense of philosophical elucidation or an essential definition of beauty.

Further, we see that, even on the lowest rungs of psychic development (in the animal world), beauty has an objective significance apart from any utilitarian relation. But even if a *genetic* dependency of the beautiful on the utile was proved, the *aesthetic* problem is not in the least solved by this. It is doubtless that all significant phenomena of the beautiful in nature and art are not connected with any practial utility either for us or even our most remote ancestors. And, in that case, the possible material utility of the primary elements into which we break down beautiful phenomena has as little significance for aesthetics as the fact that the most beautiful human body arose out of a formless embryo is indifferent to a direct feeling of beauty.

The question *What is* a certain object? never coincides with the question *Out of what* or where did this object *arise* from? The question of the descendency of aesthetic feelings belongs to the sphere of biology and psycho-physiology; but the aesthetic question of What is beauty? is not even touched by this, let alone resolved. So-called "ancient stone images" undoubtedly precede Greek statues in genetic order. But will pointing out these formless works in fact help us to comprehend the aesthetic essence of the Venus de Milo? . . . It is undoubtable that in the genetic sense, all our senses, not excluding even the higher ones—vision and hearing— are only differentiations of the sense of touch. But does this mean that an independent significance for optics and acoustics is lost? Analysis of aesthetic phenomena into primary elements, having the property of utility or pleasantness, can be very interesting; but an actual theory of the beautiful is one that has in view the true essence of beauty in all its phenomena, both simple and complex. Just as organic chemistry, with all its importance for the biologist, cannot, strictly speaking, replace botanical and zoological research for him, so too the psycho-physiological analysis of aesthetic phenomena will never obtain the significance of real aesthetics.*[2]

Formal beauty always shows itself as pure uselessness, whatever its material elements. However, this pure uselessness is valued highly by man and, as we will see further, not only by man. And if it cannot be valued as a means for the satisfaction of one or another daily or physiological requirement, then this means it is valued as a goal in itself. In beauty—even with the most simple and primary of its manifestations—we meet up with something *absolute* that exists not for the sake of another but for its own sake, so that, by its very existence, it gladdens and satisfies our soul, which, resting on beauty, becomes tranquil and is liberated from life's strivings and labors.

This ancient Greek understanding of beauty as a topic of disinterested, unselfish, and passively willed contemplation—or more simply, as pure uselessness—was renewed and disseminated not long ago by the last

---

* See L. E. Obolenskii, "A Physiological Explanation of Several Elements of the Sense of Beauty. Psycho-physiological Studies" (St. Petersburg, 1878). More pretentious, but for that also less basic, is the work of Mr. Vl. Veliamovich—"Psycho-physiological Foundations of Aesthetics. The Essence of Art, Its Social Significance and Relation to Science and Morality. (A New Experiment of the Philosophy of Art.)" Parts One and Two (St. Petersburg, 1878). As the only experiment of systematic aesthetics in Russian, this book deserves mention, but is not, however, required in criticism.

great representatives of German philosophy.³ However, everything that Schopenhauer truly says so well on this theme is in essence not more than philosophical commentary on a certain couplet, dropped in passing by Goethe:

> Die Sterne die begehrt man nicht:
> Man freut sich ihrer Pracht.⁴

There is no need to rest for long on this aspect of the matter, first, because it is exhausted by the Frankfurt thinker, and second, because it far from exhausts the question of beauty. To say that beauty is a subject of disinterested observation or an end in itself is only to say that it is not a means for secondary aims: the definition is completely reliable, but purely negative and without content. No matter how important for a thinker the quality of unselfishness and involuntariness inherent in every purely aesthetic value is, still more important and more interesting for him is the question of the true positive essence of beauty; and it is not for nothing that the poetic genius added a positive indication—man freut sich ihrer *Pracht*—to his negative indication: die Sterne die begehrt man *nicht*. Of what, precisely, does this "Pracht" (splendor) within every beautiful subject consist, strictly speaking? This is chiefly what philosophical aesthetics should resolve. As a goal in itself, beauty can serve nothing—in a practical and everyday sense it is pure uselessness; but the question of the independent content of this goal is not in the least removed by this. For what is this pure uselessness valued, for which of its proper intrinsic qualities?

We find an allusion—but only an allusion—to the truth in the well-known teaching according to which ideas (the eternal forms of things) as the objective expressions (the objectification) of the universal will constitute the essential content of beauty.⁵ There is no actual answer to the aesthetic question here—because, for this theory, all that exists is identically the objectification of the universal will; at the same time, not all that exists is identically beautiful. A view that logically compels us to acknowledge any intestinal worm to be as beautiful as Helen at the walls of Troy wastes itself in the sense of aesthetic doctrine. Abstract metaphysical points of view, incompatible with the recognition of a difference between good and evil, between beauty and ugliness, do exist; but, in resting on such points of view, it is better now not to argue moral and aesthetic topics at all.

II.

Thus, leaving abstract metaphysics to one side, we return again to the actual examples of the beautiful in nature, out of which our discussion began. The beauty of a diamond, not at all a quality of its substance (for this substance is the very same that exists in an unsightly piece of petrified coal), evidently depends on the play of light rays in its crystals. It does not, however, follow from this that the quality of beauty belongs not to the diamond itself, but to the refracted ray of light in it. For that very ray of light will not create any aesthetic impression when reflected by an unsightly object; no impression at all is obtained if it is not reflected and refracted by something.

So then, beauty, belonging neither to the material body of a diamond nor to the refracted ray of light in it, is the product of the interaction of both of them. The play of light that is captured and variegated by this body veils its crudely material appearance completely; and the dark matter of carbon is present here too, just as in coal, but only in the form of a bearer of the principle of light, which reveals in this play of colors its particular content. When a ray of light falls on a piece of coal, it is absorbed by its material substance, and the black color of the latter is the natural symbol of the fact that the light force did not overcome the dark elements of nature here.

On the other hand, if we take, for example, a simple transparent window, then here we see matter transformed into an indifferent milieu for rays of light, allowing them to pass through without any modification, not having any noticeable effect on them; and it is undoubtable that, from these two contrasting phenomena, the result obtained in the relation that occupies us is one and the same, and namely a negative one: simple transparent glass, just as black coal, does not belong to the ranks of beautiful phenomena and does not have any kind of aesthetic significance. And if such significance (in an elementary degree) inarguably belongs to a diamond, then this is evidently because neither dark substance nor light principle enjoys singular predominance in it, but they mutually penetrate one another in a certain ideal balance. On the one hand, the carbon matter here, preserving all the force of its resistance (as a solid body) distinguishes itself by contrast, becoming transparent, completely lucid, a characteristic invisible in its otherwise dark particularity. And, on the other hand, a ray of light captured by the crystal body of a diamond obtains a new fullness of phenomenal existence in it and from it, and by refraction is broken up or separated into its constituent colors in every facet; simple transparency is transformed into a complex collection of multicolored spectrums and re-flects in our eye in this new form. In this unmerged and undivided unity of matter and light both preserve their nature, but neither the one nor the other is visible in its individuality; rather, only the light-bearing matter and the embodied light are visible—lucid coal and petrified rainbow.

An absolute opposition between light and matter in their metaphysical substance and in their physical reality is impossible, and there is no need for us to maintain such an opposition. It is not possible to acknowledge light (as, for example, Schopenhauer does) as some kind of purely ideal essence; and likewise it is not possible to see in matter the naked thing-in-itself, absolutely bereft of all ideal attributes or distinctions and completely independent of all spiritual principle.[6] But no matter how anybody might philosophize about the essence of things—and, likewise, no matter what physical theories anybody might hold about atoms, ether, and motion—the relative and phenomenal contrast that undoubtedly exists between light and solid bodies, as such, is completely sufficient for our aesthetic problem. In this sense, light is in any case a supra-material, ideal agent. Thus, seeing that the beauty of a diamond completely depends on the lucidity of its substance, which captures in itself even scattered or unloosed rays of light, we should define beauty as *the transformation of matter through the embodiment in it of another, supra-material principle*. Later we will have to extend this definition and fill it with content; but its essence will remain immutable with an examination of the most complex manifestations of the beautiful not only in nature, but also in art.

And first of all, this understanding of beauty, constituted on the foundation of an elementary example of beautiful optical phenomena in nature, is fully sustained by our elementary *acoustic* example. Just as the ponderable and dark substance of carbon was expressed in diamond in the resplendent phenomenon of light, so too the material sexual instinct is expressed in the song of a nightingale in the form of harmonious sounds. In this case, the objective acoustic expression of sexual passion completely masks its material basis; it acquires an independent significance and can be abstracted from its most proximate physiological motive: it is possible to listen to a singing bird and to obtain an aesthetic impression from its singing, absolutely forgetting what prompted it to sing; precisely in the same way, in admiring the flash of a diamond, we do not need to think about its chemical substance.

But, in actual fact, just as it is necessary for a diamond to be crystallized carbon, so too it is necessary for a nightingale's song to be an expression of sexual attraction, part of which has crossed over into objective acoustic form. This song is a transformation of sexual instinct, a liberation of it from the crude physiological fact—this is animal sexual instinct embodying in itself *the Idea of love,* whereas the cries of an amorous cat on a roof are only a direct expression of a physiological essence that is not in control of itself. In this latter case the material motive predominates absolutely, while in the first it is counterbalanced by ideal form.

In this way, in our acoustic example, too, beauty turns out to be the result of the mutual action and the mutual penetration of two producers. Here, just as in the optic example, the ideal principle takes possession of the material fact and is embodied in it; and for its part, the material element, embodying in itself ideal content, is transformed and becomes resplendent.

Beauty is indeed a fact, a product of real natural processes perfected in the universe. Wherever ponderable matter is transformed into light-bearing bodies, wherever that action of a frenzied animal, aspiring to sensation, turns into a series of harmonious and rhythmic sounds—we have beauty in nature. It is absent wherever material elements of the world appear more or less *laid bare*—whether that be in the inorganic world, as crude formless matter, or in the world of living organisms, in their frenzied instinct for life. However, in the inorganic world, unpleasant objects and phenomena do not become unsightly through this, but remain simply indifferent in an aesthetic respect. A pile of sand or stone, bare earth, formless gray clouds giving vent to gentle rain—all of this, although bereft of beauty in nature, does not have in itself anything positively repulsive. The reason is clear: in phenomena of this order, universal life is found on the lowest elementary stages. It is of little substance, and the material principle has nothing in which to reveal the immensity of its resistance; it is here comparable to its sphere and makes use of the undisturbed domain of its meager existence.[7]

But wherever light and life have already been overcome by matter and universal significance has now begun to disclose its intrinsic plenitude, the unrestrained manifestation of the chaotic principle, defeating or repressing again the ideal form, naturally produces an acute impression of ugliness. And the higher on the rungs of universal development that the nakedness and frenzy of the material element appear anew, the more repulsive such manifestations are. Already in the animal kingdom we meet prominent examples of genuine ugliness. Entire branches of creation here represent only the naked embodiment of one of the functions of material life—sexual or alimentary. On the one hand, there are certain visceral intestinal worms, whose entire bodies are nothing more than sacks of the most elementary structure, containing in themselves only sexual organs, yet completely developed. On the other hand, worm-like larvae of insects (caterpillars, and so forth) seem to be one embodied instinct of feeding in all its insatiability; to a certain degree the same can also be said about giant cephalopoda mollusks. All the cited animals are undoubtedly ugly. But an extreme degree of ugliness is achieved only in the realm of the higher and most perfected natural forms: no animal can be as repulsive as a very ugly human being.

The bankruptcy (or at least insufficiency) of the popular aesthetic view that sees in beauty only a completely outward expression of inner content, indifferent to the question of what this very content consists in, is obscured by the existence of unsightly specimens in nature. In accordance with such an understanding, it follows to ascribe beauty to a mollusk or to a pig, since the body of these animals in perfection expresses their inner content, namely voracity. But it is clear precisely here that beauty in nature is not an expression of every content, but only of the content of Idea, that beauty is *the embodiment of Idea*.

III.

In the definition of beauty as *embodied Idea*, the second word (idea) eliminates the view according to which beauty can express *every* content; and the first word (embodied) rectifies as well the (still more widespread) view that finds in beauty not the actual realization, but only the apparition (*Schein*) of Idea, even though requiring for it ideal content.*[8] In the latter view, the beautiful, as a subjective psychological fact—i.e., the sensation of beauty, its manifestation or confluence in our spirit—itself represses beauty as the objective form of things in nature. Truly, beauty is an idea actually practicable, embodied in the world prior to the human spirit, and its embodiment is no less real and much more significant (in the cosmogonic sense) than those material elements in which it embodies itself. The play of rays of light in crystallized bodies, in any event, is no less real than the chemical substance of these bodies; and the modulation of birds' songs is the same natural reality as the act of reproduction.

---

* Ed. Hartmann, in his recently published voluminous and prolix "Aesthetics," has not in essence elevated himself above this view, in spite of his "transcendental realism."

Beauty, or embodied Idea, is the better half of our real world, namely that half which not only exists but also serves existence. In general, we call that which in itself is worthy of existence, "Idea." Speaking in absolutes, only an absolutely perfect or unconditional entity, completely free from every limitation and shortcoming, is worthy of existence. Particular or restricted entities, in themselves not having worthy or ideal existence, become connected to it through its relation to the absolute in the universal process, which is also the gradual embodiment of its Idea. A particular entity is ideal or worthy only insofar as it does not negate the universal, but gives it a place in itself, and exactly in the same way the general is ideal or worthy according to the extent to which it gives a place to the particular in itself. From here it is easy to deduce the following formal definition of Idea, or a worthy form of existence. It is *the absolute freedom of constituent parts in a perfected unified whole*.

The independence of the parts, or the scope of existence in various objects and phenomena, can be more or less full; the unity of the whole that this scope gives to its parts can be more or less perfect. From such relative distinctions there results a multitude of degrees in the realization of Idea, all the diversity, and all the complexity of the universal process. But, apart from the particular complexities in the process of its realization, the universal Idea in its very indissolubility is necessary from three aspects. In it are differentiated: (1) the freedom or autonomy of existence; (2) the plenitude of content, or meaning; and (3) the perfection of expression, or form. Without these three conditions there is no worthy, or ideal, existence. When considered principally from the aspect of its intrinsic unconditionality, as a desired or deigned absolute, Idea is "good"; from the aspect of the plenitude of particular attributes embraced by it, as a conceivable content for the mind, it is "true"; finally, from the aspect of its perfection or the completeness of its embodiment, as something really tangible in sensory existence, Idea is "beautiful."

Thus, it is necessary to differentiate in beauty the general ideal essence and the specific-aesthetic form in beauty just as in one of the determinate phases of the triune Idea. Only the specific-aesthetic form distinguishes beauty from truth and the good, since the ideal essence is one and the same in them—worthy existence or positive all-unity, the scope of particular existence in the unity of the universal. *This* is what we desire as the highest good, *this* is what we think of as truth, and *this* is what we sense as beauty; but in order for us *to sense* Idea, it is necessary that it be embodied in material reality. The perfection of this embodiment takes shape as beauty, as such, in its specific manifestation.

The criterion of worthy, or ideal, existence in general is the greatest independence of the parts in the greatest unity of the whole. The criterion of aesthetic worthiness is the greatest perfected and multifaceted embodiment of this ideal moment in a given substance. Of course, these criteria can coincide not at all and should be strictly differentiated in application to particular events. A perfectly weak degree of worthy or ideal existence can be embodied well in a given material to the highest degree, and an extremely imperfect expression of the most sublime ideal moments is possible in precisely the same way. In the realm of art this difference is striking, and the two criteria here—the general-ideal and the specific-aesthetic—can be confused only by completely untrained minds. The difference is less glaring in the realm of nature, but it undoubtedly exists in it as well, and it is very important not to forget this.

Let us take our two well-worn examples anew: on the one hand the intestinal worm and on the other—a diamond. The first expresses to a certain degree the Idea of life in the form of a living organism; the second, according to its ideal content, is a certain degree of lucidity of inorganic matter. But the Idea of an organic body, even if on the level of a worm, is more elevated than the Idea of a crystallized body, even if in the form of a diamond. In the latter, matter is only made lucid from without, while in the worm it is intrinsically life-giving. In a very simple organism we find an aggregate of a greater number of particular parts and a greater unity of them than in the most perfect stone; any organism is more complex and at the same time more individualized than stone.

So, according to the first criterion, an intestinal worm is above a diamond because it is of *more content*. But by applying strictly aesthetic criteria we arrive at another conclusion. In a diamond the simple and elementary Idea of a mineral made lucid (precious stone) is expressed more definitively and perfectly than the more complex and elevated Idea of organic (in particular animal) life is expressed in an intestinal worm. A diamond is an object perfect in its kind, for nowhere does such a force of strength or impermeability unite with such radiance; nowhere does one meet such a striking and subtle play of light in such a solid body. In a worm, on the contrary, we find one of the most imperfect, rudimentary expressions for the Idea of organic life in the realm to which this creature belongs. Even though a worm is already, according to the chemical composition of its tissues, a body more complex than a diamond, the *or-*

ganization of this body is most simplified and meager. Precisely in the same way, by virtue of individual unity, this most simple organism nevertheless surpasses every diamond, for it cannot in a manner similar to the latter be split indifferently while remaining itself. Yet, in an organic sense, this unity is so weak that it sometimes does not stand up even to the Idea of organism (the capability to divide into segments). Thus, from a strictly aesthetic point of view, a worm, though an extremely imperfect embodiment of its comparatively sublime Idea (an animal organism), should be placed immeasurably lower than a diamond, which, although of lowly content, is a perfected and finished expression of its Idea of stone-made-lucid.

IV.

Matter is inertness and impermeability of existence—a direct contrast to Idea, as positive all-permeability or all-unity. Only in *light* does matter free itself from its inertness and impermeability, and thus the visible world for the first time is broken up into two contrasting polarities. Light—or its weightless bearer, ether—is the elemental reality of Idea in its antithesis to solid matter, and in this sense it is the first principle of beauty in nature. Its further phenomena are conditional on the combination of light with matter. Such combination occurs of a two-fold sort: mechanical, or extrinsic, and organic, or intrinsic. Strictly light phenomena are produced by the first in nature, and phenomena of life by the second. Ancient science conjectured—and today's science proves—that organic life is a conversion of light. In this way matter becomes the bearer of beauty through the action of one and the same light principle, which at first superficially illuminates and then inwardly penetrates, organizes, and gives life.

In the inorganic world, beauty belongs either to objects and phenomena in which matter directly becomes the bearer of light or to those in which inanimate nature becomes as if animated and, in its motion, displays the characteristics of life. We leave to metaphysics the question of how much is of subjective illusion here, and how much is of life (i.e., the capacity for interior perceptions and independent motion) apart from the actual organic essences (plants and animals) that nature possesses in itself. Sufficient for us is the fact that, in the phenomena about which we speak, their beauty is conditional not on mechanistic movement, as such, but on the impression of living forces within the boundaries of aesthetic discourse.

But, first, a few words about the beauty of inorganic nature at *repose*, about beauty of a pure-light character.

The order of the embodiment of Idea, or of the phenomenon of beauty in the world, corresponds to the general cosmogonic order: in the beginning God created *the heavens*. . . . If our ancestors saw in the heavens the father of the gods, we, nevertheless, neither bowing to Svarog or Varun nor perceiving in the heavenly vault signs of a living personal being, admire its beauty no less than the pagans; consequently, it does not depend on our subjective notions, but is tied to actual attributes inherent in the expanses of the universe visible to us.[9] These aesthetic attributes of heaven are caused by light; it is "beautiful" only when illuminated. Neither on a gray, rainy day nor in a black starless night does the sky have any beauty. In speaking of this beauty, we understand precisely only phenomena of light which occur within the limits of the expanses of the universe that are accessible to our gaze.

The all-embracing sky is beautiful first as a picture of universal unity, as the expression of serene exultation, the eternal victory of the light principle over chaotic confusion, of the eternal embodiment of Idea in the entire volume of material existence. This general sense comes to light more definitely in the three main aspects of heavenly beauty—solar, lunar, and astral.

1. Universal all-unity and its physical signifier—light—in its proper activity of focus, is in the sun. Sunrise is the representation of the active victory of the forces of light. From this comes the special beauty of the sky at the moment when,

> Across the entire
> Ethereal immensity
> Is carried the universal carillon chime
> of victorious solar rays.[10]
>
> Tiutchev

The radiant beauty of the sky in bright midday—the very victory of light—is not in action but, now already achieved, in imperturbable motionless repose.

> And as the day dreams of reposing nature
> The undulating clouds pass by.[11]
>
> Fet

2. Universal all-unity from the aspect of the perception of its material nature in reflective light is in the passive feminine beauty of a moonlit night. As a natural transition from solar to lunar state—the beauty of an evening sky and setting sun [is] when a reduction of the direct central force of light rewards with a great variety of its nuances in an illuminated medium.

3. Universal all-unity and its signifier, light, in its elementary separation into a multiplicity of independent focii, embraced, however, by a general harmony—appear in the beauty of a starlit night. It is clear that in the latter, the Idea of positive all-unity is realized more fully and more perfectly than in the previous two. However, one should not forget that, just as does a direct impression from the beauty of the brilliant midday or a moonlit night, an aesthetic evaluation of this [starry] beauty embraces necessarily the entire representation of nature in a given moment. All the earthly objects and phenomena that are illuminated by the sun and moon have their own beauty strengthened by this particular illumination, in their turn magnifying the beauty of a lucid sky. While in contemplation of a starry night, the aesthetic impression is entirely delimited by the sky itself; a beauty of earthly objects merging into darkness cannot have meaning. If we eliminate this unevenness, and if we abstract from the beauty of an illuminated landscape in the aesthetic evaluation of the midday and moonlit sky, then everyone will agree that, from the three main types of sky, the starlit sky represents the greatest degree of beauty.*

Crossing over from astral infinity to the confined limits of our earthly atmosphere, we meet with beautiful phenomena that represent to different degrees the illumination of matter or the embodiment of the ideal principle in it. In this sense, clouds have independent beauty, illuminated by the morning or evening sun with varied nuances and combinations of color, as do the northern lights, and so forth. A *rainbow*—in which the dark and formless substance of water vapor is transformed in an instant into the vivid and full-spectrum revelation of embodied light and elucidated

---

* The differences that German aesthetics (especially at the time of Kant) suppose between beautiful and *awesome* (*Erhabenes*), in which a starlit sky relates to this latter aesthetic category, are well known. It seems to us that here a certain nuance of beautiful is made without sufficient foundation of the degree of an independent category contrasted to beautiful in general. However, it is not possible to ascribe any significant meaning to this terminological question; but in all cases in the Russian language we have every right to speak of the *beauty* of a starry sky.

matter—represents this Idea (of the mutual penetration of heavenly light and earthly element) more fully and more distinctly:

> How unexpected and vividly
> Across the moist heaven of blue
> An atmospheric arc has been erected
> In its momentary triumph!
> One end is thrust into forests,
> Clouds left behind by the other;
> She has captured the demi-sky
> And has grown faint in eminence.[12]
>
> Tiutchev

The beauty of a calm sea also belongs to the luminously beautiful. In water the material element is first freed from its inert and impenetrable solidity. This fluid element is a bond of earth and sky, and the significance of this appears vividly in the picture of a sea becoming calm, reflecting in itself the endless blue radiance of the heavens. Clearer still is this character of water's beauty in the smooth mirror of a lake or stream.

And luminous incarnations in solid bodies—noble metals and precious stones—should be added to the embodiments of light in gaseous matter (clouds, rainbows) and to the just-mentioned embodiments of it in liquid matter. What has been said above regarding diamonds relates here to a greater or lesser degree.

V.

We cross over from the phenomena of calm, triumphant light to the phenomena of a lively and apparently free life in the inorganic world. According to its very broadest definition, life is the play, or the free action, of particular forces and circumstances united in an individual whole. To the extent that one of the essential signs of ideal or worthy existence (which can be equally neither abstract-universal, i.e., groundless, nor incidental-particular) is expressed in this play, to the extent of its incarnation in phenomena of the material world, actual or apparent life in nature represents aesthetic significance. First of all, flowing water in the variety of its forms—brooks, mountain streams, waterfalls—is differentiated by this beauty of apparent life in the inorganic world. The aesthetic mean-

ing of this living movement is strenthened by its infiniteness, as if expressing the insatiable pangs of individual existence separated from absolute all-unity.

> A wave in parting with the sea
> Does not know calm,
> Whether it beats as a seething spring
> Or flows as a stream,
> All murmers and sighs
> In succession and in expanse
> Yearning for boundless,
> Unfathomable blue sea.[13]

And this very boundless sea in its impetuous agitation acquires new
beauty as an image of restless life, of a gigantic upsurge of elemental forces,
which cannot, however, sever the common bond of the universe and destroy its unity, except by its complementary motion, by lightning and
thunder.

> How fine you are, o nocturnal sea,
> Now sparkling—now blue-gray black!
> In moonshine as if alive
> It walks, and breathes, and splashes.
> On an endless, on a familiar expanse,
> Brilliance and motion, rumble and thunder . . .
> The sea is soaked with a dim radiance,
> How good are you in the nocturnal absence of human life!
> You great swell, you swell of sea!
> Whose holiday are you celebrating?
> Waves carry thundering and flashing,
> Vigilant stars gaze from on high.[14]
>
> > Tiutchev

Chaos, i.e., ugliness itself, is the necessary background of every earthly
beauty, and the aesthetic value of phenomena such as a stormy sea depends
namely on the fact that beneath them stirs chaos.

The motion of living elemental forces in nature has two chief nuances:
free play and terrible conflict. One and the same phenomenon of nature, the thunderstorm, can represent both the one and the other nuance,

appearing according to the conditions in which it occurs. The majestic beauty of thunderstorms, just as of a stormy sea, depends on the stirring chaos and on the excited intensity of elemental forces contesting the final triumph of luminous universal order. A thunderstorm creates a completely different impression "at the beginning of May":

> When the first spring thunder,
> As if frolicking and playing,
> Rumbles in the pale-blue sky.
> Youthful thunder peals . . .
> Now a light rain has splashed, dust flies . . .
> Hanging pearls of rain,
> And the sun gilds the fields . . .
> From the hills runs a nimble stream,
> In the forest the avian din does not quiet
> And the din of the forest, and the mountainous noise,
> All the while echoes gaily to the thunder . . .
> You speak, frivolous Heb,
> Feeding Zeus's eagle,
> Goblet of boiling thunder from the sky
> Mockingly spilled onto earth.[15]
>
> Tiutchev

And here the very same poet has a picture of an approaching storm on a summer's night, at the moment when chaotic forces still only torpidly prepare for the impending frightful struggle:

> Not yet cooled from the sultry heat
> The July night glistened,
> and over the lackluster earth
> The sky with full storm
> From sheet lightning flickered . . .
> Like heavy eyelashes
> Opened wide now and then,
> And through the fugitive sheets of lightning
> Someone's threatening pupils
> Blazed across the earth. . . .

Or better still:

Fiery sheet lightning flashes
Alternating in sparking flame,
Like demons deaf and dumb
Conduct a conversation among themselves.
According to a signal agreed upon
Suddenly the sky flashes in streaks,
And from the darkness quickly appear
Fields and far-off forests!
And here again all darkens,
All quiets in the tactful darkness
As if a secret matter
Has been resolved there up on high. . . .[16]

To the extent that we find an actual presentiment (anticipation) of life in some of the phenomena of the inorganic world (which the aesthetic significance of these phenomena is also conditional upon)—to that extent—*sound* in inorganic nature acquires a quality of beauty as expression of its own *life*. The life of material nature is inwardly penetrated by light, it absorbs and transforms it into internal motion and later communicates this movement through an external medium—in sound. Wherever this general ideal significance of sound as a living response of matter to the influence of light is not clear for us in a particular auditory phenomenon (such as the statue of Memnon, having sounded at dawn), wherever bodies reverberate not out of themselves, but only out of extrinsic and chance influences, there is no aesthetic impression obtained from sound.*[17] For all that, it also happens that certain sounds, which in their separateness have a manifestly mechanical character and therefore do not create any impression of beauty, can express in their aggregate the life of a certain collective whole and in that capacity acquire aesthetic significance. So, for example, there is nothing beautiful in the clatter of wheels on pavement; but the noise of a city, although it too is composed chiefly of similar unbeautiful sounds, creates an undoubtedly aesthetic impression in its aggregate (from afar). European cities with their indefinitely expanding environs present little convenience for such observation. But whoever has had

---

* *A note for readers concerned with logic*: it in no way follows from the fact that all beautiful sounds of inner life should be expressed, that all auditory expressions of inner life be beautiful.

occasion to approach a great eastern city, for example, Cairo, from the sides on which it is bordered by the desert, has probably hearkened with enjoyment to the auditory life of this collective animal.

In the phenomena of inorganic nature about which we already spoke (stormy sea, thunderstorm), sound enters only as one of the elements of aesthetic impression. In a raging sea, already the very form of waves displays the character of life, like their sound.

> You, my sea wave,
> Capricious wave,
> Calm or playing, how
> Full of marvelous life you are!
> Whether you are laughing at the sun,
> Reflecting the vault of heaven,
> Or crushing effortlessy and pounding
> In the wild abyss of the waters.[18]
>
> Tiutchev

According to its form and lively motion, a wave appears to the same poet as a galloping horse of the sea:

> O, zealous horse, O horse of the sea,
> With a pale-green mane,
> Now submissive, gently tame,
> Now wildly playful.
> You were raised by a tempestuous whirlwind
> In God's vast field,
> He taught you to point your ears,
> To play, to gallop freely![19]

In other cases, total *silence* in nature directly strengthens the aesthetic impression or even forms its necessary condition, as we saw above (in that same poet) in the picture of an approaching nocturnal thunderstorm. But then, in other phenomena of the inorganic world, their entire living and aesthetic significance is expressed exclusively in auditory impressions alone. Such are mournful sighs forged in the cosmic dungeon of Chaos.

> Oh why do you quarrel, nocturnal wind
> Why complain so madly?

What does your strange voice mean,
Now mutely plaintive, now noisy?
By a language understandable to the heart,
You reiterate an incomprehensible torment
And burrow into it and burst
Frantic sounds now and again!
Oh do not sing these frightful songs,
About ancient, native chaos,
How greedily the world of the nocturnal soul
Gives ear to a favorite tale.
It bursts from the mortal chest,
And thirsts to merge with the infinite,
Oh, do not awaken the slumbering storms,
'Neath them chaos stirs.[20]

Tiutchev

VI.

Impulses of elemental forces or elemental impotence, in and of themselves, are alien to beauty, yet give birth to beauty already in the inorganic world, becoming willy-nilly the material, in different aspects of nature, for more or less a clear and full expression of the universal Idea or positive all-unity.

The creative principle of the universe (Logos), reflected by matter from without as light and from within as life ignited in matter, arises in the form of distinctive animal and plant organisms and stable forms of life, which, proceeding gradually all the while to greater and greater perfection, can serve in the end as the material and the means for the actual embodiment of completely indivisible Idea.

The actual sustenance of organic forms, the material of the biological process, is taken *entirely* from the material world: these are the spoils won by the creative Mind from chaotic matter. In other words, organic bodies are only the conversion or transformation of inorganic matter, in the very same sense in which St. Isaac's Cathedral is the transformation of granite and the Venus de Milo is a transformation of marble. To recognize in living bodies a special life force present to them exclusively is the same as ascribing a special patronal force to a temple, or a special sculptural force to a statue. It is obvious that from the point of view of the actual composition in organic bodies, there is absolutely nothing besides physical and chemical elements, precisely like the point of view that sees nothing besides stone, gold, and other materials in a temple, and in the marble statue—nothing besides marble. But, from a formal aspect, in the construction of living organisms we have a new, comparatively higher degree of manifestation of the very creative principle that has already acted in the inorganic world—a new, relatively more perfected mode of embodiment of that same Idea, which has already found itself expression in inanimate nature as well, although more superficially and less definitely. The very same form of all-unity that the universal Artist casts with prominent and simple characteristics onto a starry sky or in a multi-colored rainbow, He paints delicately and in detail within plants and animal bodies.

Three main features are discerned by us in the world of organic essences: 1) the intrinsic essence or *prima materia* of life, a striving or desire to live, i.e., to feed and reproduce—hunger and love (more passive in plants, more active in animals); 2) the appearance of this life, those morphological and physiological conditions, for instance, by which nourishment and reproduction of each organic type take shape (and in connection with them, other, second-degree functions as well); and finally, 3) the biological goal—not in the sense of extrinsic teleology, but from the point of view of comparative anatomy, which defines relative to the entire organic world a place and significance of those particular forms, which in each type are sustained by nourishment and are perpetuated by reproduction. The biological goal itself, moreover, appears two-fold: on the one hand, organic types are *stages* (in part transient, in part permanent) of a general biological *process* that arrives at the creation of the human body from primitive mold; but, on the other hand, these types can be regarded as *members* of a universal organism, having an independent significance in the life of the whole.[21]

A general picture of the organic world displays two fundamental characteristics, without equal recognition of which no understanding of universal life and no philosophy of nature are possible, and consequently, no aesthetic of nature either. First, it is indubitable that the organic world is not a product of so-called spontaneous creation, or that it cannot be *directly deduced* from one absolute creative principle; for in such a case it would have had to display absolute undisturbed perfection and harmony not only in the whole, but also in all of its parts. Meanwhile, reality far from corresponds to such an optimistic conception. In this case, certain facts and discoveries of positive science have a decisive significance. Regarding the earthly organic world—especially in its paleontological history, which is sufficiently well-known in our day—we find the sharply outlined picture of a difficult and complex process, determined by the struggle of heterogenous principles, which only after long effort is resolved as a certain stable equilibrium. All this does not resemble an absolutely perfect creation, directly emanating from the creative will of a single Divine Artist: our biological history is a retarded and painful birth.*[22] We see here manifest signs of an internal struggle, jolts and convulsive concussions, blind and groping motions; an unfinished draft of unsuccessful creations—so many monstrous results and miscarriages! All these *paleozoa,* these antediluvian oddities: *megatherms, plesiosaurs, icthyosaurs, pteradactyls*—could they be perfect and direct creations of God? If they fulfilled their assignment and merited approval of the Creator, how could it happen that they gave way to forms more balanced and harmonious, and completely vanished from our earth?

Nevertheless, although the life-giving Agent of the universal process also throws away without regret his inconvenient trials, he values—and in this is the second fundamental characteristic of organic nature—not only the goal of the process, but each of its innumerable stages, only so that each stage in its measure and according to its own way will embody the Idea of life. Reconquering material step-by-step from chaotic elements for its organic works, the cosmic Mind cares for each of its spoils and abandons only those in which its victory was a sham, on which the infinity of chaos had laid its indelible print.

In general, the creative principle of nature is not indifferent to the beauty of its works. Therefore, in the animal kingdom, where positively ugly creatures are met, they either belong to specimens of *the vanished* (so-called antediluvian), i.e., cast aside by nature out of its unfitness; or they have a *parasitic* character (intestinal worms, lice, bedbugs) and are consequently devoid of independent significance, being only morbidly animated excrements of another organism; or, finally, unsightly forms belonging to the worm-like *larvae* of insects, representing only a transitional stage in the development of the whole animal. In their final form these very animals

---

* See the elucidation of this indication from a theological (biblical) point of view in my book *La Russie et L'Eglise Universelle,* 2nd ed. (Paris), pp. 248–252.

(butterflies, beetles, and so forth) are not only liberated from the disgusting appearance of a worm, but some of them even serve as completely vivid specimens of beauty in nature. And (according to general rule) only in this form—their more beautiful winged form—does the insect obtain the capacity to couple and reproduce to perpetuate its form. If larvae mated and reproduced, then they would perpetuate this unsightly animal form as the final one. But nature is not indifferent to beauty. It allows unsightly forms in the capacity of transitional stages, but for the perpetuation of its works strives to communicate to them a beauty such as is possible in each kind. True, there exist other unsightly forms apart from parasites and vermiform larvae, and even in the higher classes of the animal kingdom—for example, swine. But only the domestic fatted swine is repulsive—a *wild* pig or boar is not at all repulsive, and is even not devoid of a beauty of a kind; yet here the subject is now an abuse of man, and not a work of nature. In general, if beauty in nature (as we maintain) is the real-objective work of a complex and gradual cosmogonic process, then the existence of ugly phenomena is fully comprehensible and necessary. The most repulsive forms of the animal kingdom have served and will yet serve as corroboration and illustrations of our ideas.—After these elucidations we can turn to an aesthetic survey of the organic world.

VII.

In the plant kingdom, the ethereal light principle now not only illuminates inert matter and stimulates impulsive transitory motion in it (as in the phenomena of elemental beauty), but also *intrinsically elevates* it from within and propels it, *constantly* overcoming the force of gravity. In plants, light and material join in a concretely indissoluble combination; for the first time they permeate one another and become a single indivisible life, and this life raises the earthly element upward, compelled to reach toward the sky and sun. Between the inertness of minerals and the erratic motion of animals, this unnoticeable intrinsic movement upwards, or *growth*, constitutes the characteristic property of plants, which get their name from it as well.[23] Insofar as the light form and dark matter here for the first time organically and indivisibly merge in one whole, a plant is the first real and living embodiment of the celestial principle on earth, the first actual transformation of the earthly element. The two cosmogonic principles, which in the phenomena of the inorganic world only superficially adjoin and stimulate one another from without, are truly united here and give birth to one indivisibly dual, heavenly/earthly essence of growth.

> As if sensing the duality of life
> And covering it twice—
> They both sense the earth as home
> And entreat to the sky.[24]
>
> Fet

In the plant kingdom, life expresses itself in an objective direction, predominantly in the production of beautiful organic forms. In this first living outcome of heavenly and earthly forces, intrinsic life still only distinguishes itself weakly: this is serenely transformed earth quietly rising toward the heavens. The material principle elevated to a new degree of existence—to the stage of living essence—has not yet succeeded in developing a corresponding internal intensity, it is as if frozen in the general sense of its lucidity. Of the two inseparable, but nevertheless different, aspects of organic life in the plant world, the aspect of *organization* prevails decisively over the aspect of *life*. A plant, though alive, is still more an *organized body* than a living being: in plants, visible form is more significant than intrinsic condition. The latter exists only to a weak degree—the soul of a plant, as has already been noticed long ago, is a day-dreaming soul. Therefore, the main method for the expression of intrinsic subjective conditions—a voice—is also totally lacking in all plants; but they are endowed much more uniformly with a beauty of visible form than are animals, and, generally speaking, they surpass them in this respect. For plants, visual beauty is an actually *attained* goal; therefore, the organs of reproduction (flowers), by which, in the most significant part of the plant kingdom, a particular appearance is perpetuated, at the same time represent as well the most developed form of plant beauty in its specific character: naive, peaceful, slumbering.[25]

Since in the plant world the main point is not in intrinsic content, not in the intensity and fullness of subjective life, but in a perfected extrinsic expression (even if of a comparatively simple content), then the natural difference between the higher and lower plants is determined correspondingly to the degrees of their visible perfection or beauty; for example, the aesthetic criterion coincides here, generally speaking, with the natural-scientific, which, as we now see, is not at all observed in the animal kingdom. The two major divisions of the plant world are characterized by the presence or absence of a *flower*, that complex organ in which plant beauty is predominantly centered. Generally speaking, more beautiful plants are furnished with colors and thus comprise the higher order of phanerogamae, but plants that are devoid of colors and in general not distinguished by beauty belong to the lower order of *cryptogamae*. And, among the latter, the lowest according to structure—algae, mosses—are also the least beautiful, whereas comparatively more complex or higher ones—ferns—possess a greater degree of beauty. We see something completely different among animals. Although they too are separated into two major divisions, lower and higher—invertebrates and vertebrates—it is in no way possible to say that the higher are in general more beautiful than the lower; the aesthetic and zoologic criteria do not coincide here at all. Butterflies, which undoubtedly surpass in beauty the greater part of the higher animals, are one of the most beautiful zoological forms belonging to the order of invertebrates, and consequently to the lower of the two main divisions of the animal kingdom. And, generally speaking, among the order of vertebrates, the degree of zoological development does not correspond to the degree of beauty at all. The lowest of the four classes—fish—is very rich in beautiful forms, whereas in the very highest—mammals—such unaesthetic creatures as hippopotamuses, rhinoceroses, and whales occupy a prominent place. The most beautiful and at the same time the most musical vertebrate animals belong to the middle class—birds—and not to the higher; and in the latter class (mammals), which represents the highest degree of zoological development, a quadruped (an ape) is at the same time also the most unadorned. Evidently, in the animal kingdom beauty is not yet an *attained goal*; organic forms exist here not only for the sole sake of visible perfection, but serve as well, even chiefly, as a means for the development of the most intensive manifestations of viability. However, ultimately, these manifestations are not equilibrated and do not enter into the world of the human organism, where the greatest power and fullness of intrinsic vital conditions unites with the most perfected visible form—in the excellence of the female body, this highest synthesis of animal and plant beauty.

But if the world of animals represents (in comparison with plants) less food for direct aesthetic observation, then for the philosophy of beauty, the animal kingdom contains many especially curious and edifying data, for the analysis of which we are beholden, certainly, not to aesthetes according to profession, but to naturalists, and—at their head—the great Darwin, in his work on sexual selection. Although Darwin's goal here was to corroborate and supplement the theory of the origin of species by the path of natural selection in the struggle for existence (a subject extraneous to our current discussion), the significance of the observations and indications collected in this book (those belonging to others as well as to Darwin himself) is not exhausted with this. Many of them are interesting and important for us because they demonstrate the objective reality of beauty in nature independently of subjective human tastes.

VIII.

A potentiality—but still *just* a potentiality—of new and more perfected embodiments of the all-unity idea in beautiful forms is discovered on each new stage of universal development, with each new living extension and complexity of natural existence: we know that a substantial degree of natural existence in and of itself still does not vouch for its beauty, that the cosmogonic criterion does not coincide with the aesthetic and even finds itself partly in direct opposition to it. And this is understandable; with existence elevated to a higher degree and thus reinforced intrinsically, the elemental foundation of the universe (blind natural will) now acquires a capacity as well for a fuller and more profound subjugation to the ideal principle of the cosmos—which, in such case, also embodies in it a new, more perfected form of beauty. And, at the same time, in the chaotic element on this higher level of existence, the contrasting capacity of opposition to the ideal principle is, moreover, also reinforced by the possibility to realize this opposition on more complex and significant material.

The beauty of living (organic) creatures is more elevated, but at the same time also *rarer* than the beauty of inanimate nature; we know that positive ugliness too begins only where life begins. The passive life of plants still represents little opposition to the ideal principle, which is also embodied here in the beauty of forms pure and lucid, but of little content. The chaotic principle, fossilized in mineral and slumbering in the plant kingdom, is aroused for the first time in the soul and life of animals toward an active self-assertion, and opposes its intrinsic insatiability to the objective Idea of a perfected organism. Animals created an impression of somnambulant life on one of the German philosophers. It seems it might be more correct to compare them with the insane and with maniacs: further, we will see examples of monomania with which entire classes and types of animals are afflicted.[26] Be that as it may, distinctly imprinted both in the general paleontological history of the development of the entire animal kingdom and within the individual embryological history of each living organism is the persistent resistance of a revitalized chaos to higher organic forms, which are eternally marked in the mind of the universal Artist, who must all the while narrow the field of battle more and more for the achievement of lasting victories. And each of his new victories opens the possibility of new defeats: with every higher degree of organization and beauty attained, more powerful deviations, more profound ugliness, also appear, as a higher inverse manifestation of the original ugliness that lies at the foundation both of life and of all cosmic existence.

If, with the appearance of organic matter—animate protoplasm, in the form of the most simple, mostly microsopic, animals and plants—soil is created for new, more lasting and significant embodiments of the universal Idea in actual forms of beauty, then it is clear that in and of itself this soil has no positive relation to beauty. Universal essential ugliness announces itself here on a new stage in part with the material-passive (female) aspect in the first plants, and in part with the active-chaotic (male) aspect in the first animals. The embryos of the entire animal kingdom are as unsightly as the embryos of an individual living organism, even of the very highest one. In zoology, the first animals carry the characteristic title of unsightly or formless—*amorphozoa*. And without any doubt this stirring and motive ugliness is more repulsive than the peaceful formlessness of the first plants. But, of course, the very simplicity and insubstantiality of these *protista* does not allow them to be actual specimens of animal unsightliness. Simple formlessness alone is insufficient for this; a repulsive form is necessary. We find such a positive ugly form, serving in more or less open view as the basis of all animal organization, in the *worm*.

The form of the worm, as was already noted above, is a direct expression, or the embodiment *laid bare*, of two fundamental animal instincts—the sexual and the alimentary in all their immeasurable insatiability. This is clearest of all in those intestinal worms that feed with all their essence, with the entire exterior of their body through endosmosis (sucking), and thus do not display any organs, apart from the sexual; and these display a striking contrast with the extreme simplification of all the remaining organization in their powerful development and complex structure. Such are, for example, *acanthocephali*, in which—not speaking now about the complete absence of sensory organs—there is neither mouth nor intestine nor *anus*, but which, according to the expression of Claus, are graphically noted by "powerful sexual organs" against such a defective background.*[27] Several monstrous phenomena in sexual life itself, in the mutual relations of both sexes, correspond as well to this excessive anatomical development of sexual organs. So in *Distomum haematobium* (in the order *Tremotodes distomidae*) the male, although thicker, is shorter than the female, and always carries the latter with him in a special cavity of his abdominal part.[†] A contrasting and still more monstrous phenomenon is *trichosomum crassicauda* (*Nematodes*), in which, according to the observations of Leuckart, very undersized males in groups of two or three, and sometimes of four and five, live together within the uterine cavity of the female.[28] In the class of Annelida the ugliness of the basic specimen is alleviated a little by more complex organization, but an inordinate development and diversity of sexual organs (especially in the order *Oligochaetae*)[‡] does not allow the Idea of life any harmonious incarnation. The basic vermicular form on a much higher stage of organization is also manifestly preserved in mollusks, which Linnaeus directly related to *vermes*, and not without foundation. "From the time that the organization and development of these animals became better known, it turns out that they really have a relation to worms."[§][29] Incidentally, "according to form, cilial integument and organization, larvae of mollusks have much in common with *tricophorae*, or Loven's larvae, characteristic of many worms."[|][30] However, from an aesthetic point of view, the adult animal does not surpass its larvae at all in those specimens of mollusks that pass through a larval stage in their development. We do not see that among insects, in which the vermicular basic form (which is, according to the latest scientific opinions, in genetic affinity with Annelida)[#] in its naked ugliness is preserved only at the larval stage, and in the developed animal is concealed under a more or less beautiful winged integument.

The rudimentary worm, cloaked from without among insects, *is absorbed inwardly* among vertebrate animals: their *womb* is that same worm,

---

* Claus, "Zoology" (Russ. trans., Odessa 1888), vol. 1, p. 345.

† Ibid., p. 315.

‡ Ibid., p. 367.

§ Ibid., vol. 2, p. 1.

| Ibid., p. 6.

Ibid., vol. 1, p. 533.

not only in the etymological but also in the zoogenic sense.[31] This inter-
nally absorbed worm also obtains such predominance in a number of vertebrate animals, belonging to the class of fish and amphibians, that it im-
parts its form to the entire body of the animal. Such are, in particular,
snakes, which out of all the vertebrate animals most resemble worms, and
therefore are the most repulsive. There is no necessity to enlarge upon the
fact that this return to vermicular exterior is associated in these animals
also with an intrinsic comparison to the worm, i.e., with a new, inverse
self-affirmation of savage life in its bloodthirsty and voluptuous instinct.

The predominance of blind and limitless brutality over the Idea of
organism—that is, of the interior and exterior balance of life's elements—
is a predominance of matter over form, vividly expressed in the typical
figure of a worm; and it is only the foremost and the essential reason for ugliness in the animal kingdom. Another two, which are also of a common
character, are united with it. We know that formlessness, or instability of
form, in and of itself is something indifferent in an aesthetic sense (for example, formless and colorless clouds). But when in the animal kingdom
formlessness appears on those of its stages that already presuppose more or
less complex and stable organization, then such a relapse into elementary
protoplasm, being in direct contradiction to a given organic Idea, becomes
a source of positive ugliness. For example, snails and other slugs, apart from
the fact that they already rather clearly preserve the ugly "worm" type, are
repulsive as well according to their primitive formlessnes and spinelessness,
not at all corresponding to their comparatively complex internal organization. That very reason—the predominance of a formless mass—makes
higher animals such as whales and seals unattractive also. However, insofar
as this depends on an excessive accumulation of fat as a result of excessive
feeding here, our second reason of zoological ugliness (relapsing formlessness) coincides with the first (the brutality of animal instinct). This is fully
apparent in the case of those domestic animals that *become* formless and
unsightly as a result of artificial fattening. A third reason of ugliness in the
animal kingdom, and namely in several higher (vertebrate) animals (frogs,
apes), consists in the fact that they, remaining fully animal, resemble man
as if to caricature him. Here it is not possible to see only subjective impression alone, for, apart from the visual comparison with man, in these
animals a real anatomical presentiment (anticipation) of a higher form is
noted, one which does not correspond to the remaining characteristics of
the lower organization; and this very disparity or disharmony also constitutes an objective reason of their unsightliness.

All manifestation of animal unsightliness in its innumerable concrete variations and nuances can be placed under these three indicated formal reasons, or categories—1) excessive development of material brutality, 2) relapse to formlessness, and 3) caricatured anticipation of a higher form. But these three reasons can be, in essence, reduced to one, namely—the resistance that the material basis of life on various stages of the zoogenic process presents to the organizational forces of the ideal cosmic principle. Now, it is necessary for us to consider by what means this resistance is overcome, and beauty produced in animal nature.

IX.

The universal Artist had to work long and hard in order that ideal beauty be embodied in the realm of life—the basic matter of which is formless slime, and the typical representative, the worm. Until the appearance of animal life, terrestrial matter already had served the embodiment of a two-fold beauty—mineral and plant. And here we see that in the animal kingdom as well, prior to intrinsically overcoming the active resistance of animated matter and regenerating it in beautiful forms of higher animal organisms, the cosmic Architect uses zoological material for the production of new kinds of primal beauty, not having specifically an animal character, but partly belonging to the inorganic realm and partly reminiscent of plant forms. And, in the first place, unsightly and more or less vermicular polyps create entire forests of beautiful coral, which, according to their composition from inorganic matter, should be related to the order of minerals, but according to visible form resemble trees and flowers. To lesser degrees, that very striving to reproduce mineral-plant beauty on the foundation of animal matter in an extrinsic manner is noted in so-called starfish, sea lilies, and so forth. Further, ugly mollusks, remaining in all their repulsive formlessness, generate a hard inorganic beauty of multi-colored and multi-variegated shells; and, finally, one of these animals secretes the precious pearl.

Here in mollusks, as well as in polyps, animal life produces beauty only as an exterior inorganic deposit and dresses itself in it in a purely external way, as in a dwelling, and not in its own form. To a certain degree, the same can be said about horny deposits in certain higher animals, such as turtles; later manifestation of this kind of animal architecture we find among the class of mammals in the so-called armadillo, where it, however, loses its aesthetic significance.

We find in winged insects another less superficial relation between beautiful vestments and the animals that produce these for themselves. In place of inorganic constructions, such as corals for the polyp or shells for the mollusk, the wings of a butterfly or beetle are inseparable organic appendages to their body, and they are related to them in about the same way as flowers are to plants. Similar to the way in which plants have their sexual organs in a flower (phanerogamous), these insects also only in their winged stage achieve sexual adulthood and mate with one another. Just as it is according to organic composition and the complex structure of the wings themselves, so it is also according to their defined and close morphological relationship to the rest of the body of the insect; we should acknowledge here an aesthetic action of the generative ideal principle on animal matter that is in essence more profound and important than in inorganic shells and corals, being extrinsic to the animal body itself. However, the most beautiful butterfly too is no more than a winged worm. If the dualism between beautiful form and the ugliness of animal matter is not expressed here in all its power in the manner *of two* separate and heterogenous *bodies*, as in the mollusk and its shell, then nevertheless the duality here is not vanquished even by the perceptible form, inasmuch as the beautiful wings and the vermicular torso make up *two* sharply marked, although also organically joined, *halves* in the body of the insect.

This duality of beautiful form and ugliness of matter is overcome, finally, in the first use, at least in an exterior form, in vertebrate animals, which, absorbing into themselves their worm (or their womb), make it completely imperceptible, and at the same time the entire exterior of their body is tightly covered with more or less beautiful integument (scales, feathers, fleece, and fur). In cases when such covers in vertebrate animals are absent, as for example in frogs, this nakedness is one of the reasons for their ugliness (beyond what is indicated above).

The cosmic Artist knows that the basis of an animal body is unsightly, and he attempts in every way to cover and beautify it. His goal is not to destroy or eliminate ugliness, but that it first be covered by and then also transformed into beauty. Therefore, by enigmatic suggestions that we call instinct, he arouses animals themselves to create all sorts of membranes or envelopes from their own flesh and blood; he compels the snail to crawl into a shell constructed and whimsically embellished by it itself, a shell which for its utilitarian purpose (presupposing such) has no need at all of such a beautiful form; he compels the repulsive caterpillar to dress itself with many-colored wings that it grows for itself; and fish, birds, and beasts—to sew themselves up completely in glittering scales, multi-colored feathers, soft fleece, and fluffy fur.

But higher animals—birds and certain mammals even more (the cat family, also deer, chamois, and so forth)—apart from their beautiful exterior covers, represent as well in all their corporeal form a beautiful embodiment of the Idea of life—well-proportioned strength, a harmonious correlation of parts, and free-and-easy mobility of the whole. Under this ideal definition come all the numerous types and shades of animal beauty, the enumeration and description of which are not part of our task, but are a matter for descriptive zoology. We are also obliged to leave aside as well the question: On which paths has the generative power of the universal Artist led nature to the creation of beautiful animal forms? This question can be answered only by metaphysical cosmogyny. We can conclude our aesthetic discussion about beauty in nature with an indication of the phenomena that empirically corroborate the objective character of this beauty, as noted above.

X.

The phenomena of sexual selection that were observed by Darwin and other naturalists are completely insufficient for the explanation of the beauty of all animal forms: they relate almost exclusively only to exterior adornments or ornamental beauty in various animals. But here the matter is not in the intrinsic importance of explicable phenomena, but in the indubitable evidence of the independent objective significance of aesthetic motive, although in the most superficial of its expressions.

At a time when many rectilinear minds attempted to reduce human aesthetics to utilitarian bases in the interests of a postivistic-scientific worldview, the greatest representative of this very worldview in our century showed the independence of aesthetic motive from utilitarian goals even in the animal kingdom, and upon this positively based an authentically ideal aesthetic for the first time. This integral contribution would be sufficient to immortalize the name of Darwin, even if he was not the author of the theory of origin of species by natural selection in the struggle for existence—a theory which has determined precisely and followed up in detail one of the most important material factors of the universal process.

The life of an animal is determined by two major interests: to maintain itself by means of nourishment and to perpetuate its form by means of reproduction. This latter goal, of course, does not exist in the consciousness of the animal itself, but is achieved by nature obliquely, through the arousal of sexual attraction in heterosexual individuals. But the cosmic Artist makes this sexual attraction not only for perpetuation, but also for the adornment of given animal forms. Individuals of the energetic sex, males, pursue the female and struggle with one another on account of her; and here it turns out, says Darwin, despite all foreknowledge, that the capacity to *entice* the female in different ways has in certain cases a greater significance than the capability to defeat other males in open struggle.*

This striving *to entice* comes to light in animals even where it would least be expected. "Quiconque a eu l'occasion," says Agassiz, "d'observer les amours des limaçons, ne saurait mettre en doute la seduction déployée dans les mouvements et les allures qui preparent et accomplissent le double embrassement de ces hermaphrodites."†[32] Neither Agassiz nor Darwin explain in what the mutual enticement precisely consists here, and whether this serves any adornment of these slugs. But if snails really captivate each other with their allurements, then other mollusks that see better can have a similar and even easier effect by means of the beauty of their shells. The point is clearer in *Crustacea* and in spiders. Here certain specimens of males take on, at the time of sexual maturity, a vivid and variegated coloring that they did not have earlier and which is absent in the females.‡

"Every traveler to tropical forests has been struck by the sound which cicada males make. Females remain silent, as even the Greek poet Xenarchus noted: 'Happily live the cicada: all of them have silent wives.'"§ Fritz Müller writes to Darwin from southern Brazil that he was often present during the musical competition between two or three male cicadas who had especially clear voices and sat at a significant distance from one another. As soon as one ended his song, the other then immediately began, and in this manner they continually alternated with each other. And Darwin notes correctly that since here so much competition among males comes to light, it is completely probable that the females not only discern them by the sounds they produce, but that they, similarly to avian females, are enticed or aroused by the male possessing the most attractive voice.|[33]

---

* Darwin, *The Descent of Man and Selection in Relation to Sex* (German translation Victor Caruso, Stuttgart 1871), vol. 1, pp. 246–24 [sic].

† Agassiz, "De l'Espece et la Classification" (1869), p. 106.

‡ Darwin, *Descent of Man*, vol. 1, pp. 301–303.

§ Ibid., p. 313.

| Ibid., p. 314.

Not only was a special pre-mating coloring noted of insect wings of males belonging to the class *Neuroptera*, but in different specimens a preference of one or another color was observed.* This latter fact is important, because it shows the susceptibility and sensitivity of these insects to optic impressions as such, independent of any utilitarian significance, which in a given case, it is not possible to prove. Such an aesthetic sensitivity must be ascribed to beetles (*Coleoptera*), in which the wings are not only painted with glittering metallic colors, but are often also covered with drawn stripes, circles, crosses, and other elegant patterns—and all this only in *sighted* types; the blind *never* have decorated wings or wings covered with drawn patterns.† In several specimens in this order of insects the males are distinguished by their huge and completely changeable and freakish horns, which, as Darwin shows, undoubtedly have the character of adornment for the enticement of females.‡ Special organs for the production of sound, noted in several specimens, also serve that same purpose.§

In certain tropical specimens of the order *Lepidoptera* (butterflies), the beauty of their wings—which, according to the expression of Darwin, is not possible to describe with words |—represents that very same character, for it is undoubtable that the males principally distinguish themselves both by the glittering beauty and the variety of their wings, since the females are comparatively colorless and monotoned. This alone now shows that the beauty of wings cannot serve the utilitarian goals of *defense* in the struggle for existence (through the likening of an insect to the flower on which it sits, and so forth); females are no less in want of such a defense than males. However, there are facts which directly show that a utilitarian goal and an aesthetic-sexual goal are each present *per se*. But in many specimens it is noted that precisely the lower exterior of the wings, i.e., that which is turned outward in the sitting, most dangerous position, is completely the color of the plant on which the butterfly lands (obviously for the sake of defense); while the upper exterior, which the flitting male shows to the female during courtship, is painted and drawn with such freakish elegance that it cannot have any relation to the goals of defense.# The reader himself can

---

* Ibid., pp. 323–324.
† Ibid., p. 327.
‡ Ibid., p. 331.
§ Ibid., pp. 340–341.
| Ibid., p. 345.
Darwin, *Descent of Man*, vol. 1, p. 349.

find in Darwin still many other particular evidences that show beyond doubt the predominant action of a purely aesthetic factor here.*

Fish are also not indifferent to beauty. Only this can explain the fact that in many specimens of this class the males (in general more beautiful than the females) develop a particular beauty of colors and forms during mating.† Beyond that, despite a common opinion regarding the muteness of fish, certain specimens (for example, *Umbrina*) display indubitable musical capabilities and trumpet very loudly and sonorously—again, only males and only at the time of mating.‡

Male tritons entice their female friends with beautiful combs, and, among frogs, only the males give concerts and only at the time of courtship. These are distinguished in certain American species by a true musicality and furnish aesthetic enjoyment not only to the frog's ear, but to the human ear as well.§ In one genus of lizard (*Sitana*) male throats are supplied with a large, vividly painted (at the time of mating) leather appendage, which they spread out like a fan in front of the females.| The most aesthetic (both in the visual and in the auditory respect) class of birds represents a great abundance of facts, which prove the independent significance of beauty for these animals. Almost all of them base their conjugal success on the display of one or another aesthetic attribute, and it is noted that glittering color and capacity for sonorous singing usually do not coincide, but weakness of one of these advantages is compensated for by the development of the other.# Most curious in birds is the fact that they obviously and consciously relate to their beauty and become vain not only in front of females, but also in front of secondary observers. Darwin himself not rarely saw how the peacock strutted his attire not only before hens, but also before pigs. All natural scientists, having attentively observed birds both in the state of nature and in captivity, maintain with one voice that males find satisfaction in showing off their beauty.** In many specimens the complex adornments of males not only cannot have any utilitarian significance, but are directly harmful, for they develop in detriment to

---

* Ibid., pp. 350, 354–357, 359, 362–364, 375, 376.
† Ibid., vol. 2, pp. 6, 7, 11, 12, 13.
‡ Ibid., pp. 19, 20.
§ Ibid., p. 23.
| Ibid., p. 27.
Ibid., p. 48.
** Ibid., vol. 2, pp. 74, 76, 77, 78.

their agility—and interrupt their ability to fly or run and betray them to their pursuing enemy; but, evidently, for them beauty is more valuable than life itself.* The purely contemplative susceptibility of certain birds to the beauty of colors is proven by the fact that they pay attention and admire bright colors not only similar to themselves, but wherever they might find them, for example, on women's dresses or hats.† Diligent adornment of nests by certain birds—for example, hummingbirds, which put the finishing touches on them with the most nuanced taste—also undoubtedly proves the presence in birds of an objective-aesthetic sense.‡ Sometimes this sense even compels them to fall into scandalous extremes. So the female of the southern-African specimen *Chera progne* leaves the male if he accidentally loses the long tail feathers with which he adorns himself at the time of mating. In Vienna, Dr. Jaeger observed similar fickleness in silver pheasants.§ 34

These several indications from the mass of homogeneous facts collected by Darwin will be sufficient for us. The meaning of these facts is as simple as it is significant. Man finds certain phenomena in nature beautiful; they give him aesthetic pleasure. The majority of philosophers and scientists are convinced that this is only a fact of the subjective *human* consciousness, that in nature *itself* there is no beauty, just as there is no good and no truth in her. But here it turns out that those very combinations of form, colors, and sounds that are pleasing to man in nature, are pleasing as well to the creatures of nature themselves—to animals of all possible types and classes—and please them as powerfully, have for them as much important significance, as the maintenance and development of these useless, but sometimes also harmful (in a utilitarian sense), peculiarities underlying their specific existence. We now can in no way say that the wings of a tropical butterfly or peacock tail are beautiful only according to our subjective evaluation, for female butterflies and peacocks value their beauty precisely in the same way. But in such a case it is necessary to go farther. Because, insisting on the fact that the beauty of a rainbow or diamond has only a subjectively human character, while having allowed that a peacock tail is objectively beautiful, would be the height of absurdity. Of

* Ibid., p. 83.
† Ibid., p. 96.
‡ Ibid., p. 97.
§ Ibid., p. 105.

course, if, in a given particular case, there is no appreciative subject at all, then neither is there any sensation of beauty; yet the point is not in sensation, but rather, in the property *of an object* capable of producing homogeneous sensations in the most diverse subjects. If, in general, beauty in nature is objective, then it should also have certain general ontological foundations; it should be—on various stages and in various forms—the perceptible embodiment of one absolutely objective Idea of all-unity.

The cosmic Mind—in obvious struggle with primal chaos and in clandestine agreement with the universal Soul, or nature torn asunder by this chaos, which all the while more and more yields to the mental suggestions of the creative principle—creates in this and through this the complex and magnificent body of our universe. This creation is a *process* having two closely connected goals, a general one and a particular one. The general one is the embodiment of actual Ideas, for instance, *light* and *life*, in diverse forms of natural beauty; the particular goal is the creation of man, i.e., of that form, which, together with the greatest physical beauty, represents as well the highest intrinsic conversion of light and life that we call self-consciousness. Already in the animal world, as we just saw, the general cosmic goal is achieved with the participation and cooperation of animals themselves, through the arousal in them of certain intrinsic strivings and sensations. Nature does not manage and does not adorn animals with extrinsic material, but compels them to manage and adorn themselves, on their own. Finally, man not only already participates in the activity of the cosmic principle, but is capable *of knowing the goal* of this activity and, consequently, laboring over its achievement freely and intelligently. Just as human self-consciousness relates to the general state of animals, so beauty in art relates to natural beauty.

The Universal Meaning of Art

I.

A tree is just as beautiful when it is depicted on linen as when it grows as a plant in nature; both produce a homogeneous aesthetic impression, belong to an identical evaluation—and it is not without reason that even the word used for its expression is one and the same in both cases.[1] But if everything was limited to such visible, superficial homogeneity, would it be possible to ask: What is this reduplication of nature for? And this question has, in fact, been asked. Is it not a child's game to duplicate in a picture that which already maintains its beautiful existence in nature? The usual response to this (for example, Taine in his *Philosophie de l'Art*) is that art does not reproduce the objects and phenomena of reality themselves but only that which the artist sees in them; and the true artist sees in them only their distinctive and *model* attributes. The aesthetic element of natural phenomena, filtering through the consciousness and imagination of the artist, becomes purified from all material chance and, in this way, is strengthened and appears more vividly; beauty, which is scattered in nature in its forms and colorings, appears in a picture as concentrated,

Source: "Obshchii smysl iskusstva," *Voprosy filosofii i psikhologii* 5 (1890): 84–102. Reprinted in *Sobranie sochinenii* 6: 75–92.

condensed, and accentuated.[2] It is not possible to be absolutely satisfied now with this explanation, for the sole reason that it is completely inapplicable to entire and prominent branches of art. What phenomena of nature are "accentuated," for example, in the sonatas of Beethoven? Apparently, the aesthetic connection of art and nature is much more profound and significant. In truth, it consists not in a repetition, but in an extension of the artistic act that is begun by nature—in an impending and more complete resolution of the same aesthetic problem.

The final result of natural processes is man in a two-fold sense: first, as the most beautiful,* and second as the most conscious natural creature. In this latter capacity, man *himself*, rising out of the result, becomes an *agent* of the universal process and with this more perfectly corresponds to his ideal goal—a complete, mutual permeation and liberated solidarity of the spiritual and the material, the ideal and the real, the subjective and the objective factors and elements of the universe. But why, then, it could be asked, is the entire universal process, begun by nature and continued by man, represented to us precisely from the aesthetic aspect as the solution to some kind of artistic problem? Is it not better to acknowledge as his goal the realization of truth and the good, the triumph of higher reason and will? If, in response to this, we remember that beauty is only an embodiment in sensory forms of the same ideal content that, up until the time of such an embodiment, is called truth and the good, then this calls forth a new objection. The good and the true, a strict moralist will say, have no need of aesthetic incarnation. To do good and to know truth—is all that is necessary.

In reply to this objection we will allow that the good is realized not only in someone's personal life, but in the life of all of society: an ideal social structure is realized, full solidarity reigns—a universal brotherhood. The impermeability of egoism is abolished; everyone finds themselves in each one and each one in all the others. But if this universal mutual-permeability, in which the essence of the moral good exists, remains prior to material nature; if the spiritual principle that has defeated the impermeability of human psychological egoism cannot overcome the impermeability of matter—the physical ego—this means that this force of the good, or love, is not strong enough, that this moral principle cannot be fully realized and justified completely.

---

* I understand beauty here in a general and objective sense, namely, that the outward appearance of a man is capable of expressing a more perfected (more ideal) intrinsic content than can be expressed by other animals.

A question then appears: if the dark force of material existence finally triumphs, if it is insurmountable for the principle of the good, then is there not within it an authentic truth of everything that exists; is not that which we call "the good" only a subjective apparition? And, in fact, is it possible to speak of the triumph of the good, when society, which is constructed on the most ideal moral principles, can immediately perish in consequence of any geological or astronomical cataclysm? The absolute estrangement of moral principle from material existence is not at all detrimental to the latter, but to the former. The very existence of a moral order in the world presupposes its connection with the material order, a certain coordination between them.

But, if this is so, then does it not follow that it is necessary to search for this connection apart from any aesthetic in the direct rule of human reason over the blind forces of nature, in the absolute dominion of spirit over matter? Apparently, several important steps toward this goal have already been taken; when it is achieved, when, thanks to the achievements of applied science, we defeat, as some optimists think, not only space and time but also death itself, then the existence of moral life in the world (on the foundation of material life) will be finally secured—without, however, any relation to aesthetic concern, so that even then the declaration that *the good has no need of beauty* will remain in force. But in such a case, will the good itself *be perfected?* Indeed, it consists not in the triumph of one over the other, but in the solidarity of all. But can creatures and agents of the natural world, as well, be excluded from the list of these *all?* Then one cannot look upon them, either, as upon means or instruments of human existence only; and they also should enter as a positive element into the ideal structure of our life. If, for the sake of its *stability,* moral order must rest on material nature as upon a medium and means of its existence, then for this *fullness* and perfection it must contain in itself the material basis of objective reality as an independent part of ethical activity. Here, ethical activity is transformed into aesthetic activity; for material objective reality can be introduced into moral order only through its illumination, its inspiration, i.e., only in the form of beauty. Thus, beauty is necessary for the fulfillment of the good in the material world, for only by it is the evil darkness of this world illuminated and subdued.*

However, is not this business of "universal illumination" already perfected apart from us? Natural beauty has already enveloped the world in its

---

* On beauty as the ideal cause of the existence of matter, see my articles in "The Philosophical Principles of Integral Knowledge."

radiant veil; ugly chaos powerlessly stirs beneath the harmonious appearance of the cosmos and cannot itself cast it off either in the infinite space of heavenly bodies or in the constricted domain of earthly organisms. Should not our art only concern itself with encompassing human relations, with incarnating the true meaning of human life in tangible forms? But the dark forces in nature are not persuaded, but only defeated, by universal meaning; the victory itself is superficial and incomplete, and the beauty of nature is just a veil thrown over malevolent life and not a transformation of this life. And for this reason man, with his reasoning consciousness, should be not only the goal of the natural process, but also the means for a contrary, more profound and ample effect upon nature on the side of ideal principle. We know that the realization of this principle already has different degrees of profundity in nature itself; moreover, corresponding to each deepening of the positive aspect there is also a more profound intrinsic strengthening of the negative. If the malevolent principle acts only as gravity and inertia in inorganic matter, then in the organic world it now appears as death and decay. (Moreover, here as well, ugliness does not triumph as brilliantly in the destruction of plants as in the death and decay of animals, and among them the higher more than the lower.) And in man it expresses its most profound essence yet—apart from a greater complexity and the reinforcement of its manifestations from the physical aspect—as moral evil. But here as well the possibility of a final triumph over it and the perfect embodiment of this triumph is in imperishable and eternal beauty.

Today the refurbished ancient view that identifies moral evil with a dark subconscious physical life (of the flesh), and moral good with the reasoning light of consciousness developed in man, is widely propagated. That the light of reason is in itself a good is indisputable; but neither is it possible to call physical light evil. The meaning of one and the other in their corresponding spheres is identical. In the physical world,* the universal Idea (positive unity, the life of all for one another within One) is realized

---

* It goes without saying that I speak here about light not in the sense of visual sensation in man and animals, but in the sense of motion of weightless mediums that connect among themselves material bodies, upon which their objective existence depends for one another independently of subjective senses. The word *light* is used for brevity's sake, since various dynamic phenomena also relate to this: heat, electricity, and so forth. Moreover, we have no concern here with these or other hypotheses of physical science: the indisputable factual *difference* between the manifestations of the phenomena referred to and the manifestations of solid matter is sufficient for us.

only in a reflected sense: all objects and phenomena obtain the potentiality to exist one for another (are revealed one to another) in mutual reflections through a common weightless medium. In a similar way, all that exists is reflected in reason by means of general abstract conceptions which do not convey the intrinsic essence of things but only their superficial logical outlines. Consequently, in rational knowledge we find only a reflection of the universal Idea, and not its real presence in the known and knowable. For its actual realization, truth and the good must become the creative force in an object, transforming, and not just reflecting, reality.

Just as in the physical world, where light is transformed into life and becomes the organizational principle of plants and animals in order not only to be reflected by bodies but to become embodied in them, so too the light of reason cannot be limited by knowledge alone but must embody the conscious meaning of life artistically in a new reality that more closely corresponds to it. Of course, before one does this, before one creates in beauty, or converts a non-ideal reality into an ideal one, it is necessary to know the difference between them—to know not only in abstract reflection, but, before anything else, in the spontaneous feeling belonging to the artist.

II.

The difference between ideal—i.e., worthy and fitting—existence and unfitting or unworthy existence depends in general on the particular attachment of individual elements of the world to each other and to the whole. Existence is ideal or worthy—that which should be—when three conditions are met. First, when individual elements do not exclude one another, but on the contrary mutually situate themselves within one another, they are in solidarity among themselves; second, when they do not exclude the whole, but maintain their individual existence on a single universal foundation; third, and last, when this all-united basis—or absolute principle—does not repress and does not absorb the individual elements, but in revealing itself to them gives them full freedom in themselves. And while absolute principle exists in itself,* it appears for us not as given reality, but as an ideal, only in part realized and realizable. In this sense it becomes the final goal and absolute norm of our living reality: the will strives toward it

---

* The ground for this assertion belongs to the realm of metaphysics, not aesthetics.

as to its higher good; by it thought takes shape as absolute truth; and in part it is sensed and divined by our senses and imagination as beauty.*[3]

The same essential identity is found among these positive ideal definitions of worthy existence as among the negative principles corresponding to them. Every evil can be reduced to the destruction of mutual solidarity and balance of the parts and the whole; and every falsehood and every ugliness is also in essence reduced to this. We should acknowledge *as evil* all exclusive self-affirmation (egoism), as well as anarchic particularism and despotic unification. That is to say, evil exists when a particular or individual element asserts itself in its individuality, striving to exclude or oppress another essence; when the particular or individual elements separately or together desire to stand in place of the whole, exclude and negate its independent unity, and through this the common bond among themselves as well; and when, on the contrary, the freedom of an individual being is constricted or abolished in the name of unity.

But the very same thing, when transferred from the practical to the theoretical sphere, is *falsehood*. We call falsehood a thought that takes exclusively one of any individual aspects of existence in the name of which it negates all others; we call falsehood as well an intellectual position that gives place only to an indeterminate aggregate of particular empirical states, negating the common meaning or rational unity of the universe. Finally, we should acknowledge as falsehood abstract monism or pantheism which negates all individual existence in the name of a principle of absolute unity.[†] And ugliness is defined in the aesthetic sphere by the very same essential signs by which evil is defined in the moral sphere and falsehood in the intellectual sphere. All ugliness consists in a single part infinitely expanding and prevailing over others,[‡] where there is no unity and wholeness and, finally, where there is no free-flowing diversity. Anarchical plurality too is as contrary as deathly oppressive unity is to the

---

* Various thinkers arrive at the notion of an existing identity of beauty and the good and of the moral task of art from completely different angles and aspects. An original and talented expression of this notion is found in the recently departed French writer Guyau in his work "De l'art au point de vue sociologique." The view of Guyau is set forth by Gol'tsev in his book on art, other parts of which also merit attention.

† The falsehood of this principle in such an application of it comes to light clearly from the internal contradiction into which it, moreover, falls; for in becoming *exclusive*, unity stops being *absolute*.

‡ See examples of this in my article "Beauty in Nature."

good, truth, and beauty: any attempt to realize the latter for the senses is
reduced to the conception of an infinite desert, bereft of any individual
and definite forms of existence, that is, reduced to pure ugliness.

Ideal existence befitting merit requires identical freedom for the
whole and for the parts—consequently this is not freedom from particularities but only from their exclusivity. The fullness of this freedom requires that all the particular elements find themselves in one another and
in the whole, that each supposes itself in the other and the other in it,
that it senses in its particularity the unity of the whole and in the whole
its particularity—in a word, the absolute solidarity of all existence: God
is everything in everyone.

The fully perceptible realization of this universal solidarity or positive
all-unity—perfect beauty not only as a reflection of any idea from matter
but its actual presence in matter—presupposes first of all the most profound and the closest interaction between inward (or spiritual) and outward (or material) existence. This is a fundamental and strictly aesthetic
requirement, the specific distinction of beauty from the other two aspects
of absolute Idea. Ideal content that remains only as an intrinsic property
of spirit, its will and thought, is bereft of beauty; and the absence of beauty
is impotence of Idea. In fact, while spirit is incapable of giving to its interior content a direct outward expression, it remains embodied in material
phenomenon; and, on the other hand, until such time as matter is capable
of perceiving ideal activity of spirit, of permeating phenomena, of converting or transubstantiating in spirit, then there is no solidarity between
these chief realms of existence. And this means that in Idea itself, which
is namely the perfected solidarity of all that exists, there is in this, its phenomenon, as yet no sufficient force for the final realization or fulfillment
of its essence. An abstract embodiment of spirit incapable of creation and
a spiritless matter incapable of animation are both incompatible with
ideal or worthy existence, and both carry upon themselves the manifest
sign of their unworthiness in the fact that neither one nor the other can
be beautiful.

For plenitude of beauty, qualities are required in the following way:
1) direct materialization of spiritual essence, and 2) complete animation
of material phenomena, as the proper and inalienable form of ideal content. A third condition is joined to—or better to say, proceeds directly
from—this dual condition: during the direct and inseparable unification
in beauty of spiritual content with sensual expression, in their full mutual
penetration, a material phenomenon actually having become beautiful,

that is, really having embodied in itself Idea, it should become in the very same way as abiding and immortal as Idea itself. According to Hegelian aesthetics, beauty is the embodiment of universal and eternal Idea in particular and transient phenomena; moreover, both remain transient and vanish, as separate waves in the stream of the material process, only reflecting the radiance of eternal Idea for a moment. But this is possible only by an indifferent equanimity of relations between spiritual principle and material phenomenon. Authentic and perfect beauty, expressing full solidarity and mutual penetration of these two elements, should necessarily achieve one of them (the material) in true correspondence with the immortality of the other.

In turning to beautiful phenomena of the physical world, we find that they far from fulfill the indicated requirements or conditions of perfected beauty. First, ideal content in natural beauty is insufficiently transparent; it does not reveal here all its enigmatic profundity but displays only its general contours, so to speak, in particular concrete phenomena, the most elementary signs and attributes of absolute Idea. So light in its sensory qualities displays the all-permeability and the weightlessness of ideal principle; plants in their visible form manifest the expansiveness of life's Idea and the universal striving of the earthly spirit toward higher forms of existence; beautiful animals express the intensity of life's motives, united in a complex whole and well balanced in order to allow a free play of life forces, and so forth.

Indubitably, Idea is embodied in all this, but only in the most general and superficial way, from its extrinsic aspect. Here the animation of matter superficially corresponds to this superficial materialization of ideal principle in natural beauty. The possibility of an apparent contradiction of form with content comes from this: a malevolent beast can typically be very beautiful (the contradiction here is only apparent, namely because natural beauty, according to its extrinsic character in general, is not capable of expressing the Idea of life in its intrinsic, moral quality, but only in its superficial physical properties, such as force, swiftness, freedom of movement, and so forth).

A third essential imperfection of natural beauty is connected to this as well: since this beauty is only on the outside and in general conceals the unsightliness of material existence and does not penetrate it inwardly and completely (in all its parts), then this beauty is also preserved as changeless and eternal only *in general,* in its general patterns— kinds and forms. Each individual beautiful phenomenon and creature in its own life remains under the power of the material process, which at first breaches its beautiful form and then also completely destroys it. From the point of view of naturalism, this instability of all individual phenomena of beauty is a fateful, inescapable law. But in order to reconcile, at least theoretically, with this triumph of the all-destructive material process, it is necessary to acknowledge beauty in the world (as logical minds of this tendency do), and in general all that is ideal, as the subjective illusion of human imagination. But we know that beauty has objective significance, that it acts outside of the human world, that nature itself is not indifferent to beauty. And in such case, if it does not succeed in realizing perfected beauty in the realm of physical life, then it is not for nothing that it has arisen out of this lower realm by great labors and efforts, frightening catastrophes, and ugly, but necessary, begettings into the realm of conscious human life for a final purpose. The task, unfulfilled by means of physical life, must be fulfilled by means of human creative work.

Out of this comes a three-fold mission of art in general: 1) the direct objectivization of those most profound, intrinsic definitions and qualities of life's Idea that cannot be expressed by nature; 2) the animation of natural beauty; and through this, 3) the perpetuation of its individual phenomena. This is the metamorphosis of physical life into spiritual life, that is, into first, a life that contains within itself its Logos, or revelation, capable of being expressed directly outside itself; second, a life that has the capacity of inwardly converting or animating matter, or truly being incarnated in it; and third, a life that is free from the power of the material process and therefore remains eternal.

The highest task of art is the perfected incarnation of this spiritual fullness in our reality, a realization in it of absolute beauty, or the creation of a universal spiritual organism. It is clear that the fulfillment of this task should coincide with the conclusion of the entire universal process. While history still continues, we can have only partial and fragmentary *forewarnings* (anticipations) of perfected beauty; today's art, in its greatest works, captures flashes of eternal beauty in our current reality and extends them further, forewarns, gives presentiment of a supernatural future reality for us, and serves, in this way, as a transition and connecting link between the beauty of nature and the beauty of the life to come.[4] Art understood in this way ceases being empty amusement and becomes an important and edifying concern, not at all in the sense of didactic sermon, but rather, only in the sense of inspired *prophecy*.

That such a lofty significance of art is not an arbitrary requirement follows logically from the indissoluble bond that formerly actually existed between art and religion. Of course, we do not regard this original indivisibility of religious and artistic affairs as ideal. True, full beauty requires greater space for the human element and presupposes a higher and more complex development of social life than could be achieved in primitive culture. We view the contemporary alienation between religion and art as a transition from their ancient amalgamation to a future free synthesis. Indeed, perfected life, the anticipation of which we find in true art, will be based not on the absorption of the human element by the divine, but on their free interaction.

Now we can give a general definition of real art in its essence: *every tangible representation of any object and phenomenon from the point of view of its final, definitive status, or in light of the world to come, is artistic work.*

III.

These presentiments of perfected beauty in human art are of three kinds:

1) *Direct or magical,* when the most profound intrinsic status that connects us with the authentic essence of things and with the supernatural world (or, if you like, with the being *an sich* of all of that which exists), in breaking through all conditionality and material limitations, finds for itself a direct and full expression in beautiful sounds and words (music and, in part, pure lyric).*[5]

2) *Indirect, through intensification*—transformation of given beauty, when the intrinsically existing, eternal meaning of life, latent in particular and casual phenomena of the natural and human world and only dimly and insufficiently expressed in their natural beauty, is revealed and made clear

---

* I mean here lyric poetry (and also lyric points in certain epic poetry and drama), the aesthetic impression of which is not exhausted by the thoughts and forms that their *philological* content consists of. Lermontov likely hinted at this in certain verses:

> There are sounds—in significance
> Dark, or worthless,
> But it is impossible
> To hear them without emotion.

by the artist through the reproduction of these phenomena in concentrated, refined, idealized form: so architecture reproduces in idealized appearance certain regular forms of natural bodies and expresses the triumph of these ideal forms over the principal, anti-ideal properties of matter—weight and gravity. Classical sculpture, idealizing the beauty of the human form and strictly observing the thin, but precise, line separating corporeal and carnal beauty, foresees in artistic representation the spiritual corporeality that is sometimes revealed to us in living reality; landscape painting (and, in part, lyrical poetry) reproduces in concentrated form the ideal aspect of visible nature's complex phenomena, refining from them all material coincidence (even three-dimensional space); and religious painting (poetry as well) is the idealized reproduction of those phenomena from the history of mankind in which a higher meaning of our life was revealed in advance.

3) *Indirect, through reflection*—A final, third, and negative kind of aesthetic presentiment of impending perfected reality, of the ideal from a medium not congruous with it, typically reinforced by the artist for greater vividness of reflection. Incongruity between a given reality and Idea, or the higher meaning of life, can be of a different sort: first, a particular human reality, *in its own way* perfected and beautiful (namely in the sense of *natural* man), does not, however, satisfy the absolute ideal for which *spiritual* man and humanity are destined. Achilles and Hector, Priam and Agamemnon, Krishna, Arjuna, and Rama—are indubitably beautiful, but the more artistically represented they and their concerns are, the clearer it is *in the final analysis* that they are not real people and that it is not their exploits that constitute actual human affairs. In all likelihood, Homer—and probably the authors of Indian epics as well—did not have this notion in mind; and we should call "heroic epic" the unconscious and indistinct reflection of the absolute ideal from a beautiful human reality—but one not adequate to it—and which therefore is doomed to destruction:

> There will come a day, even sacred Troy will perish.
> And with her Priam of the spear and his entire nation.[6]

Modern poets, returning to the themes of an ancient epoch, consciously and in the form of universal truth express the idea that itself appears concretely in their examples. Such is "The Victory Celebration" of Schiller:

> All that is great on earth
> Scatters like smoke:
> Today the lot has fallen to Troy,
> Tomorrow it will fall to another. . . [7]

and even clearer (as an emphasized impression) in Zhukovsky's ballad:

> Ida has grown dark,
> Ilion has become somber,
> The figure of Atrida sleeps in the dark,
> On the plain of battle a dream. . .—etc.[8]

We find more profound attitudes toward the unrealized ideal in tragedy, where the persons portrayed are themselves permeated by the consciousness of the intrinsic contradiction between their reality and that which should be. Comedy, on the other hand, strengthens and deepens the sense of the ideal by the fact that, first, it underscores an aspect of reality that in no sense can be called beautiful, and second—it represents the persons living this reality as completely *content* with it, which aggravates their contradiction with the ideal. This *complacency*—in no way the intrinsic attribute of the subject—constitutes the essential sign of the comedic in distinction to the tragic element. So, for example, Oedipus, having killed his father and married his mother, could have been, in spite of this fact, a highly comedic person if he had related to his frightening adventures with placid complacency, finding that everything happened accidentally, that he was guilty of nothing, and therefore he could calmly utilize the kingdom that he had acquired.*

In defining comedy as a negative presentiment of life's beauty through the typical portrayal of anti-ideal reality *in its complacency*, we understand by this complacency, of course, in no way the contentedness of one or another actor with one or another particular situation, but only a general complacency with the entire given structure of life, fully shared as well by those actors who are discontented with something in a given moment. So, Molière's heroes are certainly very discontented when they are beaten with

---

* Of course, the comic element would be possible here namely because the crime was not a personally intended action. The *conscious* criminal, who is satisfied with himself and his affairs, is not tragic but repulsive, and in no way comical.

sticks, but they are completely satisfied by the order of things in which beating with sticks is one of the fundamental forms of community.

Similarly, although Chatsky in "Woe from Wit" is earnestly dissatisfied with the life of Moscow society, it is patently obvious from his speeches that he would be completely content with this life if only Sophia Pavlovna would pay him more attention, if Famusov's guests did not listen with reverence to the girl from Bordeaux, and if they did not chatter away in French: therefore, for all his discontent and even despair, Chatsky would remain an absolutely comical person even if he were altogether a living person.*[9] Sometimes moral indignation regarding some detail emphasizes a contentedness with all of bad reality; out of this a comic impression is even reinforced. So, in "The Wedding of Krechinskii," the striking comic element of one monologue is based on the fact that the character speaking, having suffered for card-sharping, finds it completely normal that some cheat at cards; and while others beat them for this, they are only indignant at the excessiveness of retribution in a given case.[10]

Apart from the indicated difference between epic, tragic, and comic elements,† if we divide all human types in artistic representation into positive and negative (as is usually done), then it is easy to see that the first should predominate in the fine arts (sculpture and painting) and the second—in poetry. For sculpture and painting have direct concern with corporeal forms, the beauty of which is already realized in reality, although still also requiring amplification or idealization; whereas the main subject of poetry is the moral and social life of humanity, infinitely far from the

---

* It has already been noted long ago in literary criticism (if I am not mistaken, by Belinsky) that the title "Woe from Wit" does not correspond at all to the content of the comedy, since Chatsky does not exhibit any singular intellect, and displays only vacuous and petty embitterment—his woe comes from a completely extrinsic and incidental circumstance. Griboedev himself could have thought differently, but this does not change the essence of the matter at all. It is apparent from recently published biographical data that in the work "Woe from Wit" there was more the operation of indirect inspiration than well-defined creative thought: Griboedev saw his comedy in a dream before he wrote it. It is all the more probable that all of his other creations—conceived but not published—are totally worthless, just as it is with the character of the hero in "Woe from Wit"—obviously invented and therefore completely lifeless in his dialogues—intended as intelligent, but in essence nonsensical.

† In the sphere of fine art, historical painting corresponds to the epic poem, and in part to tragedy, genre-painting—to comedy, but portrait art, depending on its portrayed characters, can have both an epic and tragic, as well as comic significance.

realization of its ideal. Prophetic divination and a directly creative force, which are essential for the poetic portrayal of a perfect man* or an ideal society, are not necessary in order to sculpt a beautiful body or to describe a beautiful character.[11] Therefore, apart from religious epics (which, with several exceptions, merit approval only according to design and not according to execution), the greatest poets refrained from a portrayal of directly ideal or positive types. In Shakespeare, these appear as hermits (in "Romeo and Juliet") or magicians (in "The Tempest"), but for the most part as women, and namely those possessing more of a directly natural purity than a spiritual-human moral character. And Schiller, having had a weakness for virtuous types of both sexes, portrayed them comparatively poorly.

We take Goethe's *Faust* in order to see that in the greatest works of poetry the meaning of spiritual life is realized only through the *reflection* of non-ideal human reality. The positive meaning of this lyrical-epic tragedy is revealed directly only in the last scene of the second part and abstractly recapitulated in the concluding chorus: "Alles Vergängliche ist nur ein Gleichnis," etc.[12] But where is the direct organic connection between this apotheosis and the other parts of the tragedy? The heavenly powers and "das Ewig-Weibliche" appear from above—consequently from without—and the content itself does not come to light from within.[13] The idea of the last scene is present in all of *Faust*, but it is only a reflection of the (partly real, partly fantastic) action of which the tragedy itself consists. Similar to the way that a ray of light plays within a diamond to the pleasure of the observer, but without any change of the material basis of stone, so too here the spiritual light of the absolute ideal, refracted by the imagination of the artist, illuminates dark human reality but does not at all change its essence.

Let us allow that a more powerful poet than Goethe or Schiller presented to us, in a complex poetical work, an artistic, i.e., veracious and concrete, portrayal of truly spiritual life—that which should be, which completely realizes the absolute ideal. In any case, such a marvel of art, too, not having been managed by a single poet up to the present,† would be, in the midst of present reality, only a magnificent mirage in a waterless

* The character of Christ is portrayed poetically only in the Gospels—by witnesses and chroniclers, and not by artists.

† In the third part of *The Divine Comedy*, Dante portrays heaven with characteristics, which, while perhaps truthful, are in any event insufficiently alive and concrete—an essential shortcoming which cannot be atoned for even with euphonious verse.

desert, vexing and not quenching our spiritual thirst. Perfect art in its definitive mission should embody the absolute ideal not only in imagination,
but also in actual fact—should animate and transubstantiate our real life.
If it is said that such a mission exceeds the bounds of art, then one can
ask: Who established these limits? In history we do not find them; we see
here an art that is changing—in the process of development. Some of its
branches achieve the possibility of a kind of perfection and more do not
succeed; but then new ones arise. Everyone, it seems, is in agreement with
the fact that sculpture achieved its definitive perfection with the ancient
Greeks; it is hardly possible as well to expect further progress in the realm
of heroic epic and pure tragedy.

I will allow myself to go further: I do not find particularly bold the assertion that, just as the indicated forms of art have already been perfected
by the ancients, so too modern European nations have now exhausted all
other kinds of art known to us; and if the latter has a future, then it is in
a completely new sphere of action. Of course, this future development of
aesthetic creativity depends on the general course of history; for art in
general is the sphere of the incarnation of ideas, and not their elementary
conception and growth.

4

The Meaning of Love

First Article

I.

(Preliminary observations)

The meaning of sexual love is usually assumed to be in the propagation of kind, which sexual love serves as a means. I regard this view as incorrect not only on the basis of any ideal considerations, but first of all on the basis of natural-historical facts. That the propagation of living beings can be managed without sexual love is already clear from the fact that propagation is itself managed without a division into sexes. A significant portion of the organisms of both the plant and the animal kingdom reproduces in an asexual manner: by division, budding, spores, grafts. True, the higher forms of both organic kingdoms reproduce in a sexual manner. But, in the first place, organisms propagating in this manner, both plants and (in part) animals, *can* also reproduce in an asexual manner as well (grafting

Source: "Smysl Liubvi," a series of five articles that appeared in the journal *Voprosy filosofii i psikhologii* as follows: no. 14 (1892): 97–107; no. 15 (1892): 161–172; no. 16 (1893): 115–128; no. 17 (1893): 132–147; and no. 21 (1894): 81–96. These essays were later published in book form, and were reprinted together posthumously in *Sobranie sochinenii* 7: 3–60.

in plants, parthenogenesis in higher insects).[1] In the second place—leaving the first point aside and adopting as a general rule that higher organisms propagate by means of sexual union—we should conclude that this sexual factor is connected not with reproduction in general (which can take place apart from this as well), but with the reproduction of *higher* organisms. Consequently, the meaning of sexual differentiation (*and* sexual love) should in no way be sought in the concept of generic life and its propagation, but only in the concept of the higher organism.

We find striking confirmation for this in the following grand fact. Within the range of animals propagating exclusively in a sexual manner (the vertebrate division), the higher we ascend the ladder of organisms, the lesser the power of reproduction becomes, and the power of sexual attraction, to the contrary, becomes greater. In the lowest class of this division—in fish—reproduction occurs in enormous proportions: eggs born annually to each female number in the millions; these eggs are fertilized by the male outside the body of the female, and the method by which this is done does not allow a presumption of powerful sexual attraction. Of all vertebrate animals, this cold-blooded class undoubtedly propagates more and displays loving passion less than all the others.

On the next rung—among amphibians and reptiles—reproduction is much less significant than among fish, although according to several of its forms, this class is related by the Bible, and not without foundation, to that number of creatures teeming in swarms (*sherets shirtsu*).[2] But with less reproduction, we now find among these animals more intimate sexual relations. . . . Among birds, the power of reproduction is much less not only in comparison with fish, but also in comparison, for example, with frogs; and sexual attraction and mutual attachment between the male and female achieve a development unheard of in the two lower classes. Among mammals—they too bear their young live—reproduction is significantly weaker than among birds, and sexual attraction, although less constant among the majority, is, however, at the same time much more intense. Finally, among human beings, in comparison with the whole animal kingdom, reproduction is accomplished in the lowest proportions, but sexual love achieves the greatest significance and the highest power, uniting to a superlative degree a constancy of relations (as among birds) and an intensity of passion (as among mammals). Thus, sexual love and the reproduction of kind find themselves *in an inverse relationship*: the stronger the one, the weaker the other. In general, all the animal kingdom develops in the following order from the scrutinized aspect. At the bottom is a huge power of reproduction with a complete absence of anything resembling sexual love (for lack of the very separation into sexes). Further, among the more perfected organisms, sexual differentiation appears, along with a certain sexual attraction corresponding to it. At first extremely weak, it later gradually increases to the furthest extents of organic development according to the measure of its killing the power of reproduction (i.e., in direct relation to the perfection of organization and in inverse relation to the power of reproduction); while finally, at the very top, among humans, the most powerful sexual love appears possible even with the complete exclusion of propagation. But if at the two terminals of animal life we thus find, on the one hand, reproduction without any sexual love, and, on the other hand, sexual love without any reproduction, then it is completely clear that these two phenomena cannot be placed in an indissoluble connection with one another. It is clear that each of them has its independent significance, and that the meaning of one cannot consist in being the agent of the other. The very same thing results if we examine sexual love exclusively in the human world, where it takes on, incomparably more than in the animal world, that individual character by virtue of which *precisely this* person of another sex has for the lover unconditional significance, as a unique and irreplaceable person, as an end in itself.[3]

II.

Here we meet with a popular theory, which, seeing in sexual love generally the means of a generative instinct or an implement of propagation, attempts in part to explain the individualization of the loving feeling in a human being as a certain cunning or delusion that is utilized by nature or the universal will for the achievement of its special ends. In the world of humanity, where individual particularities have much more significance than in the animal and plant world, nature (or the universal will, the will in life, or the unconscious or supraconscious universal spirit) intends not only the preservation of kind, but also the implementation within its boundaries of a multitude of possible individual or aspectual types and individual natures. But besides this general aim—the manifestation of a possible full variety of forms—the life of humanity, understood as a historical process, has as its objectives the elevation and perfection of human nature. For this, not only is it required that there be as ample a diversity of specimens of humanity as possible, but that there appear in the world *the best* of its specimens, which are valued not only in themselves as individual types, but also according to their impact upon the advancement and improvement of others. Thus, for the propagation of human kind, the force—whatever we may call it—that drives the universal and historical process is interested not only that human persons continuously arise according to their kind, but also that *these* definite, and as far as possible significant, individualities come into being. And for this, a procreation by means of the chance and indifferent union of individuals of different sex is now insufficient: a combination of individually *constructive* procreators is necessary for individually constructive reproduction; and consequently, general sexual attraction, which serves reproduction of kind in animals, is also insufficient. Since, in humanity, the situation does not just concern the production of progeny in general, but also the production of *this* most appropriate progeny for universal purposes, and since a given person can produce this required progeny not with every person of the opposite sex, but only with one particular person, this one person then should also have for him a special attractive force, should seem to him to be somehow exclusive, irreplaceable, natural, and capable of imparting the highest bliss. And this is simply that individualization and excitement of the sexual instinct by which human love is distinguished from animal love, but which, just as with the other, is aroused in us by an alien, perhaps even supreme, power for its own ends, extraneous to our personal consciousness. This instinct is aroused as an irrational fateful passion that takes possession of us, disappearing like a mirage as the necessity in it passes.*[4]

If this theory were true, if the individualization and exhilaration of the loving feeling had their entire point, their single reason and aim, outside this feeling—*to wit:* in the requisite (for universal ends) properties of progeny—then from here it would logically follow that the degree of this loving individualization and exhilaration, or the power of love, is found in direct relation to the degree of typicality and significance of the progeny that proceeds from it: according to this theory, the more important the progeny, the stronger the love of parents would have to be; and, in reverse: the stronger the love that connects two given people, the more remarkable the progeny we would have to expect from them. If the loving feeling is generally aroused by the universal will for the sake of the requi-

---

* I have set forth the general essence of a view repudiated by me, not dwelling on minor variations it produces in Schopenhauer, Hartmann, and others. In a recent booklet, "The Basic Motive Force of Heredity" (Moscow, 1891), Valter attempts by means of historical facts to prove that great people are the fruit of intense mutual love.

site progeny and is only *an agent* for the purpose of its production, then it is clear that in each given instance the force of the agent utilized by the cosmic prime mover should be proportionate to the importance for it of the attained end. The more the universal will becomes interested in the product that has to appear in the world, the stronger it should attract the two necessary procreators one to another and connect them.

Let us assume that the situation concerns the birth of a universal genius, who has a huge significance in the historical process. Obviously, the supreme power that directs this process becomes interested in this birth many times more strongly than with others, insofar as this universal genius is a rarer phenomenon compared with ordinary mortals; and consequently, the sexual attraction by which the universal will (according to this theory) secures for itself, in this case the attainment of the end so important to it, must be stronger than usual as well. Of course, the defenders of the theory can repudiate the idea concerning the exact quantitative relation between the importance of a given person and the force of his parents' passion, since these subjects do not allow for precise measurement; but it is completely inarguable (from the point of view of this theory) that if the universal will *becomes extraordinarily interested* in the birth of any person, it must take *extraordinary measures* for the guarantee of the desired result (that is, according to the sense of the theory, it must arouse in the parents an *extraordinarily intense* passion, capable of shattering all obstacles to their union).

In reality, however, we find nothing of the kind, no correspondence between the strength of loving passion and the value of progeny. First of all, we encounter a fact completely inexplicable for this theory—that the most intense love quite frequently occurs as unrequited, and not only does not produce any great progeny, but no descendents at all. If, in consequence of such love, people shave their heads and become monks or commit suicide, then what did the universal will, having become interested in progeny, even bother for? Yet even if the ardent Werther* had not killed himself, his unhappy passion still remains an inexplicable enigma for the theory of specialized progeny.[5] The extraordinarily individualized and impassioned love of Werther and Charlotte showed (from the point of view of this theory) that it is precisely with Charlotte that he should have

---

* Here and further I elucidate my argument with examples chiefly from great works of poetry. They are preferable to examples from real life, since they represent not separate phenomena, but entire categories.

produced especially important and necessary progeny for humanity, and for the sake of which the universal will awakened in him this unusual passion. But how then could this all-knowing and all-powerful will not surmise or not be capable of acting in the desired sense on Charlotte as well, without the participation of whom Werther's passion was completely pointless and unnecessary? For a teleologically active substance, "love's labour lost" is total nonsense.[6]

Especially intense love for the most part is unhappy, and unhappy love quite usually leads to suicide in one form or another; and each of these multitudinous suicides from unhappy love manifestly refutes the theory according to which intense love is only aroused at all in order to produce, at whatever cost, the desired progeny, the importance of which is marked by the intensity of this love; whereas, in fact, in all these cases the intensity of love precisely excludes the very possibility not only of valuable progeny, but of any descendents whatsoever.

Instances of unrequited love are too usual and ordinary to see in them only an exception that can be abandoned without consideration. Indeed, if it were thus, it would assist little in the matter, for even in those cases where love appears especially intense from both sides, it does not lead to that which is required by the theory. According to the theory, Romeo and Juliet should have, corresponding to their great mutual passion, given birth to some very great man—at least a Shakespeare. But in fact, as everybody knows, it was the other way around: it was not they who created Shakespeare, as should have followed according to the theory, but he them, and moreover without any passion—by means of asexual creation. Romeo and Juliet died, as do also the majority of passionate lovers, not having given birth to anyone; but Shakespeare who gave birth to them, was born, like other great people as well, not of a madly enamoured couple, but of an ordinary, everyday marriage (and although he himself experienced intense loving passion—as is apparent, by the way, from his sonnets—no remarkable progeny resulted from this). For the universal will, the birth of Christopher Columbus was, perhaps, even more important than the birth of Shakespeare; but we know nothing about any special love of his parents; yet we do know about his especially intense passion for Donna Beatrice Enriques; and although he had by her an illegitimately born son, Diego, this son produced nothing great, but only wrote a biography of his father, which any other could have carried out as well.

If the entire meaning of love is in progeny and the supreme power directs matters of love, then why does it, in place of striving to unite the lovers, on the contrary and as if intentionally, impede this joining, as if its mission is precisely to remove at whatever cost the very possibility of progeny from true lovers? It forces them out of fateful misunderstanding to bury themselves in crypts, drowns them in the Hellespont, and by all other means leads them to an untimely and childless end.[7] And in those rare instances when intense love does not take a tragic turn, when a loving couple happily lives to old age, it remains, for all that, barren. A reliable poetic flair for reality compelled both Ovid and Gogol to deprive Philemon and Baucis as well as Afanasii Ivanovich and Pulkheria Ivanovna of progeny.[8]

It is not possible to acknowledge a direct correspondence between the intensity of individual love and the value of progeny when the very existence of progeny in the presence of such a love is only a rare fortuity. As we have seen, (1) intense love quite usually remains unrequited; (2) in requital, intense passion leads to a tragic end, not resulting in the production of progeny; (3) happy love, if it is very powerful, also usually remains fruitless. And on those rare occasions when an unusually intense love produces progeny, they turn out to be very commonplace. It is possible to establish as a general rule, from which there is almost no exception, that a special intensity of sexual love either does not grant progeny at all, or grants only the kind whose importance does not at all correspond to the intensiveness of the loving feeling and the exceptional character of the relations engendered by it.

To see the meaning of sexual love in expedient procreation means to acknowledge this meaning only where love itself does not exist at all, and where it does exist, to remove from it any meaning and all justification. Compared with reality, this supposed theory of love turns out to be not an explanation, but a rejection of every explanation.

III.

The force directing the life of humanity—which some call the universal will, and others the unconscious spirit, and which in fact is Divine Providence—without doubt manages opportunely the birth of providential people necessary for its ends, arranging in a long series of generations the necessary combinations of procreators in view of future products, not only the most proximate, but the remotest as well.[9] The most diverse means are used for this providential selection of procreators; but love in a special sense (i.e., extraordinary, individualized, and impassioned sexual attraction) does not belong among the number of these means. In this case, as always, biblical history, with its truly profound realism, which does not exclude but embodies the ideal meaning of facts in their empirical details, gives truthful and edifying evidence for every man with a historical and artistic sense, independent of religious faith.

The central fact of biblical history, the birth of the Messiah, more than any other assumes a providential plan in the selection and union of successive procreators; and indeed, the chief interest of biblical stories concentrates on the multifarious and miraculous destinies by which the births and unions of the "god-sires" were arranged.*[10] But in the entire complex system of means that determined in a series of historical phenomena the birth of the Messiah, there was no place for love in a special sense. Of course, love is encountered in the Bible, but only as an independent fact and not as an instrument of the Christogonical process.[11] Holy scripture does not say whether Abram marries Sarai on the strength of ardent love.†[12] But, in any event, Providence waited until this love would cool completely in order to produce a child of faith—and not out of love, but out of centenarian parents. Isaac married Rebecca not out of love, but according to a decision and plan arranged by his father beforehand. Jacob loved Rachel, but this love turns out to be unnecessary for the descendancy of the Messiah. He must descend from a son of Jacob—Judah—who is brought forth not by Rachel but by Leah, who is unloved by her husband.[13] For the procreation of an ancestor of the Messiah in a given generation, the union of Jacob precisely with Leah was essential; but, in order to achieve this combination, Providence does not arouse in Jacob any intense, loving passion toward the future mother of a "god-procreator," Judah.[14] Not violating the freedom of heartfelt feeling, the supreme power lets him love Rachel, but uses means completely of another kind for Jacob's essential union with Leah: the self-interested cunning of a third person, Laban, who is devoted to his familial and economic interests.[15] For procreation of the Messiah's remote ancestors, Judah himself must, in spite of his first progeny, join in old age with his daughter-in-law Tamar. Since such a union was not at all in the order of things and could not have taken place under ordinary conditions, the end is achieved by means of an extremely strange adventure, highly seductive for superficial readers of

---

* Chiefly, Sts. Joakim and Anna are referred to in this way in ecclesial language, but other ancestors of the Blessed Virgin also sometimes carry this title among ecclesial writers.

† Apparently, this is excluded by the well-known adventure in Egypt, which would have been psychologically impossible with intense love.

the Bible.[16] There cannot even be any talk about any kind of love in this adventure. Neither is it love that joins the Jerichoan prostitute Rahab with a Hebrew visitor.[17] At first, she gives herself to him according to her profession, but later the chance connection is validated by her faith in the power of a new God and the hope of his protection for herself and her own. Nor was it love that joined David's great-grandfather, the old man Boaz, to the young Moabitess Ruth; and Solomon was born not out of a real profound love, but only out of the chance, sinful caprice of an aging sovereign [David].[18]

In sacred history, just as in common history, sexual love is not a means or an instrument of historical goals; it does not serve humankind. Therefore, when a subjective feeling says to us that love is an independent good, that it has a special, absolute value for our personal life, corresponding to this feeling is also the fact that intense individual love in objective reality never exists as a subordinate instrument of generative ends, which are achieved in spite of it. In common history, just as in sacred history, sexual love (in the proper sense) plays no role and does not exert a direct effect on the historical process: its positive significance must be rooted in individual life. Just what kind of meaning does it have here?

Second Article

I.

Sexual love is the supreme blossom of individual life in both animals and man. But since generative life decisively outweighs individual life in animals, then even the highest intensity of the latter goes only to the benefit of the generative process. Sexual attraction is not only the means for simple procreation or reproduction of organisms, but with the help of sexual competition and selection, it serves the procreation of *more perfect* organisms. An attempt was made to ascribe just such a significance to sexual love in the human world as well, but, as we have seen, completely in vain. For in humanity, individuality has an independent significance and cannot be in its most powerful expression only an instrument of the ends of a historical process external to it. Or, better said, the true end of the historical process is not of such a kind that human personality can serve it only as a passive and transient instrument.

Conviction in the unconditional value of man is not based on self-conceit or on the empirical fact that we do not know another more perfect being in the natural order. The unconditional value of man consists in the absolute form (image) of a rational consciousness, without doubt peculiar to him. While recognizing, as animals themselves also do, the conditions endured and experienced by him, and observing among them one or another connection, and on the basis of this connection anticipating by force of mind the conditions of the future, man has *over and above this* the capacity to evaluate his conditions and actions and all facts in general, not only in their relation to other isolated facts but also to universal ideal norms. Above and beyond the phenomena of life, his consciousness is also formed by a *sense of truth*. Considering his actions with this higher consciousness, man can infinitely perfect his life and nature *without leaving the boundaries of human form*. And therefore, he is indeed the supreme being of the natural world and the effective end of the world-creative process.[19] For, apart from Being, which alone among all others is the eternal and absolute truth, that which is capable of perceiving and realizing in itself the truth is supreme, not in a relative but in an absolute sense. What rational foundation is it possible to invent for the creation of new, in essence more perfect, forms when there is already a form capable of endless self-perfection, empowered to accommodate the entire plenitude of absolute content? With the appearance of such a form, further progress can consist only in new degrees of its own development, and not in its replacement by any creatures of another type, other unprecedented forms of being.

In this there is an essential difference between the cosmogonic and the historical process. The first gradually creates (until the appearance of man) newer and newer types of being, while some of the former ones are destroyed as unsuccessful experiments and others coexist together with a new external form and randomly collide among themselves, not forming any effective unity owing to the absence in them of a general consciousness that would connect them among themselves and with the cosmic past. Such a general consciousness appears in humanity. In the world of animals, the succession of the higher forms from the lower forms, in all its regularity and expediency, is for animals an absolutely extrinsic and alien fact which for them does not exist at all: an elephant and a monkey can know nothing about the complex process of geological and biological transformations that caused their appearance on earth. A comparatively high degree of development of individual and isolated consciousness does not signify here any progress in general consciousness, which is just as absolutely absent in these intelligent animals as in a dumb oyster. The complex brain of a higher mammal serves the self-illumination of nature in its integrity as little as rudimentary nervous ganglia serve any worm. In humanity, on the contrary, universal consciousness proceeds through heightened individual consciousness, religious and scientific. The individual mind here is not only an organ of solitary life, but an organ of recollection and conjecture for all of humanity, and even for all of nature as well.

The Hebrew who wrote: *this is the book of the generations of heaven and earth* (*elle tol'dot hashamaim ve haarets*), and further: *this is the book of the generations of man* (*ze sefer tol'dot haadam*), did not only express his personal and national consciousness, for through him shone forth in the world for the first time the truth of universal and all-human unity.*[20] And all further progress of consciousness consists only in the development and embodiment of this truth. It is not possible for him to vacate, and there is no point in him vacating, this *universal* form: and what else can the most complete astronomy and geology do but establish fully the genesis of the heavens and the earth. Exactly in the same way, the supreme objective of historical knowledge can be only to establish "the book of the generations of man" (that is, a genetic, continuous connection in the life of humanity). And, finally, our creative activity cannot have a higher goal than to embody in tangible forms this unity of the heavens, earth, and man, created and proclaimed from the beginning. *All truth*—the positive unity of everything—was from the beginning placed in the living consciousness of man and is gradually carried out in the life of humanity with conscious continuity (for a truth *that does not recall kinship* is not truth). Thanks to the limitless extensibility and indissolubility of his continuous consciousness, man, left to himself, can achieve and realize the entire, limitless fullness of existence, and thus no higher types of beings are necessary or possible to replace him. Within the boundaries of his given reality, man is only a part of nature; but he constantly and consistently breaches these boundaries. In the products of his mind—religion and science, morality and art—he comes to light as the center of a universal consciousness of nature, as the soul of the world, as the realized potential of absolute all-unity; and consequently, above him can be only the most absolute in its perfected act, or eternal existence, i.e., God.

---

* If it is said that these words are divinely inspired, then this is not an objection, but only a translation of my thought into theological language.

II.

The advantage of man over other creatures of nature—the faculty to per-
ceive and to realize truth—is not only generic, but also individual: *every*
man is capable of perceiving and realizing truth, each one can become a
living reflection of the absolute whole, a conscious and independent organ
of universal life. There is truth (or the divine image) in the rest of nature
as well, but only in its objective commonality, unknown to individual creatures; it fashions them and acts in them and through them as a fateful
force, as a law of their existence unknown to the creatures themselves, a
law to which they submit involuntarily and unconsciously. For they themselves, in their inner sensations and consciousness, cannot rise above their
given fragmentary existence; and they find themselves only in their particularity, separated from *everything,* and consequently, outside of truth. Therefore truth, or universality, can triumph here only in the replacement of
generations, in the tenure of kind and in loss of individual life, which does
not accommodate in itself truth. Human individuality, however, is not
abolished by truth, but is preserved and strengthened in its triumph, precisely because human individuality can accommodate truth in itself.

But in order that an individual being find in truth—in all-unity—its
justification and affirmation, a consciousness of truth alone on its part is
insufficient. This being must exist in truth; but an individual man, just
as an animal, does not exist in truth originally and spontaneously: he finds
himself as an isolated element of the universal whole and he affirms this,
his fragmentary existence, in egoism as the whole for himself; and he wants
to be the "all" himself and to exist completely separate from everything—
outside truth. As the actual practical and fundamental principle of individual life, egoism directs and permeates its entirety, determines in it everything concretely; and therefore, in a theoretical consciousness of truth
alone, it can in no way outweigh and abolish it. Until the living force of
egoism in man meets another living force opposed to it, consciousness of
truth is only a superficial illumination, the flash of an alien light. If man
could in this sense only accommodate truth, then the connection of his
individuality with it would not be intrinsic and indissoluble; his own being,
remaining as an animal outside truth, would be as the animal, doomed (in
its subjectivity) to destruction, being preserved only as an idea in a thought
of absolute Mind.

Truth, as a living force that takes possession of the inner essence of
man and effectively leads him out of false self-affirmation, is called love.
Love, as the effective abolition of egoism, is a valid justification and re-

demption of individuality. Love is more than rational consciousness, but without it love would not be able to act as an intrinsic redemptive force, ennobling, and not abolishing, individuality. Man can differentiate his own self (that is, his true individuality) from his egoism thanks only to rational consciousness (or consciousness of truth). And therefore, in sacrificing this egoism and giving himself over to love, he finds in it not only a living, but a vivifying force as well; and he does not lose together with his egoism his individual essence, but to the contrary, immortalizes it. Owing to the absence of a proper rational consciousness in the world of animals, the truth that is realized in love, but does not find in animals an intrinsic point of rest for its activity, can act only bluntly as an extrinsic and portentous force, controlling them as blind instruments for universal ends alien to them. Here, love appears as a unilateral triumph of the general, the generic over the individual, inasmuch as, in animals, their individuality coincides with egoism in the spontaneity of fragmentary existence, and therefore perishes together with it as well.

III.

In general, the meaning of human love is *the justification and redemption of individuality through the sacrifice of egoism*. On this common foundation we can also resolve our special problem: to explain the meaning of sexual love. It is not without reason that sexual relations not only are called love, but also by general acknowledgment represent love, for the most part appearing as a type and ideal of every other love (see the Song of Songs and Revelation).

The falsehood and evil of egoism consist not at all in the fact that a man appreciates himself too highly and attaches to himself unconditional significance and infinite value: in this he is correct, because every human subject—as an independent center of living forces, as the potential (possibility) of infinite perfection, as a creature capable of accommodating absolute truth in its consciousness and in its life—every man in this capacity has absolute significance and value, is something absolutely irreplaceable, and cannot evaluate himself too highly. (In the words of the Gospel: What will a man give in exchange for his soul?)[21] The lack of one's acknowledgment of this unconditional significance is tantamount to a renunciation of human worth; this is the fundamental error and source of every unbelief: he is so fainthearted that he is unable to believe even in himself—how can he believe in anything else? The basic falsehood and evil of egoism is not in this absolute self-consciousness and self-appreciation of a subject, but in the fact that while attributing to itself justly an unconditional significance, it unjustly rejects others in this significance. Acknowledging itself as the center of life, which it in fact is, it ascribes others to the circumference of its objective reality, reserving for them only an extrinsic and relative value.

Of course, in the abstract theoretical consciousness, any man whose reason is not impeded always allows a full equality of the rights of others with himself; but in the living consciousness, in his intrinsic feeling and in actual practice, he affirms an infinite difference, a complete incommensurability between himself and others: he in himself is everything, they in themselves are—nothing. Meanwhile, and precisely in such an exclusive self-affirmation, a man cannot in fact be that which he affirms himself to be. That unconditional significance, the absoluteness that he in general justly acknowledges for himself but unjustly removes from others, has in itself only a potential character—it is only a possibility that requires its realization. God *is* everything (that is, possessing in one absolute act all positive content), the entire plenitude of being. Man (in general, and every individual man in particular), being actually only *this one* and not *the other,* can *become* everything only by removing in his consciousness and life the external barrier that separates him from another. "This one" can be "everything" only *together with others;* only together with others can he realize his unconditional significance—to become an inseparable and irreplaceable part of the all-united whole, an independent, true, and distinctive organ of absolute life. True individualilty is a certain fixed mode of all-unity, a certain fixed manner of perception and assimilation of all else to oneself. In affirming himself outside of everything else, man by the same token strips his own existence of meaning, removes from himself the true content of life, and transforms his individuality into empty form. Thus, egoism in no way is self-consciousness and self-affirmation of individuality, but the opposite—self-negation and ruin.

The metaphysical and physical, historical and social conditions of human existence in every way modify and assuage our egoism, assuming strong and multifarious barriers against its disclosure in pure form and in all its horrible consequences. But this entire complex system of obstacles and correctives, predetermined by Providence and implemented by nature and history, leaves untouched the very foundation of egoism, which constantly peers out from under the covers of personal and social morality, and on occasion is also displayed in full plainness. There is only one force that can from within and at root undermine egoism, and actually does undermine it: namely love, and chiefly sexual love. The falsehood and evil of egoism consist in the exclusive acknowledgment of the unconditional significance of self and in its denial in others. Reason shows us that this is unfounded and unjust, and to all intents and purposes love directly abolishes such an unjust attitude, compelling us, not in abstract consciousness but in an inner feeling and in the viable will, to acknowledge for ourselves the unconditional significance of the other. In perceiving the truth of another not abstractly, but materially, in love, in transferring the center of our life beyond the boundaries of our empirical self in practice, we by the same token manifest and realize our own truth, our unconditional significance, which consists also precisely in the capacity of crossing the boundaries of our actual phenomenal objective reality, in being capable of living not only in ourselves, but in another as well.

Every love is a manifestation of this capacity, but not every love realizes it to an identical degree, not every love identically and radically undermines egoism. Egoism is not only a real force, but a fundamental one that has rooted itself in the very deepest center of our existence, and from there permeating and embracing all our reality—a force continuously acting in all the particulars and details of our being. In order to undermine egoism in a genuine way, it is necessary to counterpose to it a love just as concretely defined that permeates all our being, absorbing everything into it. The other, who must liberate our individuality from the shackles of egoism, must have a correlation with all this individuality, must be just as real and concrete, fully objectified by the subject, as we ourselves are. And at the same time, the other must differ from us in everything in order to be truly the other (i.e., having all the essential content that we also have, having it by other means, in another form); so that every manifestation of our essence, every living act we encounter in this other corresponding but not identical manifestation, the attitude of one to the other, is a full and continual interchange, a full and continual affirmation of self in the other, a perfect interaction and intercourse. Only then will egoism be undermined and abolished not only in principle, but in all its concrete reality. Only at that, so to speak, chemical joining of two elements, homogeneous and equivalent, but *all-round* different according to form, is the creation of a new human being, an authentic realization of true human individuality, possible (both in the natural order and in the spiritual order). We find such a union, or at least the most proximate possibility to it, in sexual love, which is why we attribute to it exclusive significance as the necessary and irreplaceable foundation of all further perfection, as an inevitable and permanent condition under the auspices of which only man can effectively exist in truth.

IV.

Recognizing fully the great importance and the lofty merit of other kinds of love, which false spiritualism and impotent moralism would like to substitute for sexual love, we see, however, that only the latter satisfies two fundamental requirements, without which a resolute abolition of self in a complete and vital intercourse with another is not possible.[22] Either homogeneity (and equality and cooperation between the lover and the beloved) or an all-round distinction of properties that make up one another is lacking in all other kinds of love.

So, in mystical love, the object of love at long last amounts to an absolute indifference that devours human individuality; here, egoism is abolished only in a wholly insufficient sense in which it is abolished when a man falls into a state of deep sleep (with which the union of the individual soul with the universal spirit is compared and sometimes even directly identified in the Upanishads and Vedas).[23] Not only can there be no vital intercourse between a living man and the mystical "Abyss" of absolute indifference, according to the complete heterogeneity and incommensurability of these two quantities, but there cannot even be a simple compatibility: if there is an object of love, then there is no lover—he vanished, lost himself, became immersed as if in a deep sleep without dreams; and when he comes to, the object of love vanishes and, in place of absolute indifference, a multi-hued variegation of actual life is restored against a backdrop of personal egoism adorned with spiritual pride. History knows, however, of mystics and entire schools of mysticism where the object of love was understood not as absolute indifference, but assumed concrete forms that allowed this object relations. But—very much remarkably— these relations received here the quite distinct and consequently mature character of sexual love. . . .[24]

Parental love—maternal in particular—both by intensity of feeling and by concreteness of the object, approaches sexual love, but for other reasons cannot have equal significance to it for human individuality. It is conditional on the fact of propagation and on the law of the replacement of generations with that which predominates in animal life, but does not have, or in any event ought not to have, such significance in human life. In animals, the subsequent generation directly and quickly annuls its predecessors and lays bare the senselessness of their existence, only in order to be immediately, in its turn, laid bare in the same senselessness of existence by its own broods. Maternal love in humanity, which sometimes attains a high degree of self-sacrifice that we find in a hen's love, is a remnant of this order of things, undoubtedly necessary for the time being. In any event, it is without doubt that in maternal love there cannot be full mutuality and vital intercourse now, because the lover and the beloved belong to different generations; because for the latter, life is in the future with new independent interests and problems, in the midst of which representatives of the past are only as pale shadows. It is enough that parents cannot be for children the aim of life in the sense in which children exist for parents.[25]

Of course, setting her entire soul on the children, a mother sacrifices her egoism, but she at the same time also loses her individuality; and even if maternal love upholds individualism in them, it preserves and even strengthens egoism. Apart from this, in maternal love there is not a proper acknowledgment of unconditional significance of the beloved, an acknowledgment of its true individuality, because, although for the mother her child is dearer than anything, it is only precisely as her child, and not otherwise—just as is the case with other animals. That is to say that, here a supposed acknowledgment of the unconditional significance of another in reality is conditional upon an extrinsic physiological connection.

Still less can the remaining kinds of sympathetic feelings have a claim to take the place of sexual love. Friendship between persons of one and the same sex lacks an all-round formal distinction of qualities making up one another. But if, nevertheless, this friendship achieves a particular intensity, then it changes into an unnatural surrogate of sexual love. As for patriotism and love of humanity, these feelings, in all their importance, cannot in themselves concretely and vigorously abolish egoism, owing to the incommensurability of the lover and loved one. Neither humanity nor even the nation can be for an individual man as concrete an object as he himself. It is certainly possible to sacrifice one's life for the nation or humanity, but to create out of oneself a new human being, to manifest and realize true human individuality on the basis of this extensive love is not possible. Here the real center still remains one's old egoistic *I*, and the nation and humanity belong to the periphery of consciousness as ideal objects. The same should be said about love for science, art, etc.

Having indicated in a few words the true meaning of sexual love and its advantages before other related feelings, I should explain why it is so feebly realized in reality, and show how its full implementation is possible. I will attend to this in subsequent articles.

THIRD ARTICLE

I.

The meaning and value of love as feelings consist in the fact that love compels us effectively to acknowledge in *another,* with all our being, the unconditional, central significance that, on the strength of egoism, we sense only in ourselves. Love is important not as one of our sensations, but as the transfer of all of our life's vital interest from ourselves into another, as the transposition of the very center of our personal life. This is characteristic of every love, but chiefly of sexual love.* It differs from other kinds of love both by greater intensity, a more captivating character, and by the possibility of a fuller and all-round mutuality. Only this love can lead to a true and indissoluble union of two lives in one, and only concerning this love is it said in the word of God: And the two will become one flesh (that is, will become one real essence).[26]

The feeling requires such a wholeness of union, inherent and definitive, but the matter usually does not go farther than this subjective requirement and striving; indeed, even that turns out to be only transient. In practice, in place of the poetry of an eternal and intrinsic union arises only a more or less prolonged, but nevertheless temporary, a more or less intimate, but nevertheless extrinsic, superficial drawing together of two isolated beings in the constricted framework of everyday prose. The object of love does not preserve in reality that unconditional significance attached to it by an amorous reverie. To an outsider's view, this is clear from the very beginning; but the involuntary tinge of ridicule that unavoidably accompanies an outsider's attitude to lovers turns out to be only an anticipation of their own disappointment. The pathos of the loving attraction passes at once or little by little, and it is yet good if the energy of altruistic feelings that manifested themselves in it is not wasted in vain, but, having lost its concentration and lofty enthusiasm, is only transferred in a fragmented and diluted way to children, who are born and raised for a repetition of the very same deception. I say deception—from the point of view of *individual* life and the unconditional significance of human personality— while fully acknowledging the necessity and expediency of procreation

---

* I call sexual love (for want of a better name) the exclusive attachment (both reciprocal and unilateral) between persons of different sex, capable of being with one another in the relation of man and wife, not at all predetermining in this the question concerning significance of the physiological aspect of the matter.

and the replacement of generations for the progress of humanity in its collective life. But, properly speaking, love does not apply here. A coincidence of intense loving passion with successful procreation is only an accident, and a rare one at that; historical and everyday experience without doubt shows that children can be successfully born, ardently loved, and splendidly educated by their parents even if the latter were never in love with one another. Consequently, the social and universal interests of humanity connected with the replacement of generations do not at all require the lofty pathos of love. And in the meantime, this finest of its blossoms turns out to be a poor flower in individual life. The primary point of love here loses all its meaning when its object descends from the loftiness of the absolute center of immortal individuality to the level of a coincidental and easily replaceable means for procreation of a new—maybe a little better, and maybe a little worse, but in any case, relative and transient—generation of people.

Thus, if one looks only at that which usually occurs, at the actual result of love, then it must be acknowledged as a reverie that temporarily takes possession of our being and vanishes, not getting down to any business whatsoever (since procreation is not properly a matter of love). But upon recognizing by virtue of its obviousness the fact that the ideal meaning of love is not implemented in reality, should we then acknowledge it as *infeasible?*

According to the very nature of man, who, in his rational consciousness, moral freedom, and capacity for self-perfection possesses infinite possibilities, we do not have the right to consider infeasible beforehand any task whatsoever, provided it does not contain within itself an intrinsic, logical contradiction or inconsistency with the general meaning of the universal and expedient course of cosmic and historical development.

It would be completely unfair to deny the feasibility of love only on the basis that it has hitherto never been realized; indeed, much else has once found itself in just this situation: for example, all the sciences and the arts, civil society, and control of the forces of nature. Even the most rational consciousness, before becoming an actuality in man, was only a vague and unsuccessful aspiration in the world of animals. How many geological and biological epochs passed in unsuccessful attempts to create a brain capable of becoming an organ for the embodiment of rational thought! For man, love is, for the time being, the very same thing that reason was for the world of animals: it exists in its beginnings or rudiments, but not yet in actual practice.[27] And if vast worldwide epochs—witnesses to infeasible reason—did not prevent it finally from being realized, then all the more the infeasibility of love in the course of a relatively few millenia endured by historical humanity in no way gives the right to conclude anything against its future realization. It ought only to be recalled that if the reality of rational consciousness appeared in man, but not by means of him, then the realization of love, as the supreme step to the proper life of man himself, should arise not only in him, but *through him* as well.

The task of love consists in *justifying in practice* the meaning of love, which at first was given only in feeling; a combination of two given restricted beings is required, such that it would create from them an absolute ideal personality. This task not only does not contain in itself any intrinsic contradiction and any inconsistency with universal meaning, but is directly given by our spiritual nature, the particularity of which consists precisely in the fact that man can, remaining as himself, in his own proper form, accommodate absolute content, become absolute personality. But in order to become imbued with absolute content (which in religious language is called eternal life or the Kingdom of God), the human form itself must be restored in its entirety (integrated). In empirical reality, the human being, as such, does not exist at all—it exists only in a certain one-sidedness and restrictiveness, as male or female individuality (and already on this basis all other distinctions evolve). But a true human being in the fullness of its ideal personality obviously cannot be only male or only female, but must be the highest unity of both.[28] The proper, most immediate task of love is to realize this unity or to create a true human being as a free unity of the male and female principle, preserving their formal solitariness, but having overcome their essential discord and disintegration. Examining the conditions required for its actual resolution, we will become quite convinced that only the nonobservation of these conditions leads love to habitual breakdown and compels us to acknowledge it as illusion.

II.

The first step to the successful resolution of any problem is its conscious and faithful presentation: but the problem of love has never been consciously presented and, therefore, has never been resolved as it should. Love has been viewed and is viewed only as a given fact, as a state (normal for some, unhealthy for others) that is endured by a human being, but that does not oblige one to anything. True, two problems are appended here: physiological possession by the beloved person and everyday union with him—of the two, the latter imposes certain obligations—but here now the matter obeys the laws of animal nature, on the one hand, and the laws of a civic way of life on the other; and love, from the beginning and to the end, left to its own, vanishes like a mirage.

Of course, love is first of all a fact of nature (or a divine gift), a natural process emerging independently of us; but from here it does not follow that we could not and must not consciously relate to it and, by our own initiative, direct this natural process toward higher aims. The gift of speech is also a natural attribute of man; just as with love, language is not contrived. However, it would be extremely sad if we related to it only as to a natural process that occurs in us of itself; and if we spoke as the birds sing, we would give ourselves up to natural combinations of sounds and words for the expression of feelings and notions involutarily passing through our soul, but not making of the language instruments for the consistent realization of certain thoughts, of means for the attainment of rational and consciously purveyed goals. In an exclusively passive and unconscious attitude to the gift of speech, neither science nor art nor a civic way of life could be cultivated; indeed, even language itself, in consequence of the insufficient application of this gift, would not have evolved and would have remained in its rudimentary manifestations alone. Whatever significance *speech* has for the formation of human community and culture, love has the very same and an even greater significance for the creation of true human individuality. And if, in the first realm (community and culture), we note indubitable, although slow, progress, while human individuality from the beginning of historical time up to the present remains invariable in its actual limitations, then the first cause of such a difference is the fact that we relate to verbal activity and to the production of speech gradually more and more consciously and by our own initiative; but love remains as before, completely in the dark realm of vague fits of passion and involuntary attractions.

As the true assignment of speech consists not in the process of speaking in itself, but in *what* is being spoken — in the revelation of the reason of things through speech or understanding — so too the true assignment of love consists not in the simple experience of this feeling, but in that which takes place by means of it — in the act of love. It is insufficient for one to feel for oneself the unconditional significance of the beloved object, but actually necessary to give or to communicate to the beloved this significance, to unite with it in the actual creation of absolute individuality. And just as the lofty task of verbal activity is already predetermined in the very nature of words, which inevitably represent common and static concepts and not separate and transient impressions (and consequently, already in themselves being a connection of many into one, lead us to an understanding of universal meaning), in a very similar manner the lofty task of love is also already forecast in the loving feeling itself, which inevitably, before every realization, introduces its object into the sphere of absolute individualilty, sees it in an ideal world, and believes in its unconditionality. Thus, in both cases (both in the realm of verbal knowledge and in the realm of love), the task consists not in inventing out of oneself anything completely new, but only in consistently conducting further and bringing to a conclusion that which is already given rudimentarily in the very nature of the act, at the very basis of the process. But if speech has evolved and continues to evolve in humanity, then people have remained and continue to remain, relative to love, up to the present time in the presence of natural rudiments alone; and indeed, these are understood poorly in their true meaning.

III.

Everyone knows that in love there occurs a special *idealization* of the beloved subject, which appears to the lover to be completely in a light other than the one in which people outside see him or her. I speak here of light not only in the metaphysical sense; the point here does not only concern a particular moral and intellectual evaluation, but also a special sensual perception: the lover actually *sees*, visually perceives, what others do not. Even for him, by the way, this amorous light soon vanishes; but does it follow from here that it was false, that this was only a subjective illusion?

The true essence of each human being, and man in general, is not exhausted by his given empirical phenomena—rational and established grounds cannot be contrasted to this situation from any point of view. For the materialist and sensualist, no less than for the spiritualist and idealist, that which seems is not identical to that which is; and when the matter concerns two distinct kinds of seemingness, then the question is always legitimate as to which of these kinds most coincides with that which is, or better, that which expresses the nature of things. For that which seems to be, or appearance in general, is an actual relation or interaction between the seer and the seen and, consequently, is defined by their mutual properties. The external world of a man and the external world of a mole—both consist only of relative phenomena or appearances; however, hardly anyone will seriously doubt the fact that one of these two seeming worlds is superior to the other, corresponds more to that which is closer to truth.

We know that man, apart from his animal and material nature, has yet an ideal nature that connects him with absolute Truth, or God. Besides the material or empirical content of his life, each man contains within himself the divine image (that is, a particular form of absolute content). This divine image is perceived by us theoretically and abstractly in reason and through reason, but in love it is perceived concretely and vividly. And if this revelation of ideal being, usually shut off by material phenomena, is not restricted in love by inner feeling alone, but becomes sometimes tangible in the sphere of external sensations as well, then the more significance we should acknowledge for love as the principle of the perceived restoration of the divine image in the material world, as the source of embodiment of the true ideal of humanness. The power of love, converting into light, transforming and inspiring the form of extrinsic phenomena, reveals to us its objective potency; but that is why it is now up to us: we ourselves must understand this revelation and avail ourselves of it, so that it not be left as a fleeting and enigmatic flash of some mystery.

The spiritually physical process of the restoration of the divine image in material humanity in no way can be effected on its own, apart from us. Its beginning, as with all the best in this world, emerges from what is for us the dark realm of unconscious processes and attitudes; the seed and roots of the tree of life are there, but we must grow it by our own conscious action. A passive receptiveness of feeling is sufficient for a start; but then active faith is necessary as moral exploit and labor, in order to hold on to, strengthen, and develop this gift of serene and creative love, in order to embody in oneself and in another the divine image by means of it, and to create one absolute and eternal individuality from two finite and mortal beings. If the idealization peculiar to love inevitably and involuntarily shows us the distant ideal image of a beloved object through an empirical manifestation, then, of course, this is not so that we only be in love with it; this is also so that we might transform, according to this true image, a reality that does not correspond to it — transform it by the power of true faith, of real imagination and real creative work, and that we embody in it as well an actual phenomenon.

But who has ever thought anything similar concerning love? The knights and minnesingers of the Middle Ages, in their intense faith but feeble rationality, contented themselves with the simple identity of a love ideal with a given person, closing their eyes to the obvious discrepancy.[29] This faith was as firm, but just as fruitless, as the stone upon which the famous knight von-Grunvalis sat "at the castle of Amali . . . always in the same position."[30]

Medieval love was, of course, also connected with a thirst for exploits apart from a faith that compelled one only to contemplate reverently and to praise exaltedly the imaginarily personified ideal. But these martial and destructive exploits, not having any relation to the ideal that had inspired them, could not lead to realization of the ideal. Even the pale knight who completely devoted himself to the impression of heavenly beauty that had been revealed to him, not confusing it with earthly phenomena, was inspired as well by this revelation only in actions that served more to the detriment of foreigners than the utility and glory of the "eternal feminine."

> Lumen coeli! Sancta Rosa!
> he, wild and ardent, exclaimed.
> And his threat struck
> The Muslims like thunder.[31]

Of course, there was no need to have "visions, incomprehensible to the mind" for the defeat of the Muslims. But this bifurcation between heavenly visions of Christianity and "wild and ardent" forces in real life weighed upon the entire medieval knighthood, until, finally, the most famous and last of the knights, Don Quixote de la Mancha, having slain many rams and broken not a few wings off windmills (but not at all able to bring a dairymaid from Toboso near to the ideal of Dulcinea), arrived not at a true, but only at a negative, consciousness of his error. And if that typical knight remained faithful to the end to his vision and "died as a madman," then Don Quixote crossed over from madness only to a sorrowful and hopeless disillusionment in his ideal.

This disillusionment of Don Quixote was chivalry's bequest to the new Europe. It operates in us even up to the present day. Amorous idealization, having ceased being a source of insane exploits, inspires no exploits at all. It turns out to be only an allurement that compels us to desire physical and common everyday control, and that vanishes as soon as this completely non-ideal goal is achieved. This light of love does not serve anyone as a guiding beam to a lost paradise; it is gazed upon as a fantastic illumination of a brief, amorous "prologue to heaven," which then nature very much opportunely extinguishes as completely unnecessary for the ensuing terrestrial presentation. In fact, this light actually extinguishes the weakness and involuntariness of our love, which distorts the true course of the matter.

IV.

Common, extrinsic, and, particularly, physiological unions do not have a positive relation to love. Such unions occur without love, and love occurs without them. They are necessary for love not as its indispensable condition and independent aim, but only as its final culmination. If this culmination is set as a goal in itself prior to the ideal practice of love, it ruins love. Every extrinsic act or fact is, in itself, nothing; love is something only thanks to its meaning, or Idea, as the restoration of the unity or the integrity of human personality, as the creation of absolute individuality. The extrinsic acts and facts connected with love are nothing in themselves: their significance is determined by their associations to that which constitutes love itself and its practice. When a zero is placed after a whole number, it increases it by ten times, but when it is placed prior to it, this diminishes or reduces it by as much, removing from it the character of a whole number, transforming it into a decimal fraction; and the more of those zeroes that preface the whole number, the smaller the fraction and the closer it gets to zero itself.

The feeling of love in itself is only an impulse, suggesting to us that we can and must recreate the integrity of the human essence. Each time this holy spark is ignited in the human heart, the entire groaning and suffering creation awaits the first revelation of the glory of the sons of God.[32] But without the action of the conscious human soul, the divine spark is extinguished and a beguiled nature creates new generations of the sons of man for new hopes.

These hopes are not being fulfilled so long as we do not want to acknowledge fully and realize completely all that true love requires and all that is contained in its Idea. To begin with, two facts stop us short at a conscious attitude to love and an actual resolution to fulfill its mission. Apparently, this dooms us to impotence and justifies those who consider love as an illusion. In the feeling of love, according to its fundamental meaning, we affirm the unconditional significance of another individual, and through this the unconditional significance of our own individuality as well. But absolute individuality cannot be *fleeting,* and it cannot be *vacant.* The inevitability of death and the emptiness of our lives are completely incompatible with the elevated affirmation of individuality of self and other that is contained in the feeling of love. This feeling, if it is intense and entirely conscious, cannot be reconciled with certainty in the forthcoming decrepitness and death of the beloved person as well as one-self. Meanwhile, the unquestionable fact that people have always died and continue to die is accepted by everyone, or almost everyone, as an un-conditionally incontestable law (so that, even in formal logic, this con-viction is used for the construction of a model syllogism: "all people are mortal, X is a person, therefore X is mortal"). Many, it is true, believe in the immortality of the soul; but it is precisely the sensation of love that shows better than anything the insufficiency of this abstract faith. A dis-embodied spirit is not a human being, but an angel. However, we love the human being, the whole human individuality, and if love is the source of lucidity and inspiration for this individuality, then it necessarily requires the preservation of it as such; it requires eternal youth and the immor-tality of this particular human being, of this embodied living spirit in a corporeal organism. An angel or pure spirit has no need of illumination and inspiration; only flesh is illuminated and inspired, and it is the neces-sary object of love. It is possible to imagine anything one wants, but it is possible to love only something living and concrete; and, in truly loving it, it is not possible to be reconciled with the certainty of its destruction.

But if the inevitability of death is incompatible with true love, then immortality is completely incompatible with the emptiness of our life. For the majority of humankind, life constitutes only shifts of difficult mechani-cal labor and coarsely sensed pleasures that deafen consciousness. And that minority which has the possibility of actively concerning itself not only with the means, but also with the ends of life, instead utilizes its freedom from mechanistic labor chiefly for senseless and immoral pastimes. I have nothing to add concerning the emptiness and immorality—involuntary and unconscious—of all this would-be life, after its magnificent reproduc-tion in "Anna Karenina," "The Death of Ivan Illych," and "The Kreutzer Sonata." * 33 In returning to my subject, I will point out only an obvious consideration: that for *this kind* of a life, death is not only inevitable, but even extremely desirable. Is it possible, without horrific sadness, even to imagine the infinitely continuing existence of any high-society lady, or any sportsman, or card player?

---

* Our "society"—and among that number ladies of high society—read these works, in particular "The Kreutzer Sonata," with delight. But hardly one of them after such reading turned down any invitation to a ball—this is how difficult it is to alter the practical functioning of the social sphere with ethics alone, even in perfect artis-tic form.

The incompatibility of immortality with *this kind* of existence is clear at first glance. But more attention will oblige us also to acknowledge the same incompatibility with respect to others, even those who appear more imbued with being. If, in place of a high-society lady or a gambler, we take, at the opposite pole, great people—geniuses—who have endowed humankind with immortal works or altered the fate of nations, then we will see that the content of their life and its historical fruits have significance only as gifts once and for always, and would lose all meaning with the infinite continuation of the individual existence of these geniuses on earth. The immortality of works, obviously, does not at all require, and even in itself excludes, the continuous immortality of the individual that produced them. Can one imagine Shakespeare eternally creating his dramas or Newton eternally continuing to study celestial mechanics—not to mention, even, the absurdity of the endless continuation of the activity for which Alexander the Great or Napoleon became famous? It is obvious that art, science, and politics, while giving content to different aspirations of the human spirit and satisfying the temporal historical requirements of humanity, do not at all impart an absolute, self-complacent content to human *individuality*, and therefore also do not have need of its immortality. Only love has need of this, and only it can achieve this. True love is that which not only affirms in subjective feeling the unconditional significance of human individuality in another and in oneself, but also justifies this unconditional significance in reality, effectively saves us from the inevitability of death, and fills our life with absolute content.

Fourth Article

I.

"Dionysus and Hades—are one and the same," said the most profound thinker of the ancient world.[34] Dionysus, the youthful and prosperous god of material life and the full intensity of its turbulent forces, the god of aroused and fruitful nature—is the same as Hades, pale lord of the gloomy and silent kingdom of departed shadows. The god of life and the god of death are one and the same. This is a truth, inarguable for the world of natural organisms. The abundance of life's forces simmering in an individual being is not its own life; it is an alien life, a life of a sort that is indifferent and merciless to it, and that is, for it, death. In the lower divisions of the animal kingdom this is quite clear; here individuals exist only for the purpose of bringing forth progeny, and then they die. In many varieties they do not survive the act of procreation; they die on the very spot. In others they survive only for a very short time. But if this connection between birth and death, between preservation of kind and destruction of the individual, is the law of nature, then, on the other hand, nature itself gradually limits and weakens this law more and more in its progressive development. The necessity for the individual to serve as a means for the maintenance of kind and to die after the fulfillment of this service remains, but the effect of this necessity appears less and less spontaneously and exclusively according to the perfection of organic forms and the increasing independence and consciousness of individual beings. Thus, the law of the identity of Dionysus and Hades (of generic life and individual death—or the law of opposition and struggle between kind and individual) acts more intensely on the lower levels of the organic world, and with the development of higher forms gradually weakens more and more. And if this is so, then with the manifestation of an absolutely supreme organic form, which envelops the individual self-conscious and self-initiating being and which disengages itself from nature and relates to nature as to an object (and consequently is capable of intrinsic freedom from procreative requirements), should not the end of this tyranny of kind over individual be at hand with the appearance of such a being? If, in the biological process, nature gradually aspires more and more to restrain the law of death, then should not man in the historical process completely countermand this law?

It is clear in itself that while man procreates like an animal, he also dies like an animal. But, on the other hand, it is just as clear that simple restraint from the procreative act does not at all deliver one from death: persons who preserve their virginity die; eunuchs also die. It is also clear that neither the one nor the other enjoys even a special durability. Death in general is the disintegration of a creature, the decay of the factors that constitute it. But the division of the sexes into male and female components of the human essence—a division not eliminated by a superficial and fleeting union in the reproductive act—is already, in itself, a state of disintegration and the beginning of death. To be in sexual distinction means to be on the path to death, and whoever cannot or does not want to leave this path must, according to natural necessity, traverse it to the end. He who sustains the root of death inevitably partakes of its fruit as well. Only the undivided human being can be immortal, and if physiological union cannot really restore the wholeness of the human essence, then this means that the spurious union must be exchanged for a true one and not replaced by any restraint from joining (that is, in no way by striving to hold a divided, disintegrated, and consequently mortal human character in statu quo).[35]

In what then does true union of the sexes consist, and how is it realized? Our life is so far from truth in this respect that only the less extreme, the less scandalous, abnormality is taken here for the norm. Before going further, it is necessary to elucidate this somewhat more.

II.

There have recently appeared in the psychiatric literature of Germany and France several books intended for specialists, dedicated to what the author of one of them has called psychopathia sexualis (i.e., multifarious deviations from the norm in sexual relations).[36] Apart from their special interest for law and medical students, these works and the patients themselves are of interest from yet another aspect. And this aspect is one that certainly neither the authors nor the majority of readers have thought about, *to wit*: what is striking in these treatises, written by respected scholars who are probably of irreproachable morality, is the absence of any clear and express understanding about a norm of sexual relations, about what is proper in this realm and why. Consequently, the definition of deviations from the norm (the very subject of these researches) turns out to be grasped casually and arbitrarily. The sole criterion turns out to be the singularity of the phenomena: those attractions and acts in the sexual realm that are comparatively rare are acknowledged as pathological deviations requiring treatment, and those that are routine and generally accepted are assumed as the norm.

Along with this confusion of norm with customary deviation, the identification of that-which-should-be with that-which-commonly-occurs at times reaches high comedy here. So, in a casuistic part of one of these works, we find beneath some numbers a repetition of the following therapeutic consultation: the invalid is compelled in part by persistent medical advice, but chiefly by hypnotic suggestion, to occupy his imagination with the idea of a naked female body or other indecent pictures of a *normal* sexual character (sic); and the treatment is recognized as having been successful and recovery complete if, under the influence of this artificial arousal, the patient begins, willingly and effectively, to visit *lupanaria* [brothels] frequently. . . .[37] It is surprising that these respected scientists were not restrained, even if only by the simple consideration that, the more successful this kind of therapy, the more obviously the patient can be put in need of turning for help from one medical specialty to another, and that the triumph of a psychiatrist can cause big problems for a dermatologist.

The perversions of sexual love studied in medical books are important for us as an extreme development of the same thing that has come into everyday, customary use in our society and is considered permissible and normal. These unusual phenomena represent the same scandal that is inherent in our customary relations in this realm, only in more glaring form. It would be possible to prove this by an examination of all particular perversions of sexual sensation. But I hope that in this matter I will be forgiven the incompleteness of argumentation; and I will allow myself to be restricted to one more common and less loathesome anomaly of the realm of sexual sensation. In many persons, almost always of the male sex, this sensation is aroused chiefly, and sometimes even exclusively, by one or another part of a creature of the other sex (such as, hair, hand, foot) and even by extrinsic objects—certain parts of clothing, etc. This anomaly has received the title of fetishism in love. The abnormality of such fetishism consists, obviously, in the fact that a part is set in place of the whole, a member in place of the essence. But if the hair or feet that arouse a fetishist are parts of a woman's body, then surely this body itself in all its composition is only a part of a woman's essence; and yet the very numerous lovers of a woman's body in itself are not called fetishists, are not recognized as insane, and do not undergo any treatment. In what then is the distinction here? Is it really in the fact that the hand or foot represents a smaller surface area than the body?

If, in principle, the sexual attitude in which a part is set in place of the whole is abnormal, then people who in one way or another buy the body of a woman for the satisfaction of a sexual requirement, and by the same token separate the body from the soul, should be acknowledged as abnormal in a sexual respect—psychiatric invalids, fetishists in love, or even necrophiliacs. And in the meantime, these living-but-dying lovers-of-deadness are considered normal people, and almost all humanity passes through this second death.[38]

In full concordance with philosophical understanding, the unrepressed conscience and the un-calloused aesthetic sense condemn every sexual attitude based on the separation and isolation of the lower animal sphere of the human essence from the higher. And outside of this principle, it is impossible to find any firm criterion for a distinction between what is normal and what is abnormal in the sexual realm. If the need in certain physiological acts has a right to satisfaction whatever the cost only because it is a need, then the need of the "fetishist in love," for whom the single longed-for object in a sexual respect turns out to be a just-laundered but not-yet-dry apron hanging on a clothesline,* has absolutely the very same right to satisfaction.[39] Even if a difference is found between this eccentric and any chronic visitor of brothels, then it goes without saying this difference will be in favor of the fetishist. Attraction to a wet apron is without doubt natural and genuine, for it is not possible to invent any false motives for this, whereas many people visit brothels not at all because they really have a need, but out of false hygienic considerations, out of the imitation of bad examples, under influence of intoxication, etc.

Psychopathic manifestations of sexual feelings are usually condemned on the basis that they do not correspond to the naturally designated sexual act, namely, procreation. To hold that a freshly laundered apron, or even a worn shoe, can serve for the procreation of progeny would be, of course, a paradox; but hardly less paradoxical would be the assumption that an institution of public women corresponds to this goal. "Natural" depravity, obviously, is just as contrary to procreation as "unnatural" depravity, so that from this point of view, as well, there is not the slightest basis to consider one of them normal and the other abnormal. If, finally, one dwells on the point of view of harm to self and others, then, certainly, a fetishist who cuts locks of hair from strange ladies or steals handkerchiefs from them[†] will inflict damage upon a stranger's property and upon his reputation. But can this harm be compared with that which is caused by the unhappy popularizers of the terrible contagion that constitutes the rather typical after-effect of the "natural" satisfaction of "natural" need?

III.

I say all this not in justification of the unnatural, but in condemnation of the supposedly natural methods of satisfaction of sexual sensation. In general, speaking of naturalness or unnaturalness, it ought not be forgotten that the human being is a complex creature, and what is natural for one of the principles or elements constituting it may be unnatural for the other and, consequently, abnormal for the entire human being.

For man, as an *animal*, the unrestricted satisfaction of his sexual need by means of a certain physiological action is completely natural, but man as

---

* See Binet, "Le fetishisme en amour," also Krafft-Ebing, "Psychopathia sexualis."
† Ibid.

a moral being finds this act repugnant to his higher nature and is *ashamed* of it. As a *social* animal, it is natural for man to restrict a physical function relative to other persons by the requirements of the socio-moral *law*. This law restricts and shuts off animal function from without, and makes it the means for a social aim—cultivation of the marriage union. But the essence of the matter does not change from this. The marriage union is still based on a superficial material joining of the sexes: it leaves the human being-animal in its previous disintegrated, halved state, which necessarily leads to the further disintegration of the human essence, that is, to death.

If, beyond his animal nature, man were only a socio-moral being, then out of these two struggling elements—identically natural for him—the former would claim the final triumph. The socio-moral law and its basic objectification—the family—bring the animal nature of man to restrictions necessary for generative progress; they make mortal life orderly, but do not reveal the path of immortality. An individual being becomes just as exhausted and dead in the socio-moral order of life as if it had remained exclusively under the law of brute life. An elephant and a raven turn out to be even significantly more durable than a virtuous and cautious man himself.* But apart from animal nature and socio-moral law, there is in man yet a third, higher principle—spiritual, mystical, or divine. Here as well, in the realm of love and sexual relations, it is the "stone the builders rejected" that "has become the cornerstone."[40] Prior to physiological joining in animal nature, which leads to death, and before lawful union in the socio-moral order, which does not deliver from death, there must be union in God, which leads to immortality because it does not only restrict the mortal life of nature by human law, but regenerates it by

---

* Concerning recent doctrines of death and the fear of death, it is necessary to note that apart from fear and indifference—identically unworthy of the thinking and loving being—is a third attitude: struggle and triumph over death. The matter concerns not one's own death, about which morally and physically healthy people, of course, worry little, but about the death of others, beloved beings, toward which a dispassionate attitude is not possible for the lover (see the Gospel of John 11:33–38).

Resignation in this respect would be the requirement of reason only in the event that the death of a man would be the absolutely inevitable outcome. But this has always only been presupposed and never proven, and not without cause, for to prove this is impossible. Of course, there is no argument about the fact that *under certain conditions* death is necessary; but there is not even a shadow of rational foundation to think that these conditions alone are possible, that to alter them is forbidden, and that, consequently, death is an *absolute* necessity.

the eternal and non-decaying power of grace. This third, but in true order, first, element (with requirements peculiar to it) is completely *natural* for the human being in its entirety, as a creature participating in the supreme, divine principle and interceding between it and the world. And the two lower elements—animal nature and the social law—just as natural in their place, become *unnatural* when they are taken separately from the higher one and are assumed in place of it. Not only is every incoherent satisfaction of sensual needs (similarly to animals) devoid of higher spiritual illumination unnatural for man (apart from the various monstrous phenomena of sexual psychopathy), but those unions between people of different sex who are *joined* and upheld *only* on the basis of the civil law—exclusively for moral-social aims without a proper spiritual, mystical principle—are also unworthy of man and unnatural as well. Yet from the point of view of the undivided human being, just such an unnatural transposition of these relations also predominates in our life and is acknowledged as normal. And all condemnation is transferred to the unhappy psychopaths of love, who only drive this same generally acknowledged and reigning perversion to amusing, scandalous, sometimes disgusting, but for the most part comparatively harmless extremes.

IV.

The manifold perversions of the sexual instinct with which psychiatrists occupy themselves are only marvelous varieties of the general and all-permeating perversion of these relations in humanity, of the perversion by which the kingdom of sin and death is maintained and perpetuated. Although the three natural relations or contacts between the sexes (that is to say, contact in brute life, or according to the lower nature; then everyday moral contact, or under law; and finally, contact in spiritual life, or union in God) all exist in humanity, they are realized unnaturally—namely, separately one from the other—inversely to their true meaning and order of succession and in an unequal degree.

That which in truth should be in the last place—the physiological animal bond—appears in our reality in the first place. It is recognized as the foundation of the entire matter, whereas it should be only its utmost conclusion. For many here the foundation coincides with the end: they do not go farther than animal relations. For others, the socio-moral super-structure of the lawful marriage union arises from this broad foundation. Here the mediocre middle is accepted as the summit of life; and that which should serve free, intelligent expressions of eternal unity in a temporal process becomes the involuntary conduit of senseless material life. And then, finally, pure spiritual love remains for a select few as a rare and exclusive phenomenon. In pure spiritual love, all actual content is already removed beforehand from other lower contacts, so that it has to be satisfied with a dreamy and sterile tenderness devoid of any real objective and vital aim. This unfortunate spiritual love reminds one of the little angels of ancient artwork, who only have a head and little wings and nothing more. These angels do not do anything owing to a lack of hands, and cannot move forward since their little wings have sufficient strength only for the purpose of maintaining them motionless at a certain height. Spiritual love too finds itself in just such an elevated but extremely unsatisfied situation. Physical passion has before it a definite, though ignoble, act; the lawful marriage union, though of mediocre value, also fulfills the act. But in spiritual love, as it has hitherto appeared, there is wittingly absolutely no act, and thus it is not surprising that a majority of sensible people "glaubt an keine Liebe oder nimmt's für Poesie."[41]

This exclusively spiritual love is, obviously, the very same anomaly as an exclusively physical love and an exclusively socially acceptable union. The absolute norm is the restoration of the wholeness of the human essence; and, in any case, whether this norm is violated in one or another respect, an abnormal, unnatural phenomenon occurs as a result. A supposedly spiritual love is not only an abnormal phenomenon, but also completely aimless, because the very best outcome of the separation of the spiritual from the sensual, to which it aspires, occurs with death. However, true love is not a feeble imitation and forewarning of death, but a triumph over death; not a separation of the immortal from the mortal and the eternal from the temporal, but a conversion of the mortal into the immortal, a conception of the temporal into the eternal. False spirituality is a denial of the flesh; true spirituality is its regeneration, redemption, and resurrection.

V.

"On that day God created man, in the image of God he created him, male and female he created them."

"This is a great mystery, but I am talking about Christ and the Church."[42]

The mysterious divine image in which the human being is created originally refers to the true unity of its two fundamental aspects, male and female, and not to any separate part of the human essence. Just as God relates to his creation and Christ relates to His church, so too a husband must relate to his wife.[43] As much as these words are generally well known, their meaning is little understood. As God creates the universe, as Christ establishes the church, so man must create and establish his female complement. It is, of course, an elementary thesis that man represents the active and woman the passive principle, that the former must informatively influence the mind and character of the latter. Yet we have in mind not this superficial aspect, but that "great mystery" about which the Apostle speaks. This great mystery represents an important analogy, although not an identity, between human and divine relations.

Indeed, the establishment of the church by Christ is already distinguished from the creation of the universe by God, as such. Whereas God creates the universe out of nothing (that is, from a pure potential of existence, or emptiness), consequently, filling (i.e., conceiving) real forms of intelligible things out of a divine act, Christ establishes the church from material already diversely formed and animated and, in some of its parts, self-initiated, to which it is necessary only to communicate the principle of new spiritual life in a new, higher sphere of unity. Finally, for his creative activity, man has, in the person of woman, material equal to himself in degree of actualization, before which he utilizes not actual perfection, but only the potential advantage of initiative, only the right and the duty of a first step on the path to perfection. God relates to the creation as everything to nothing (i.e., as absolute fullness of being toward the pure potential of being); Christ relates to the church as actual perfection toward the potential of perfection, being formed into actual perfection. And the relation between husband and wife is the relation of two distinctly acting but identically imperfect potentials, achieving perfection only by a process of cooperation. In other words, God receives nothing from the creation for himself (that is, no accretion) but gives everything to it; Christ receives from the church no increase in the sense of perfection, but gives perfection to it all; yet He does receive from the church an increase in the sense of the completeness of His collective body. Finally, man and his female alter ego mutually fulfill one another not only in a real, but also in an ideal sense, achieving perfection only through cooperation.[44] Man can fundamentally restore the divine image in the living object of his love only at the same time that he restores this image in actual practice as well; and for this he does not have the strength in himself, for if he had, then he would not be in need of restoration. Not having it in himself, he must receive it from God. Consequently, the man (the husband) is a creative, fundamental principle relative to his female complement not in himself, but as an intermediary or conveyor of divine power. Strictly speaking, Christ also creates not by some separate power of His own, but by the very same creative power of Divinity; but being himself God, He possesses this power by nature and *actu*; we, however, possess it by grace and adoption, having in ourselves only the possibility (potential) for its conception.

In proceeding to the exposition of the fundamental factors in the process of the realization of true love (that is, in the process of the integration of the human essence, or the restoration in it of the divine image), I foresee the bewilderment of many: Why climb to such inaccessible and fantastic heights concerning such a simple thing as love? If I considered the religious norm of love fantastic, then I certainly would not even suggest it. Precisely in the same way, if I had in mind only *simple* love (i.e., customary, commonplace relations between the sexes—that which exists, and not that which should exist), then I certainly would restrain myself from any discussions of this subject. Without a doubt, such simple relations belong to those things about which someone once said: it is not good to do this, yet worse to talk about it. But love, as I understand it, is, on the contrary, an unusually complex matter, obscured and muddled, requiring a fully conscious analysis and investigation, in which it is necessary to be concerned not about simplicity, but about truth. . . . A rotten stump is undoubtedly simpler than a many-branched tree, and a corpse is simpler than a living human being. A simple attitude to love concludes with that conclusive and extreme simplification called death. Such an inevitable and unsatisfactory end of "simple" love prompts us to search for another, more complex, source for it.

VI.

The matter of true love is first of all based on *faith*. The radical meaning of love, as was already shown, consists in the acknowledgment of another as a being of unconditional significance. But in its empirically objective reality, which is subject to real sensual perception, this being does not have any unconditional significance: it is imperfect according to its merit and fleeting according to its existence. Consequently, we can affirm for it an unconditional significance only by faith, which is a notice of things hoped-for, an uncovering of invisible things.[45] But what is faith related to in the present case? What does it properly mean to believe in the unconditional and, by the same token as well, infinite significance of this individual person? It would be as absurd as it is blasphemous to affirm that it possesses absolute significance in itself, as such, in this its particularity and taken separately. Of course, the word "worship" is quite common in the sphere of loving relations, but then the word "insanity" also has its legitimate application in this realm. Thus, observing the law of logic, which does not allow the identity of contradictory attributes, and also the precept of true religion, which forbids idol worship, we must by faith in the object of our love understand the affirmation of this object as something that exists in God, and in this sense possesses infinite significance. It goes without saying that this transcendental attitude toward one's other, this mental conversion of it to the divine sphere, presupposes the very same attitude toward oneself, the very same conversion and affirmation of oneself in the absolute sphere. I can only acknowledge an unconditional significance for a given person or have faith in him (without which true love is impossible) by affirming him in God, consequently, by having faith in God himself and in myself as one having the center and root of my existence in God. This triune faith is now a certain intrinsic act; and with this act, the first ground is laid toward the true reunification of man with his other and the restoration in him (or in them) of the image of the triune God. The act of faith in actual conditions of time and place is prayer (in the fundamental, not technical sense of this word). The indivisible union of self and other in this respect is the first step toward true union. In itself this step is small, but without it anything further and greater is impossible.

Since for God, who is eternal and indivisible, everything is together and immediate, all is in one, then to affirm any individual being in God means to affirm it not taken separately, but in everything, or more precisely—in the unity of everything. Yet since this individual being in its given reality does not enter into the unity of everything, but exists separately as a materially isolated phenomenon, then the object of our faithful love necessarily is distinct from the empirical object of our instinctive love, although indivisibly tied to it. This is one and the same person in two distinct forms, or in two different spheres of existence—ideal and real. The first is still only an Idea. But in real, faithful, and seeing love, we know that this Idea is not our arbitrary contrivance, but that it expresses *the truth* of the object, only not yet realized in the sphere of extrinsic, real phenomena.

Although it shines through the real phenomenon in clearer view in instants of loving pathos, this true Idea of the beloved object appears at first only as an object of the imagination. The concrete form of this imagination, the ideal image in which I wrap the beloved person in a given moment, is of course created by me; but it is not created out of nothing, and the subjectivity of this image, as such (i.e., its appearance here and now before the eyes of my soul), not at all proves the subjective (i.e., for me only the existential) character of the imagined object itself. If for me, finding myself on this side of the transcendent world, a certain ideal object appears only as the product of my imagination, this does not prevent its full reality in another, higher sphere of existence.[46] And, although our real life is outside this higher sphere, our mind is not completely alien to it, and we can have a certain speculative comprehension of the laws of its existence. And here is the first fundamental law: if, in our world, distinct and isolated existence is a fact and actuality, and unity is only a concept and idea, then there, on the contrary, reality belongs to unity—or, more precisely, all-unity—and distinction and isolation exist only potentially and subjectively.

And from here it follows that the objective reality *of this* person in the transcendent sphere is not individual in the sense of local, real existence. There (i.e., in truth), an individual person is only a radiant beam of the living and the real, but an indivisible beam of a single, ideal luminary Body—of the essence of all-unity. This ideal person, or personified Idea, is only an individualization of all-unity, which is indivisibly present in each of these its individualizations. Thus, when we imagine the ideal form of a beloved object, under this form is communicated to us the essence of all-unity itself. But how then should we conceive of it?

VII.

In distinguishing His other (i.e., everything that is not Himself) from Himself, God, as one, unites with Himself this everything, representing it to Himself altogether at once in absolutely perfected form, consequently, as a single whole. Since here an eternal void (pure potential) perceives the fullness of divine life, this *other* unity, distinct but not indivisible from the original divine unity, is relative to God a passive, feminine unity. But, if *at the foundation* of this eternal femininity lies a pure nothing, then for God this nothing is eternally concealed by a perceived image of absolute perfection from divinity. This perfection, which for us is still only being realized, is for God (i.e., in truth) already real. That ideal unity to which our world aspires and which constitutes the aim of the cosmic and historical process, cannot be just somebody's subjective conception (for whose?). It truly exists as the eternal object of divine love, as His eternal other.

In preceding our love, this living ideal of divine love contains in itself the mystery of its idealization. Here the idealization of the lower essence is at the same time the incipient realization of the higher, and herein lies the truth of loving pathos. However, full realization—transformation of the individual female essence into a beam of eternal divine femininity, indivisible from its radiant source—will become actual (not only subjective, but also objective) reunification of the individual human being with God, a restoration in it of the living and immortal divine image.

The object of true love is not simple, but two-fold: firstly, we love that ideal essence (ideal not in the abstract sense, but in the sense of belonging to another, higher sphere of objective reality), which we must introduce into our ideal world; and, secondly, we love the natural human essence that provides the living, personal material for this realization, and which is idealized through this—not in the sense of our subjective imagination, but in the sense of its actual objective change or regeneration. Thus, true love is indivisible, both *ascending* and *descending* (*amor ascendens* and *amor descendens*, or those two Aphrodites that Plato distinguished well, but foolishly isolated—*Aphrodite Ourania* and *Aphrodite Pandemos*).[47] For God, His *other* (that is, the universe) has always had the form of perfected femininity, yet He wants not only that this form be for Him, but that it also be realized and embodied for each individual essence capable of uniting with it. Eternal femininity itself, which is not only a passive form in the divine mind, but a living spiritual essence possessing the entire plenitude of force and action, aspires to such realization and embodiment as well. The entire universal and historical process is a process of its realization and embodiment in a great variety of forms and degrees.

In truly understood and truly realized sexual love, this divine substance receives a means for its definitive, utmost embodiment in the individual life of a human being and a method for the most profound and, at the same time, extrinsic, really tangible union with it. From here come those flashes of unearthly blessing, that waft of otherworldly joy, through which even imperfect love is conducted, and which make even imperfect love the greatest enjoyment of people and gods—*hominom divomque voluptas*.[48] From here, however, also come the most profound sufferings of love, powerless to hold its true object, and gradually becoming more and more distanced from it.

Here, that element of adoration and boundless devotion—which is so peculiar to love and has so little sense if it relates only to its earthly object taken separately from the heavenly—receives its legitimate place as well.

The mystical foundation of the two-fold (or better said, bilateral) character of love resolves the question and the possibility of the repetition of love. The heavenly object of our love is only one—always and for everybody one and the very same—eternal divine femininity. Yet since the task of true love consists not only in bowing to this higher object, but in realizing and embodying it in another, lower essence of that very feminine form (which is not of an earthly nature), then it is only one of many, and its sole significance for a lover, of course, *may* also be fleeting. But the questions of why and *whether* it *should* be thus are already resolved in each individual case and depend not on the single and changeless mystical foundation of the true loving process, but on other of its moral and physical conditions, which we should consider as well.

FIFTH ARTICLE

I.

An involuntary and immediate feeling reveals to us the meaning of love as the highest manifestation of individual life, which is found in uniting our own infiniteness with another being. But is this momentary revelation enough? Is it really too little to actually feel one's unconditional significance just once in life?

> And I know having gazed at the stars awhile,
> That we looked at them as gods, you and I.[49]

It is hardly enough even for a single poetic feeling, but the *consciousness of truth* and the *will in life* cannot be completely reconciled on this point. Just a *momentary* infinity is an unendurable contradiction for the mind, and suffering for the will a blessing only in the past. There are those flashes of a different world after which

> Still darker is the gloom of daily life
> Than after glaring autumn heat-lightning.[50]

If these flashes are only a deception, then even in reminiscence they can call forth only shame and the bitterness of disappointment; but if they were not a deception, if they revealed to us some reality that later was shut off for us and vanished, then why ever should we reconcile ourselves with this disappearance? If that which was lost was true, then the task of consciousness and volition is not in the acceptance of the loss as decisive, but in understanding and removing its cause.

The most proximate cause (as was in part shown in the preceding article) consists in perversion of the loving attitude itself. This begins very early: hardly does the original pathos of love succeed in showing us the rim of a different, better reality, with another principle and law of life, than we immediately strive to utilize the enthusiasm of the energy that results from this revelation—not for going further, whither it calls us, but only in order to take root more deeply and to become established more lastingly in the former ugly reality over which love just lifted us. We accept the good news from the lost paradise—news of the possibility of its recurrence—as an invitation finally *to become naturalized* in the land of exile, the sooner to enter into a full and hereditary possession of one's small part of a field with all its thistles and thorns.[51] The breach of personal confinement that marks loving passion and constitutes its fundamental meaning results as a matter of fact only in the *egoism of two together,* then of three, etc. This is still certainly better than egoism on one's own, but the dawn of love revealed completely different horizons.

As soon as the vital sphere of loving union is carried over into material reality, such as it is, then immediately the very order of unity is distorted by the corresponding form. Its "otherworldly" mystical foundation, which so intensely gave notice about itself in primary passion, is forgotten as a fleeting exultation, and that which should be only its utmost conditional manifestation is acknowledged as the most desired, essential aim and first condition of love. This latter, physical union, which is set in place of the former and thus stripped of its *human* meaning and returned to animal significance, makes love not only powerless against death, but itself inevitably becomes a moral grave for love much earlier than a physical grave will claim lovers.

An explicit personal opposition to such an order of things is more difficult to achieve than to comprehend: this is possible to point out in a few words. To abolish this ugly order of living phenomena, it is first of all necessary to acknowledge it as abnormal, affirming by the same token what is the other, normal order, in which everything superficial and incidental is subordinated to the inner meaning of life. Such an affirmation should not be baseless; not abstract principle, but other experience— *experience of faith*—should be contrasted to the experience of superficial sensations. The former is incomparably more difficult than the latter, for it is conditional more upon inner activity than perception from without. We enter into a real correlation with the realm of the truly existing, and through this into a true correlation with our "other," only by consistent acts of conscious faith. Only on this foundation can that unconditionality of the other person for us (and consequently, also the unconditionality of our union with him), which spontaneously and unaccountably is revealed in the pathos of love, be held and consolidated in the consciousness; for this loving pathos comes and goes, but the faith of love remains.

But in order not to remain as dead faith, it is necessary for it to defend itself continuously against the actual milieu where senseless chance creates its dominion in a game of animal passions and, even worse, human ones.[52] In faithful love there exists only a defensive weapon against these hostile forces—patience to the end.[53] In order to merit its bliss, it must take up its cross. It is not possible to preserve true love in our material surroundings if it is not understood and accepted as moral deed. It is not for nothing that the Orthodox Church in its ceremony of *marriage* commemorates the saintly *martyrs* and compares matrimonial crowns to their crowns.

Religious faith and moral deed protect the individual man and his love from being swallowed up by the material environment during his life, but do not give him triumph over death. The inward regeneration of the loving feeling and the reform of perverted relations of love do not correct or countermand the ugly law of physical life in the external world, nor within man himself. He *realistically* remains as before, as a restricted being subjected to material nature. His inner—mystical and moral—union with a complementary individuality can overcome neither their mutual separateness and impenetrability nor their common dependence on the material world. The last word remains not with a moral deed, but with the ruthless law of organic life and death; and people who have defended the eternal ideal to the end die with human dignity, but bestial impotence.

While an individal deed is limited only by its most proximate object— by the reform of a personal, perverted relation between two beings—it necessarily remains without decisive success in this immediate concern as well. For the evil with which true love collides—the evil of material sepa-rateness, of the impenetrability and extrinsic struggle of two beings intrin-sically making up each other—is a particular, although also a typical, case of common perversion to which our life is subjected, and not only ours, but the life of the entire world as well.

The solitary man can actually be redeemed (that is, can be reborn and immortalize his individual life in true love) only conjointly, or together with all. He has the right and duty to defend his individuality from the ugly law of common life, but not to divide his good from the true good of all the living. Although it is a fact that the most profound and intensive manifestation of love is expressed in the mutual relations of two beings fulfilling one another, in no way does it follow that this mutual relation could separate and isolate itself from everything else as something self-sufficent. On the contrary, such isolation is the ruin of love; for sexual love in itself, in all its subjective significance, turns out to be (objectively) only fleeting, an empirical phenomenon. Precisely in the same way, it does not follow from the fact that the perfect union of such solitary beings will always remain the foundation and true form of individual life, that this living form, locked in its own individual completeness, must exist as void; when, on the contrary, and according to the very nature of man, it is designated for and capable of filling itself with universal content. Finally, if the moral meaning of love requires the reuniting of that which has been unjustly separated, requires the identity of self and other, then to separate the objective of our individual perfection from the process of universal unification would be contrary to this moral meaning of love it-self, even if such a separation were physically possible.

II.

Thus, every attempt to seclude and isolate the individual process of re-generation in true love is met with a three-fold insuperable barrier. Our individual life with our love, which is separated from the process of uni-versal life, inevitably turns out to be: firstly, physically unsound, powerless against time and death; next, intellectually empty, contentless; and, finally, morally unworthy. If the imagination can vault over a physical and logical obstacle, then even it must halt before a moral impossibility.

Let us suppose something absolutely fantastic—let us suppose that a man so empowered his spirit by consistent concentration of consciousness and volition, and so purified his corporeal nature by ascetic exploit, that he actually restored (for himself and for his complementary "other") the true wholeness of human individuality and achieved full spirituality and immortality. Will this regenerated individuality enjoy its lonely bliss in an environment where everything as before suffers and perishes? But let us go further. Let this regenerated couple receive the capacity to communicate to all others its higher state; this is, of course, impossible insofar as it is conditional upon personal moral deed, but let this be something of the sort of a philosopher's stone or an elixir of life. And now, all those living

on earth are cured of their wickedness and illnesses, all are free and immortal. But in order to be happy as well, they need yet another condition:
they must forget their fathers, forget the real initiators of this, their good
fortune; because no matter what fantastic significance is attributed to personal exploit, it would still be necessary that thousands and thousands of
generations in their combined collective labor create the culture and the
moral and intellectual constructs without which the task of individual regeneration could not have been not only fulfilled, but even conceived.
And these billions of people who laid down their lives for others will rot
in their graves, and their useless descendants will indifferently enjoy their
happiness gratis! But in moral terms this would assume running wild and
still worse, because even primitives respect their ancestors and preserve
links with them. How then can this final and highest state of humanity be
based on injustice, thanklessness, and forgetfulness? Man, having achieved
higher perfection, cannot accept such an unmerited gift; if he is not in a
condition to rip away from death *all* its spoils, he would be better off rejecting immortality.

> Break this goblet, a wicked bane is concealed in it.[54]

Happily, all this is only an arbitrary and idle fantasy, and the matter
will never reach such a tragic experience of our *moral* solidarity with the
whole world, because of the physical impossibility of the *private* resolution
of a problem of such vital importance by an individual man or an individual generation. Our regeneration is indissolubly linked with the regeneration of the universe, with the reorganization of its forms of space and
time. A true life of individuality, in its full and unconditional significance,
is realized and immortalized only in the corresponding development of
universal life, in which we can and must actively participate, but which is
not created by us. Our personal concerns, insofar as they are true, are the
common concern of the whole world—the realization and individualization of the all-unity Idea and the spiritualization of matter. It is being prepared by the cosmic process in the natural world, continues and is being
perfected by the historical process in humanity. Our *ignorance* concerning the multilateral connection of concrete particulars in the unity of
the whole leaves us with this freedom of action, which, with all its consequences, already entered into the absolute universal plan long ago.

The all-unity Idea can be definitively realized or embodied only in the
plenitude of perfected individualities. So the final aim of the entire busi-

ness is the highest development of each individuality in the fullest unity of all; and this necessarily includes in itself our life's aim as well, which we, consequently, have neither the motive for nor the possibility of separating or isolating from the universal aim. We are necessary to the world as much as it is to us; the universe has long been interested in the preservation, development, and perpetuation of all that is really necessary and desirable for us, of all that is positive and worthy in our individuality; and it is left to us only to take more conscious and active participation as much as possible in the general historical process—for ourselves and for all others *indivisibly*.

III.

In our world, corporeal objective reality is opposed to true existence, or the all-unity Idea. This is the same objective reality that suppresses, by its senseless persistence, our love, as well, and does not allow its meaning to be realized. The chief property of this corporeal objective reality is a *twofold impenetrability:* (1) impenetrability *in time*, by virtue of which every successive moment of objective reality does not preserve in itself the previous one, but excludes or displaces it from existence, so that everything new in the midst of matter takes place at the cost of the former, or is damaging to it; and (2) impenetrability *in space*, by virtue of which two parts of matter (two bodies) cannot occupy one and the same place at once (i.e., one and the same part of space), and necessarily displace one another. Thus, that which lies at the foundation of our world is objective reality in a state of decay, objective reality broken into fragments, and moments that exclude one another. Here is the kind of deep soil and broad foundation that we must accept for that fateful division of beings, in which exists all the distress of our personal life as well. The objective of the world process is as simple in the understanding as it is complex and difficult in concrete realization: to defeat this dual impenetrability of bodies and phenomena and to make the extrinsic, actual environment conformable to the intrinsic all-unity Idea.

The apparent predominance of the material basis of our world and life is still so great that many conscientious but slightly one-sided minds think that nothing at all exists apart from this corporeal, objective reality in its diverse variations. However, without speaking here about the fact that the acknowledgment of this visible world as the only one is an arbitrary hypothesis, which it is possible to believe in but impossible to prove, and without leaving the boundaries of this world—it must nevertheless be acknowledged that materialism is wrong even from a factual point of view.

Actually, even in our visible world, much exists that is not only a variation of materially objective reality in its spatial and temporal impenetrability, but is even a direct negation and annulment of this very impenetrability. Such, in the first place, is universal *gravity*, in which parts of the corporeal world do not exclude one another, but, on the contrary, strive to join and find room reciprocally. For the sake of preconceived principle, it is possible to construct pseudo-scientific hypotheses one upon another; but for rational comprehension, it will never be possible to explain factors of a directly opposite property out of the attributes of inert matter: neither the uniting of gravity to space, nor the deduction of attraction from impenetrability, nor the understanding of striving as indolence, will ever be possible.[55] And meanwhile, without these nonmaterial factors, even the most simple physical existence would not be possible. Indeed, matter in itself is only an indeterminate and incoherent aggregation of atoms to which, more magnanimously than soundly, motion that is purportedly inherent to them is imparted. In any event, for a definite and permanent unification of corporeal particles in bodies, it is necessary that their impenetrability, or in other words, absolute incoherence, be replaced to a greater or lesser degree by a positive interaction between them. Thus, our whole universe, as well, inasmuch as it is not a chaos of uncoordinated atoms but a single and coherent whole, presupposes above its subdivided material another form of unity (and an active force as well, subduing elements opposed to it). The unity of the corporeal world is not corporeal unity—such a thing cannot be at all, this is a *contradictio in adjecto*.[56] Formed by the antimaterial (and from the point of view of materialism, antinatural) law of gravitation, a universal body is a real-ideal, psycho-physical whole; or bluntly (in accord with the thought of Newton concerning *sensorium Dei*), it is a *mystical body*.[57]

Beyond the force of universal gravitation, ideal all-unity is realized in a spiritual-corporeal manner in the body of the universe by means of light and other related phenomena (electricity, magnetism, heat), the character of which is found in such manifest contrast with the properties of impenetrable and inert matter that even materialistic science is evidently in need of recognizing here a special kind of semicorporeal substance, which it calls ether. This is weightless material, impenetrable and all-penetrating—in a word, *nonmaterial matter*.

Our real world is sustained by these embodiments of the all-unity Idea—gravitation and ether; and matter in itself (i.e., the mortal totality of inert and impenetrable atoms) is only conceived by abstracted reason, but is not observed and is not revealed in any reality. We do not know a moment such that the present reality would belong to material chaos and cosmic Idea would be a feeble shadow lacking in density; we only assume such a moment as a point of departure for a universal process in the boundaries of our visible universe.

Now in the natural world, everything belongs to Idea; but its essence requires that not only everything belong to it, everything be joined to it or embraced by it—but *that it itself belong to everything;* that everything (i.e., *all* particular and individual essences, and consequently *each* of them as well) actually possess ideal all-unity, join it to itself. Perfect all-unity, according to its very conception, requires full equilibrium, equality of worth, and equality of rights between one and all, between the whole and the parts, between the common and the individual. The plenitude of Idea requires that the greatest unity of the whole be realized in the greatest independence and freedom of particular and isolated elements—in themselves, through them, and for them. In this tendency, the cosmic process approaches the creation of animal individuality, for which the unity of Idea exists in the image of *kind,* and is experienced with full force in the moment of sexual attraction. This is when the intrinsic unity, or commonality with another and with "everything," is concretely embodied in relation to a solitary person of another sex, which is this complementary "everything"—in one. The individual life of the animal organism itself now contains in itself a certain likeness—although restricted—of all-unity, inasmuch as here is realized the full solidarity and mutuality of all particular organs and elements in the unity of a living body. But just as this organic solidarity *in* an animal does not cross the boundaries of its corporeal composition, so also *for* it the form of the complementary "other" is completely restricted by the very same isolated body with the possibility only of material, partial union. And therefore, supratemporal infinity, or the eternity of Idea, which acts in the vital creative force of love, takes on here an ugly rectilinear form of limitless propagation (that is, repetition of one and the same organism in a monotonous replacement of solitary, temporal existences).

Although the direct line of generational propagation is in essence preserved in human life, thanks to the development of consciousness and conscious intercourse, it guides the historical process gradually in a more and more extensive circuit of social and cultural organisms. These social organisms are produced by the same vital creative force of love that gives rise to physical organisms as well. This force directly creates the family, and the family is the formative element of every society. Notwithstanding this genetic connection, the relation of human individuality to society is essentially different from the relation of animal individuality to kind: man is not a fleeting specimen of society. The unity of the social organism *really coexists* with each of its individual members, has an objective reality not only in it and through it, but also *for* it, and is found with it in a definite connection and correlation: social and individual life mutually penetrate one another from all aspects. Consequently, we have here a much more perfect form of the embodiment of the all-unity Idea than in a physical organism. At the same time, here begins from within (out of consciousness) a process of integration in time (or *against* time). Notwithstanding the replacement of generations that continues in humanity as well, there are now principles of the immortalization of individuality in the religion of ancestors—at the basis of every culture—in tradition, in the memory of society, in art, and finally in historical study. The imperfect, experimental character of that immortalization corresponds to the imperfection of human individuality and society themselves. But progress is unquestionable, and the definitive task becomes clearer and more proximate.

IV.

If the root of deceptive existence consists in impenetrability (that is, in the mutual exclusion of beings by one another), then true life is living in another as in oneself, or finding in another a positive and unconditional fulfillment of one's essence. The basis and type of this true life is and always will remain sexual, or conjugal, love. But its proper realization is impossible, as we have seen, without a corresponding transformation of the entire extrinsic environment (i.e., the integration of individual life necessarily requires the very same integration in the spheres of social and universal life). A certain distinction, or separation of life spheres, both individual and collective, will never and should not ever be abolished, because such a universal merger would lead to indifference and emptiness, and not to a fullness of existence. True union presupposes the true separateness of those uniting (such that, by virtue of which they do not exclude, but mutually assume one another, finding fullness of their own life in each other). Just as in individual life, two beings—distinct, but equal in rights and equal in worth—serve one another not as negative boundary but as positive complement, precisely the very same must also be in all spheres of collective life. Every social organism must be for each of its members not an external boundary of its action, but a positive support and complement—just as for sexual love (in the sphere of personal life), the solitary "other" is at the same time everything, so too, on its part, the social *everything,* by virtue of the positive solidarity of all its elements, must for each of them appear as a real unity, as if it were the other living being that complements it (in a new, broader sphere).

If the relations of individual members of society to one another should be fraternal (and filial—with respect to past generations and their social representatives), then their connection with entire social spheres—local, national, and finally, the universal sphere—should be still more instrinsic, multilateral, and significant. This connection of the active human prin-ciple (personal) with the embodied all-unity Idea in the social, spiritually corporeal organism must be a living *syzygy* relation.*[58] The attitude of true human individuality—not only to its most proximate social milieu, to its nation, but also to all of humanity—is neither to submit to one's social sphere nor to exercise dominion over it, but to be with it in a loving inter-action, to serve for it as an active fertilizing source of advancement, and to find in it a plenitude of vitally important conditions and possibilities. In the Bible, cities, countries, the Israelite nation, and then all of regenerated humanity, or the universal church, as well, are represented in the form of female individuality; and this is not a simple metaphor. In no way does it follow from the fact that since the form of the unity of social bodies is not tangible for our external senses, then it does not exist at all: indeed, for a separate brain cell and for a blood corpuscle, our own corporeal form is also completely intangible and unknown; and if we, as individuals capable of the fullness of being are distinguished from these elementary individuali-ties not only by a greater clarity and breadth of rational consciousness, but also by a greater strength of creative imagination, then I do not see the ne-cessity of renouncing this advantage. Be that as it may, with form or with-out form, it is first of all required that we relate to the social and universal milieu as to a real living being with which we, while never merging to in-distinction, find ourselves in the most proximate and fullest interaction. Such an extension of the syzygy relation to the spheres of collective and universal existence perfects individuality itself, communicating to it the unity and fullness of living content, and by the same token, elevates and immortalizes the fundamental, individual form of love.

---

* From the Greek *syzygy*—combination. I am compelled to introduce this new expression, not finding in the existing terminology another, better one. I will note that the gnostics utilized the word *syzygy* in another sense and that, in general, the use of a certain term by heretics still does not make it heretical.

Undoubtedly, the historical process is being effected in this direction, gradually destroying false or insufficient forms of human union (patriarchal, despotic, unilaterally individualistic) and, at the same time, gradually becoming more and more proximate not only to the unification of all humanity, as a solidary whole, but also to the establishment of the true syzygy form of this all-human union. As to the measure of how the all-unity Idea is realized through the consolidation and improvement of their individually human elements, the forms of false division, or impenetrability of beings in space and time, perforce weaken and are diminished. But for their full abolition and for a definitive immortalization of all individualities, not only present but past as well, it is necessary that the process of integration cross the boundaries of social, or properly speaking, human life, and join to itself the cosmic sphere from which it emerged. In the arrangement of the physical world (the cosmic process) the divine Idea only adorned the kingdom of matter and death with a shroud of natural beauty from without: through humanity, through the activity of its universally rational consciousness, it must enter into this kingdom *from within*, in order to vivify nature and immortalize its beauty. In this sense, it is necessary to change the relation of man to nature. He must establish with it, as well, that syzygy unity by which his true life in the personal and social realms is determined.

V.
Nature has hitherto been either an all-powerful despotic mother of an infant humanity or a foreign slave to it—a thing. In this second epoch, only poets alone somewhat preserved and upheld at least an unconscious and timid feeling of love toward nature as toward a being with equal rights, which had or was capable of having *life in itself*. True poets always remained prophets of a universal restoration of life and beauty, as one of them remarked so adeptly to his confreres:

> Only with you do fleeting daydreams
> Reflect in the soul with old friends,
> Only with you do fragrant roses
> *Eternally* sparkle with tears of rapture.
> From everyday, colorless, stuffy bazaars
> How joyful to see the subtle colors,
> In your transparent-atmospheric rainbows
> The caresses of a native sky appear to me.[59]

This goal, the establishment of a truly loving, or syzygy relation of man not only to his social, but also to his natural and universal surroundings, is clear in itself. It is not possible to say the very same about the paths of its attainment for an individual man. While not going into premature, and therefore dubious and improper, details, it is possible, based on the solid analogies of cosmic and historical experience, to hold with confidence that every conscious human activity, being determined by the Idea of universal syzygy and having as a goal to embody the all-unity ideal in one or another sphere, by the same token actually produces or liberates real spiritually corporeal currents. These currents are gradually getting control over the material environment, are inspiring it and embodying in it, one way or another, forms of all-unity—living and eternal likenesses of absolute humanness. But the strength of this spiritually corporeal creation in man is only the transformation or *inward conversion* of that same creative force that, in nature, being directed outward, produces an ugly infinity of the physical propagation of organisms.

Having associated individual sexual love with the truth of the essence of universal life in the Idea of universal syzygy, I have fulfilled my direct task—to determine the meaning of love, since by the meaning of any subject is understood precisely its intrinsic connection with universal truth. As for certain social problems I had to touch upon, I intend to return to them again.

5

A First Step toward
a Positive Aesthetic

I.

To the vast number of recent literary reactions has now been added another reaction in favor of "pure" art, or "art for art's sake." While some of
these reactions are evoked by opposite extremes, others are not elicited by
constructive motive. This one undoubtedly belongs to the first category—
to a category of *pardonable* reactions; everyone has memories of the opposite extreme that evoked it. But is this an inevitable fate for us—to neu-
tralize one untruth with another and subject our intellectual development
badly and "hard-heartedly" to the contrived law of retribution: an eye for
an eye and a tooth for a tooth? If, as they usually say, each error *naturally*
calls forth another, its opposite, then for man as a rational being, submit-
ting to such a natural process of errors is not entirely natural—it is much
more natural for him to place in opposition to every error the pure and
simple truth; and besides, this is also more fruitful.

Source: "Pervyi shag k polozhitel'noi esteteki," *Vestnik Evropy* 1 (1894): 294–302.
Reprinted in *Sobranie sochinenii* 7: 69–80.

When, for example, writers who proclaimed Pushkin "a vulgarian" asked in confirmation of this notion the question: "What benefit has Pushkin's poetry brought, and what benefit will it bring?", the objection was: "Pushkin—was a priest of pure art, of beautiful form; poetry need not be utile, poetry is superior to utility!"[1] Such words respond neither to the adversary nor to the truth, and only mutual misunderstanding and contempt are left as a result. And, meanwhile, a real and just response is so simple and near: No, the poetry of Pushkin, taken as a *whole* (for it is necessary to measure with a "just yardstick") brought great benefit and continues to do so, because its perfect beauty of form reinforces the action of the spirit embodied within it, and this spirit is alive, good and elevated, as he himself testifies in the famous lines:

> And I will long be held dear by the people for the fact,
> That I awakened good sentiments with lyre,
> That in this cruel century I glorified freedom,
> And appealed for mercy to the fallen. . . .[2]

Such a just response would even have been appropriate and convincing in the event that the adversary would have understood under "utility" in this hyperbole only material utility, requiring "stove pots" from poetry. For, in such an event, it would not be difficult to explain that, although good sentiments in themselves are also insufficient for the provision of all the people with necessary domestic utensils, *without* such sentiments it would not be possible even to speak of a similar utilitarian enterprise in the absence of inducements intrinsic to it. In that case, only a continuous war for pots would have been possible, and in no way their fair distribution for general usage.

If advocates of "art for art's sake" understand by this only that artistic creativity is a special activity of the human spirit that meets a particular requirement and has its own sphere, then they certainly would be correct; but then, for them, it would be nothing to raise a reaction as well in the name of a truth against which nobody would argue seriously. However, they go much farther; they do not limit themselves to the justified claim of a specific peculiarity of art or independence of those *means* by which it acts. Rather, they disclaim any vital connection of it with other human activities and any necessity of *subjecting* it to vital common aims of humanity, regarding it as somehow locked up in itself and absolutely self-sufficient; in place of a legitimate *autonomy* for the artistic sphere, they propagate *aesthetic separatism*. But even if art were just as necessary for all humanity as breathing is for an individual man, the latter essentially depends on the circulation of the blood, on the activity of nerves and muscles, and it is subordinated to the life of the whole; and even the most excellent lungs will not revive him when other vital organs are stricken. The life of the whole does not exclude, but on the contrary requires and assumes, the relative independence of the parts and their functions—but any particular function in its separateness is not and cannot be absolutely self-sufficient.

The following subtle distinction, made by some of the advocates of aesthetic separatism, is useless for them as well. Let us allow, they say, that in our common life art is connected with other activities, and all of them together are subordinated to the final goal of historical development; but this connection and this goal, finding themselves outside the boundaries of our consciousness, are fulfilled by themselves and apart from us—and consequently they cannot define our relation to one or another human activity. Out of this comes the conclusion: let the artist be only an artist, think only about excellence aesthetically, about the beauty of form, and let nothing consequential exist for him in the world besides this form.

Reasoning similar to this, having in mind the exaltation of art, actually diminishes it profoundly—making it similar to a factory worker who all his life must only make certain wheels of a watch mechanism, but has nothing to do with the whole of the mechanism. Of course, service to a pseudo-artistic form is much *more palatable* than factory work, but for the rational consciousness palatability alone is too meager.

And what is this conviction in the fateful "unconsciousness" of the historical process, in the absolute unknowability of its goals, based on? If a definite, fully adequate, concrete, and workable conception regarding the final status of humanity is required, then of course such a conception is accessible to no one—and not so much because of the limitation of the human mind as because the very understanding of *absolutely final* status as the conclusion of a *temporal* process contains in itself hardly removable *logical* difficulties. However, such an impossible conception about an inconceivable subject is of no utility. A general understanding about the direction of the historical process is completely sufficient for conscious participation in it; in other words, it is enough to have an ideal conception of the *maximum* quantity, mathematically speaking, that the *variable* quantities of human progress undoubtedly and continuously approach but, according to the nature of things, can never coincide with. And anyone, not excluding even an aesthetic separatist, can obtain a completely clear understanding about the ideal end toward which history is *actually* moving if only he turns for directions, not to preconceived opinions and bad instincts, but to conclusions that come out of historical fact, for which reason vouches and to which the conscience attests.

In spite of all the vacillation and the zigzagging of progress, in spite of all of today's exacerbation of militarism, nationalism, anti-Semitism, terrorism, and so on and so forth—for all that, the fact that the *resultant force* of history is going from cannibalism toward love of fellowman, from lawlessness to justice, and from hostile disconnection of particular groups toward *universal solidarity* remains doubtless. To prove this would mean to lay out a comparative course of universal history. But for conscientious pessimists perplexed by the retrograde phenomena of the present epoch, it will be enough to recall that these phenomena themselves clearly show the irrevocable force of general historical advancement.

Here are two examples from totally different spheres, but leading to one and the same moral. In Germany there appeared a talented writer (unfortunately, he turned out to be mentally ill) who began to preach that compassion is a base feeling, unworthy of a person who respects himself; that morality is suited only to slave natures; that there is no such thing as humanity, but there are masters and slaves, demi-gods and demi-cattle; that to the former all is permitted, and the latter are obliged to serve as instruments for the former, and so forth.[3] But is that correct? These ideas, in which and by which the subjects of Egyptian pharaohs and Assyrian kings once believed and lived—ideas for which even now Beganza in Dahomey and Lobengula in Matabeland fight with their last ounce of strength—have been received in our own Europe as something unusually original and fresh, and in this capacity everywhere have had a *grand succès de surprise*.[4]

Does this not prove that we have not only been able to survive but to forget as well that which our ancestors lived by, so that their worldview would obtain for us now the fascination of novelty? And the fact that similar envisaged resuscitations of dead ideas are never and nowhere frightening for the living at all is already visible out of just one consideration: besides the two classes of people indicated by Nietzsche—haughty masters and humble slaves—there has developed everywhere yet a third class—that of not-humble slaves, i.e., those who have ceased being slaves—and thanks to the propagation of printing and many other inescapable and in-evitable evils, this third class (which is not limited by *tiers-état* alone) grows so thick that it has already absorbed the two others. These people have no intention of returning to humility and slavish submissiveness of their own free will, and nobody can compel them in any way—at least not until Antichrist and his prophet arrive with deceptive wonders and signs; and this final disguised reaction of Dahomeyan ideals too will be sufficient only for a little while.[5]

A second example of how reactionary phenomena testify to true prog-ress is the character of today's militarism: with all the vast armaments and with such an extraordinary exacerbation of national rivalry and enmity, there is an unprecedented indecisiveness to starting a war! Everybody involuntarily senses and understands that, with today's multilateral *inter-connectedness* among diverse parts of humanity, it will not be possible to localize armed conflict; and that the unprecedented vastness of forces in numbers of armies and deadliness of weapons represents war in all its yet unprecedented horror, making its repetition insufferable morally and ma-terially. This means one of two things: either, in spite of all the militarism, war for all that will not ensue; or, if it begins, then it will be the *last one*. Militarism will devour war. Armed internecine political strife among na-tions will inevitably diminish, as did permanent internecine strife among separate regions and cities within countries.[6]

Local history shows here and there how, by difficult, tangled, and not infrequently crooked paths, the land gathered around national leaders, and how little by little national consciousness grew and developed. But universal history too shows us how, by still more difficult and complex paths, *the entire earth*, all of humanity, *gathers around* an invisible but pow-erful center of Christian culture; and how, in spite of any obstacles what-soever, the consciousness of universal unity and solidarity continually grows and strengthens. This analogy between the national and the uni-versal "gathering of the land" could be advanced yet further, but I limit myself to only manifest and inarguable features.

And so history (and consequently, the entire universal process as well) has a goal that we undoubtedly know—an all-embracing goal, which is at the same time sufficiently defined so that we can consciously participate in its attainment; for relative to any human idea, feeling, and concern, it is al-ways possible according to reason and conscience to resolve whether it is in agreement with the universal ideal of solidarity or contradicts it, whether it is directed toward the realization of true all-unity or counteracts it.* And, if so, then where is the right for any kind of human activity to be separated from the common activity, to retire into oneself, to declare oneself as being one's own intrinsic and unique goal? And in particular, where are the rights of aesthetic separatism? No: art is not for art's sake, but for the realization of the plenitude of life, which necessarily includes in itself also the special element of art—beauty—not as something separate and self-sufficient, but in a vital and intrinsic connection with all the remaining content of life.

The first step toward a true positive aesthetic is to repudiate the fantastic alienation of beauty and art from the common activity of universal life; to acknowledge that artistic activity does not have in itself some kind of special supreme object, and only serves the common vital goal of humanity *in its own way,* by its own means. In Russian literature this step was taken nearly forty years ago by the author of an aesthetic treatise, which (together with other, less important, though also interesting, studies by that same writer) has been reprinted precisely now; and this is very apropos in view of the revival among us of aesthetic separatism.

In desiring to indicate the positive significance and merit of this old but not yet out-of-date treatise, neither do I close my eyes at all to its many particular shortcomings or to the general incompleteness of the views represented by it. At the time, many were convinced that the author of "The Aesthetic Relations of Art to Reality" had spoken the final word in this realm. I am so far from a similar frame of mind that I emphasize at once the opposite: he spoke only the *first,* and not at all the final, word of true aesthetics. But I consider it unjustified to require from the one who did this that he bring everything to conclusion, and I think that the inevitable inadequacy of the first step by itself will be eliminated when further steps are made.

II.

If our author subjects art to reality, then this is certainly not in the sense in which other of his contemporaries did, declaring that "boots are more im-

---

* I call true, or positive, all-unity that in which one exists not on account of everyone or to their detriment, but to the benefit of all. A false, negative unity represses or absorbs the elements entering into it and itself turns out in this way to be *futility;* true unity protects and strengthens its elements, being realized in them as *a plenitude* of being.

portant than Shakespeare." He maintains only that the *beauty* of real life is superior to the beauty of artistically created fantasies.*⁷ At the same time, he stands up for the reality of beauty against Hegelian aesthetics, for which the excellent "appears only as an apparition" resulting from the inscrutability of a perspective and not illuminated by philosophic thought, before which the apparent fullness of an Idea's manifestation in an individual object (i.e., beauty) disappears. So "the higher that a thought is developed, the more the excellent vanishes before it, and, finally, for absolutely developed thought only the true exists, but the excellent does not."†

In contrast to such a view, our author recognizes beauty as the essential property of actual objects and insists on its factual reality—not only for man, but also in nature and for nature:

> Understanding the excellent as the plenitude of life, we should acknowledge that a striving toward life, which permeates all nature, is at the same time a striving toward the production of the excellent as well. If we must in general see not a goal in nature, but only results, and therefore cannot call beauty the goal of nature, then we cannot but call it the essential result, toward the production of which the forces of nature are directed. Non-premeditation or unconsciousness of this tendency does not at all interfere with its reality, just as the unconsciousness of geometrical striving in a bee or the unconsciousness of striving toward symmetry in the force of growth does not at all interfere with the correctness of the hexahedronal cell structure of a honeycomb or the symmetry of the two halves of a leaf.‡

The author dedicated a significant part of his treatise to detailed evidence of the idea "that a product of art can have an advantage over reality in two or three worthless respects, and by necessity remains far lower than it in its essential properties."§ There is much that is naive in the broad argument (pp. 38–81)—one must not forget that this is a youthful

---

* "Estetika i poeziia," *Sovremennik* (1854–1861), published by M. N. Chernyshevsky (St. Petersburg, 1893), p. 81.

† Ibid., pp. 2–3. In these words it is less that the Hegelian point of view is simply set forth than that it "vanishes into fresh water"; but the essence of the matter is transmitted completely faithfully.

‡ Ibid., pp. 42–43.

§ Ibid., p. 80.

dissertation. Some points of dispute are asserted without adducing any proof, and other inarguable things are proved with pedantic complete-ness. But all these shortcomings and extraneous things should not shut us off from that which *is faithful* in the idea demonstrated—it is faithful to such a degree that the reader is unsatisfied with the author's diffuse prose, and can find a short, yet more precise expression of that same view at an opposite pole of our literature, in this poem by Fet:

> To whom goes the crown: to the goddess of beauty,
> *Or to the mirror of its image?*
> The poet is embarrassed when you marvel
> At his rich imagination.
> Not I, my friend, but God's world is rich:
> In a speck of dust he coddles and multiplies *life*,
> And the poet cannot retell
> What one of your gazes expresses.[8]

But, if this is so, then what is the significance and mission of art? Our author approaches this question from a realistic angle. Having refuted the opinion that art creates perfect beauty that does not exist in reality, he notes: "In works of art there is no perfection; he who is dissatisfied with real beauty can be satisfied still less by the beauty created by art. And so, it is not possible to agree with the usual explanation of the significance of art; but in this explanation are hints that can be called correct if they are expounded upon in an appropriate manner. Man is not satisfied by the ex-cellent in reality, to him little of reality is excellent—this is the essence and veracity of the standard explanation, which, being erroneously un-derstood on its own, is in need of explanation."*

The author's own explanation is unsatisfying, and I will not dwell on it. Neither will I begin to defend all the seventeen theses with which his dissertation concludes. Its main content is reduced to two tenets: 1) Ex-isting art is only a weak surrogate of reality, and 2) Beauty in nature has an objective reality—and *these* theses *will remain*. Their assertion in a trea-tise constrained by the limitations of the special philosophical outlook of the author (he was at that time an extreme follower of Feuerbach), does not

---

* Ibid., p. 89.

resolve the issue but only presents another task; yet a faithful position is a first step toward resolution. Further fruitful work in the sphere of aesthetics that should connect artistic creativity with the higher goals of human life will be possible only on the foundation of these truths (the objective nature of beauty and the insufficiency of art), and in no way through a return to artistic dilettantism.

6 ✍

The Fate of Pushkin

I.

There are topics about which it is possible to have an incorrect or insufficient understanding without it being directly harmful to life. Although these topics themselves can have an actual, practical and great significance, the concern of truth relative to them is only intellectual, scientific-theoretical. Until the end of the seventeenth century when the renowned Lavoisier analyzed the composition of *water* as being of two elementary gases—oxygen and hydrogen—people everywhere, even scientists, understood it incorrectly; they considered water a simple body, a homogeneous element. What Lavoisier did had great theoretical importance—it is not for nothing that modern scientific chemistry springs from him. And, of course, by virtue of his discovery, chemistry also exerted an indirect influence as well on everyday life (with respect to its material interests), which good chemistry can serve more successfully than bad chemistry.

But Lavoisier's analysis of *water* as such cannot have a *direct* impact of any practical significance. In order to wash oneself, to water animals, to

Source: "Sud'ba Pushkina," *Vestnik Evropy* 9 (1897): 131–156. Reprinted in *Sobranie sochinenii* 9: 33–61.

turn mill wheels, or even to move a locomotive, water alone is necessary—and not a knowledge of its composition or its chemical formula. We make use of light and heat precisely in the same way, completely independent of our knowledge or ignorance, or our correct or incorrect understandings in the realm of astronomy and physics. In all similar events, experiential knowledge about an object's superficial properties is sufficient for its every-day utilization, completely independent of a precise theoretical percep-tion of its nature; and the greatest scientist cannot have any advantage here over the ignoramus and the primitive.

But there are topics of a spiritual order, the vital significance of which is directly determined for us by the *understanding* we have about them, apart from their essential real properties. The present essay is concerned with one of these topics.

Although not material or tangible, there is something called *fate* that is nevertheless absolutely real. I now understand by the term fate the *fact* that the course and outcome of our life depend on something apart from ourselves, on some *surmounting necessity* to which we should willy-nilly subordinate ourselves. As a fact, this is inarguable; the *existence* of fate in this sense is acknowledged by all thoughtful people, independently of any difference in views and degrees of education. It is only too apparent that a person's power—even that of the most stubborn and energetic person—over the course and outcome of his life has very restricted limits. However, at the same time, it is easy to see that the power of fate, with all its imper-ishable force over a person *from without,* is conditional upon the energetic and personal cooperation of the person himself *from within.* Since we con-trol the intrinsic agents, reason and will, then the power that determines our existence, which we call fate, even if independent of us in essence, can, however, act in our life only through us, only under condition of one or another attitude to it on the part of our conscience and will. Our own personal attitude *necessarily* goes into the configuration of this *necessity,* by which our life's events are directed. And this attitude, in its turn, is neces-sarily tied to *how* we understand the governing power in our life, so that *our concept* of fate is also one of the conditions *of its action* through us. This is why the *constant* of fate is more important for us than knowing the chemi-cal composition of water or the physical laws of heat and light.

A stable concept of fate is so important to people everywhere that from earliest times it was a given and was accessible to everyone. But even the most constant of constants is not taken on faith by anybody today; the present is distinguished from earlier epochs by a peculiar development, if not of mind, then of intellectual requirements; authenticity must be deduced by means of reason and out of given experience.

An entire metaphysical system corroborated by complex historical and sociological research would be required for a complete and methodical justification of constancy in the concept of fate that we find in the universal beliefs of humanity. In this brief essay I desire only to dilute certain erroneous popular opinions about this important topic and to allude to the reliable character of that which is called fate, with the help of one vivid and—especially for us Russians—proximate historical example.

II.

In contemporary literature and in everday discourse, the word *fate* is usually conveyed by more or less negative epithets: "hostile" fate, "blind" fate, "pitiless" fate, "cruel" fate, and so forth. The "mockery" and "irony" of fate are articulated less acutely, but for all that with a certain disapproval. All these expressions assume that our life depends on some kind of power, at times indifferent and undifferentiating, and at times even directly hostile and malicious. In the first case, the understanding of fate merges with a popular understanding of *nature*, for which indifference serves as the common epithet:

> And let youthful life play
> At the tomb's entry,
> And *indifferent* nature
> Radiate eternal beauty.[1]

When this property—indifference—is emphasized in the concept of fate, then by "fate" no more than a law of the physical world is strictly understood.

In the second case—when fate is spoken of as a hostile force—the understanding of fate comes close to a demonic comprehension, the hellish principle in the world, whether it is represented in the form of an evil spirit of religious systems or in the form of a senseless universal will, as in Schopenhauer.

Of course, both the one and the other exist in reality—both a law of indifferent nature as well as an evil satanic principle in the universe—and we have business with both of them. But is it these forces that we *ultimately* depend on; is it they that determine the common course of our life and resolve its outcome—is it they that constitute our fate?

A force governing the life of people and controlling the course of events certainly acts with equal necessity everywhere and always; all of us are alike subjected to fate. But there are people and events upon which fate acts in a particularly manifest and *palpable* manner; they are even directly called *fateful* or resigned; and, of course, it is easier than anything for us to discern the actual essence of this subjugating force.

Although, *in general,* it has long been clear to me that the decisive role in our existence does not belong either to "indifferent nature" or to the spiritual power of evil, and though I have been firmly convinced in the truth of a *third* view, I could not for a long time relate to it certain particularly fateful events. I was convinced that they, too, are somehow permanently explained from a reliable point of view, but I *did not see* this explanation and could not be reconciled with incomprehensible facts in my soul. In them was sensed some kind of mortal offense, as if there was the direct action of some kind of hostile, mischievous, gloating force.

The death of Pushkin created such an impression more acutely than anything else. I do not recall a time when the cult of his poetry was alien to me. Not yet able to read, I still knew much of his work by heart, and this cult only thrived with the years. It is no wonder that the fateful death of Pushkin in the flowering of his creative forces seemed to me a flagrant untruth, an insufferable offense, and that fate acting here was not connected with the conception of a beneficent force.

Meanwhile, after turning my thoughts again and again to this tormenting theme and its long-known facts, and thanks to documents promulgated after 1880 (especially those after 1887 in which new details were acknowledged), I finally had to arrive at a sad consolation:

> An enemy did not take away his life—
> He fell *by his own* power,
> A sacrifice of ruinous rage—[2]

by his own power or, better to say, by his own *rejection* of the moral power that was accessible to him and the use of which was for him facilitated in every way.

Neither the aesthetic cult of Pushkin's poetry nor the heartfelt delight produced by the best traits in the image of the poet himself assuage our acknowledgment of the truth—that he ended his earthly walk of life in conformity with his own will. The opposite view, apart from its lack of historical foundation, would be degrading for Pushkin himself. Is it really not degrading for a great genius to be the idle plaything of extrinsic, alien influences, and issuing forth besides from people for whom sufficiently contemptuous expressions are not to be found both in this genius himself and among his admirers?

The chief mistake here is in the fact that genius is taken only for some kind of marvel of nature, and the point that here we have a *man* of genius is forgotten. According to his nature, he towers above ordinary people—this is inarguable. But, according to nature as well, even ordinary people tower over many other creatures, for example, animals; and if this *comparative* elevation *obligates* every ordinary man to observe his human dignity and by this justify his natural advantage over animals, then the loftier gift of genius obligates one *all the more* to guard this more elevated, if you like, superhuman dignity. While not insisting too much on this gradation, which is made complex by circumstances of another sort, one should say in any event that a man of genius is obligated at least to the protection of a certain minimal—even if the lowest—degree of moral human dignity, similar to how we require from the most ordinary man at least those virtues to which even animals have a capability, as for example, parental love, gratitude, loyalty.

To maintain that genius has absolutely no obligation to anything, that all is permitted to genius, that he can without detriment to his high calling remain all his life in the mire of lower passions—is crude idolatry, fetishism that does not account for anything and is itself accounted for only by the spiritual feebleness of its advocates.[3] No! if genius is nobility according to advantage or a lofty degree of nobility, then according to advantage it obligates to a higher degree: noblesse oblige. We will take a serious look at the life and fate of Pushkin from the point of view of this moral axiom.

III.

I would wish more than anything that my opinion not be understood in the sense of prescribed ethics, indicting the poet for his moral dissolution and ready to maintain that he perished as punishment for his sins against "virtue," in the narrow sense of this word.

Strong sensuality is the material of genius. As mechanistic movement is converted to heat, and heat to light, so the spiritual energy of creativity in its actual manifestation (in order of time, or process) is a *conversion* of the lower energies of the sensual soul. And just as a strong development of heat is necessary for the creation of a *powerful* light, so too a high degree of spiritual creativity (according to the law of restricted, earthly life) assumes a strong development of sensual passions. A higher manifestation of genius requires not customary impassivity, but the definitive overcoming of powerful passion, triumph over it at a decisive moment.

And Pushkin possessed the natural conditions for such a triumph. A clear and straightforward intellect was united in him with an unbridled sensual nature. Pushkin was not at all a thinker in the realm of speculation, just as he was not a practical sage either; but he possessed to an elevated degree a sound understanding of vital moral truths, the meaning of truth. His mind was well balanced, stranger to all morbid deviations. He could protect the clarity and precision of conscience amidst the most fiery passion; and if it is possible to reproach him for something in this regard then, indeed, only in the excessive sobriety and straightforwardness of opinion, in the absence of any practical or everyday *idealism*. All his highly principled energy was exhausted by poetic images and sounds, *by a brilliant regeneration of life in poetry;* and only prose, common sense, and wit accompanied by gay laughter were left for ordinary life itself, for everyday practice.

Such a bifurcation between poetry—i.e., life creatively illuminated—and practical or real life is sometimes striking in Pushkin. People who were formerly unfamiliar with biographical details about him certainly found much that was unexpected in the latest editions of his correspondence.

One of our poet's best and most popular verses speaks about a woman who, at "the magical instant" of first acquaintance, impressed him "as a fleeting vision, as the brilliance of pure beauty"; that is why the time of parting with her was for him an oppressive series of hollow and gloomy days, and only a new rendezvous revived for his soul "both divinity and inspiration, and life, tears, and love." The person to whom this verse related had long been known, and a reader of Pushkin formerly had ample foundation to imagine, if not this lady, then, in any case, the poet's attitude toward her in the loftiest ideal illumination. But after the appearance in print of certain letters about her, it now turns out that her image in the poem "I Recall a Magical Instant" is not even what in Hegelian aesthetics is called *Schein der Idee*, and sooner resembles that which in juridical language is designated as "a witting communication of false information."[4] In an intimate letter, written almost at the same time as the poem, Pushkin speaks candidly about this very lady, but now "our whore of babylon,

Anna Petrovna" appears in place of the brilliance of pure beauty awakening the soul and reviving divinity in it.

I hasten to warn of a possible misunderstanding. No one has any business regarding what kind of lady the one made famous by Pushkin was in reality. Although I am totally convinced that he was strongly exaggerating and that the apocalyptic image was not at all a trait of this good woman, that's not the point. If it turned out that a real monster of immorality was openly accepted by some poet for the brilliance of pure beauty and sung of in such a sense, then the poetical work would lose nothing as a result, not only from the point of view of poetry, but from the point of view as well of the personal and vitally important dignity of the poet himself. An error in hypocrisy is not being presented; but in the present case, it is impossible not to see a certain hypocrisy, although certainly not in the crude sense of this word. In representing an ordinary woman as an elevated, unearthly creature, Pushkin himself clearly noted and sharply expressed his deceit immediately here, even exaggerating it. The poet's acquaintance was, of course, neither the brilliance of pure beauty nor the whore of babylon, but was "simply a pleasant lady" or perhaps even "a pleasant lady in all respects."[5] But in the exaggeration of her censure it is remarkable that there is not heard in Pushkin any bitterness of disillusionment, which would speak for the vital sincerity and integrity of the former passion—the blunt reference is stated in the tone of gay joking, in complete contrast to the style of the verse.

Another of Pushkin's verses, directed at that same person, bears more semblance to reality, but even it contradicts the tone and expressions of his letters.

> When sensational rumour
> Dishonours your youthful years
> And according to the verdict of the world,
> You have lost the right to honour;
>
> Alone amidst the frigid mob,
> I share your sufferings
> And pray for you a fruitless
> Supplication to an unfeeling idol.
>
> Yet the world . . . does not alter
> Its cruel condemnations

It does not punish errors,
But demands secrets for them.

Worthy of equal contempt are
Its vainglorious love
And hypocritical persecution—
The heart is prepared to oblivion;

Do not drink the excruciating poison;
Abandon the brilliant, stifling circle
Abandon the senseless amusements:
One friend is left to you.[6]

It is impossible, in actual fact, not to pity the profound unhappiness of this woman: she was left with only one friend and defender from "cruel condemnations"—and even that one called her the whore of babylon! What condemnations must they have been!

IV.

If inspiration is not acknowledged as an independent source of poetry, then in comparing the verse "I Recall a Magical Instant" with Pushkin's prosaic reference, it is possible to draw only one conclusion: that the lines are simply invented, that their author never saw that image and never experienced the sentiments expressed there. But in denying poetical inspiration, it is better not to speak of poets at all. And it should be clear for those acknowledging inspiration and sensing its power in this work that Pushkin really experienced that which was said in these verses at *the moment of creativity*; he really saw the brilliance of pure beauty, really felt the revival of divinity within himself. But this ideal reality existed for him only at the moment of creativity. Returning to life, he immediately stopped believing in the experienced illumination, immediately recognized in it only the deception of imagination—"the deception that elevates us"—but for all that a deception and nothing more. The visions and feelings that arose in him pertaining to certain persons or events and that comprised the content of his poetry were not ordinarily connected with these people and events in his routine life at all, and he did not in the least feel the burden of such an incoherence, such an impassable abyss between poetry and everyday practice.

The reality given in everyday experience is undoubtedly in profound contradiction to the ideal of life revealed to faith, philosophic speculation, and creative inspiration. There are three possible ways out of this contradiction. It is possible to renounce the ideal directly as idle invention and deception and to acknowledge fact, which contradicts ideal requirements, as *the definitive and sole* reality. This is the way out of moral skepticism and misanthropy—a view that can be respectable when sincere, as for example in Shakespeare's Timon of Athens, but which does not bear logical criticism. Actually, if ugly reality were the sole reality, then how would it be possible for man *to feel the burden* of this, his single reality, to reproach and deny it? A creature in a homogeneous milieu—for example a man in the atmosphere above ground or a fish in water—does not feel the pressure of this milieu. When a true misanthrope really suffers from moral indignation of the human milieu, then he thereby witnesses to the authentic power of the ideal living within him—his suffering is already the source of another, better reality.

A second way out of the contradiction between ideal and bad reality is *Don Quixotism*, in which ideal notions control a person to such a degree that he, with absolute candor, either does not see the facts contradicted by it or counts these facts as phantom and deceit. For all the nobility of such idealism, its unsoundness does not require any explanations after Cervantes' satire.

The third, and evidently common, way out could be called *practical idealism*. It consists in not closing one's eyes to the ugly side of reality, but not elevating it to a principle, to something absolute and irrevocable either. It consists *in noting real rudiments or inclinations of that which should be in that which is* and relying upon these, as yet insufficent and incomplete, but nevertheless actual manifestions of the good, as upon an existence already given. It consists in helping to protect the growth and triumph of these good principles, and gradually drawing reality nearer to the ideal more and more, and, through this, embodying a higher revelation in the facts of our life. Such practical idealism is applicable and obligatory for societal, individual, and even the most intimate relations alike. Certainly, something completely different would have happened both for him [Pushkin] and for her, and his inspired verse would have had not only poetic, but vital significance as well—if the poet had rested on the actual rudiments of elevated dignity (which in essence should have been included, suggesting to him pure images and sentiments, even if only for an instant) instead of taking comfort from an exaggerated contrast between "the brilliance of pure beauty" and the "whore of babylon"; and if he had not rejected everyday life in that which he saw and felt in the moment of inspiration, but resolved to protect and multiply these tokens of something better and to base his attitudes toward this woman on them. But now, in evaluating these lines, though the artistic beauty remains, it is not possible to be completely indifferent to the circumstance that, in a real historical sense and from the point of view of Pushkin himself, they give only unnecessary confirmation of Aristotle's words that "poets lie a lot."[7]

All possible ways out of the contradiction between poetic ideal and everyday reality alike remained alien to Pushkin. Happily, he was neither misanthrope nor Don Quixote; but unhappily, he either did not know how or did not want to become a practical, ideal, and active servant of good and a reformer of reality. He noted the contradiction with total clarity, but somehow reconciled himself with it easily: pointing to it as to a fact and beautifully characterizing it (for example in the poem "Until a Poet Is Necessary"). He did not even suspect—until his last, mature years—that in this fact there is a problem requiring a solution. The acute discord between creative and everyday motives seemed to him somehow decisive and irrevocable, and it did not offend the moral ear, which apparently was less sensitive than the poetic ear.

Relations with women occupied a very large place in the life and poetry of Pushkin; and although these relations did not in every case give him occasion for apocalyptic likenesses, the irreconcilable duality between the idealism of creativity and the extreme realism of everyday opinions appears everywhere. In the extensive correspondence with his wife, we will not even find a hint of the "prayerful reverence before a shrine of beauty" spoken about in a poem to Natalia Nikolaevna Gonchareva.

V.

According to Pushkin's own testimony, there were two different and unconnected essences within him: the inspired pagan priest of Apollo, and the vainest of the vain children of the world. The lofty essence did not appear immediately; his poetic genius came to light gradually. In his early works we see a playfulness of wit and formal poetic talent, the effortless reflections of everyday and literary impressions. He himself characterizes such creativity as the "affectionate sounds of madness, laziness, and passions." But a great poet quickly grew within the frivolous youth, and he soon began to repress the "vain child of the world." By his thirtieth year, a "restless attraction of something for which his soul thirsted" appears resolutely in Pushkin—a dissatisfaction with the play of dark passions and its luminous reflections in effortless images and delicate sounds. "He became acquainted with a voice of other desires, he became acquainted with a new sorrow." He realized that "service to the muse does not tolerate vanity," that "the beautiful must be sublime"; i.e., that before it can be pleasant, beauty must be worthy, that *beauty is only the palpable form of truth and the good.*[8]

If Pushkin had lived in the Middle Ages, he could have gone into a monastery after having achieved this realization, in order to connect his vocational calling with the straightforward cult of that which is absolutely worthy. It would have been easy for him to distance himself from the world, the reform and revival of which, as we know, he did not believe in. In the conditions in which a Russian poet of the nineteenth century found himself, it was more convenient and more secure to select another kind of asceticism: he married and became the father of a family. With this, a period of unbridled sensual passions, which could have crushed a not-yet-strong creative gift instead of nourishing it, passed happily for him. *This* temptation seemed insufficiently strong to overcome his genius, and he was able in time to place a limit on the immensity of his lower instinct and to direct his material life into a channel. "He became acquainted with the voice of other desires, became acquainted with new sorrow."

But in becoming the father of a family, Pushkin, out of necessity, more closely than formerly, connected himself with a social life, with the social milieu to which he belonged; and here a new, more subtle, and dangerous temptation awaited him.

Having reached maturity, Pushkin clearly acknowledged that the mission of his life was a service "which does not tolerate vanity," a service to all that is beautiful, which "must be sublime." Since he remained within society, his service to beauty inevitably took on the character of *public* service, and it was necessary for him to establish his *proper* relation to society.

But having isolated poetry (too much even) from everyday relations, Pushkin did not want to separate here the legitimate consciousness of his higher poetic calling and his intrinsic advantage over others—which gave him his genius. He did not want to separate this legitimate feeling of his worth as a great poet from the personal petty passion of ambition and conceit. If Pushkin stood above others by virtue of his genius and was correct in acknowledging this eminence, then in his conceited vexation he attacked others from his summit, stood *against* others—that is, on a level with them—and, through this, lost all justification for his vexation as well. It now turned out to be only the ugly passion of enmity and spite.

VI.

Self-love and conceit are properties of all people; their total elimination is not only impossible, but very likely undesirable as well. Important stimulators of human activity would grow numb; this would be dangerous while humanity must live and act upon the earth.

I have read among the patristic writings—the Limonaria of St. Sophronius, Patriarch of Jerusalem—the following story. A novice monk came to a well-known ascetic, asking him to direct him to the path of perfection. Tonight — said the elder — go into the churchyard and eulogize the deceased who are buried there, and afterwards come back and tell me how they received you. The next day the monk returns from the churchyard: — I followed your command, father! All night long I eulogized these deceased with a loud voice, praised them as holy, blessed fathers, great and righteous people and pleasing to God, luminaries of the universe, mines of information, salt of the earth; I ascribed to them every virtue, about which I've only read in Holy Scripture and in ancient Greek books. — Well, all right. How did they express their pleasure to you? — In no way, father: They observed silence the whole time; I heard from them not a single word. — Very surprising, said the elder, but here is what you do: tonight go back there again and curse them until the morning, the more zealously the better; with this they will probably begin to speak. — The next day the monk again returned with a report: — I reviled them and defamed them in every possible way, called them unclean dogs, vessels of the devil, apostates; I compared them to all the evildoers from the Old and New Testaments, from Cain-the-fratricide to Judas-the-betrayer, from the savage Gibeonites, to Ananias and Sapphira, and from Valentinianism to the newly-brought-to-light monothelitism.[9] — Well, all right. How is it you withstood their wrath? — No wise, father! They were silent the whole time. I even put my ear to the graves, but nobody as much as stirred. — Well, now you see, said the elder: You have ascended the first rung of angelic life, which is obedience; you will only achieve the summit of this life on earth when you are as indifferent as these corpses to both praise and insult.

For Pushkin, too, the ideal of perfection presupposed a complete mortification of self-love and conceit: "Praise and slander accepted indifferently. . . ."[10] But to await such an ideal's actual realization or to require it would be, of course, unjust. Remaining in the world, he rejected the practice of supraworldly perfection, and it would be pitiful if the poet of luminous life gave chase as well after a perfection of the deceased.

But one could and should have required and expected from Pushkin that which, according to right, is expected and required by us from any rational man in the name of human dignity — one could and should have awaited and required from him that, remaining in his self-love and even giving one expression or another to it when he had the chance, he did not attach to it *substantial* significance, did not accept it as a motive of important resolutions and acts, so that he could always say about the passion of self-love, as of every other passion as well: I have it, and it does not have me. To a lesser extent, Pushkin tied his genius to this, his service to majestic beauty, his own words finally obliging, when, turning to his hero with reproach he says that he:

> Had to prove himself
> Not as a ball of prejudices,
> Not as an ardent boy, as a soldier
> But as a man with honor and with an intellect.[11]

Pushkin did not fulfill this least duty.

VII.

Allowing the *power* of vanity over his soul, Pushkin strived to justify it by the sense of his elevated calling. This fraudulent justification of undignified passion inevitably placed him in a false relation to society, called forth and maintained in him contempt toward others, then alienation from them, and finally, enmity and spite against them.

Already in the sonnet "To the Poet," the height of self-consciousness merges with arrogance, and the requirement of dispassion — with an offended and insulted expression of alienation. "You are — a tsar, live alone!"[12]

This was taken from Byron, it seems: the solitude of kings. But the loneliness of tsars consists not in the fact that they live alone—which strictly speaking does not happen—but in the fact that they have *amid others* a singular situation. This is the loneliness of mountain summits.

> Montblanc—a monarch of neighboring mountains:
> They have crowned it.[13]
>
> Byron's "Manfred"

Nobody, not even a genius, could remove *this* loneliness on his own, just as it is not possible to remove from Montblanc its 14,000-foot height. It is not necessary to point out or emphasize such loneliness of genius; it goes without saying. But is it a cause for contempt and alienation? The sun too is alone in the sky; but for all that it lives and it *vivifies*, and no one will see a symbol of haughty detachment in this.

And such arrogance did not become the sun of our poetry either. With the advance of maturity, not just a consciousness of his genius, but a religious consciousness calling him to *other* sentiments and opinions awakened and clarified within him. Formerly, his unbelief was more of frivolity than of conviction, and it passed together with other frivolous passions. That which he spoke about Byron applied even more to himself: "this skepticism was only a temporary capriciousness of the mind, sometimes running contrary to inner conviction, to spiritual faith."

The poet had a dual foundation in the consciousness of his genius and in Christian faith; a foundation more than sufficient for him to hold onto an elevation in life unassailable by petty enmity, slander, and gossip—at an elevation that was equally remote from un-Christian disdain for those close to him and undignified semblance to the mob alike. But we see that Pushkin constantly vacillated between arrogant disdain and petty irritation against the society surrounding him; this degenerated into caustic personal pranks and epigrams. In his relations with inimical persons, there was nothing either of genius or of Christianity—and the real key to understanding the disaster of 1837 lay in this.

VIII.

According to the opinion of Pushkin himself—repeated by the majority of critics and historians of literature—the "world" was hostile toward him and

persecuted him. The *evil fate* from which the poet purportedly perished—
embodied here in "society," "the world," "the mob"—generally lay within
this notorious *milieu,* whose fateful predestination, it seems, consists only
in "tormenting" people.

If one analyzes this opinion in all its expansiveness, it turns out to
be baseless in the extreme. Pisarev's criticism all the while still weighs over
Pushkin, only without the clarity and consistency of this excellent writer.
It would seem that people of a directly opposite tendency to Pisarev related
to him with "murderous" contempt, as they did to all the activity of the
sixties. They actually apply the method of Pisarev's criticism to their idol—
to Pushkin—but from the opposite end and in a much more absurd way.

Pisarev repudiated Pushkin because he was not a social and political reformer. The requirement was baseless, but the fact was completely
true. Pushkin really was not a reformer. Not abandoning the poor critical
method—of *arbitrary* requirements and *casual* criteria—Pushkin's contemporary adorers reason thus: Pushkin was a great man, and since *our criterion* of true greatness is given in the philosophy of Nietzsche and requires from a great man to be a teacher of the cheerful wisdom of paganism
and a prophet of a new or rejuvenated cult of the heroes, then Pushkin
was indeed such a teacher of wisdom and such a prophet of the new cult,
for which he in fact suffered from the dull and vile mob. Although the requirements here are other than in Pisarev, the bad method is in essence
the very same one, presenting to the great poet its personal or partisan demands. Pisarev's criticism can be reduced to the following syllogism: Maj.:
the great poet should be a prophet of radical ideas; Min.: Pushkin was not
such a prophet; C.: ergo—Pushkin was a useless good-for-nothing. Expressed here in the conclusion is a subjective evaluation, crudely untrue,
but logically flowing from the application to the *actual* Pushkin of an arbitrary standard seized by the critic: he indicates something about our poet
that, while factually true, was completely malapropos regarding what he
did not actually possess.

The judgments of the most recent Pushkin-o-maniacs can be expressed, in their turn, in the following syllogism: Maj.: a great poet should
be the embodiment of the Nietzschean idea; Min.: Pushkin was a great
poet; C.: ergo—Pushkin *was* the embodiment of the Nietzschean idea.
This syllogism is just as formally correct as Pisarev's, but you see an *essential* difference in the deceased critic's usage: a false *evaluation* was expressed only in his conclusion, while a *false fact* becomes firmly established
in theirs. In reality Pushkin embodied Nietzschean theory as little as he

embodied applied radicalism. But Pisarev, measuring Pushkin against the yardstick of radical tendencies, clearly saw and candidly announced that he does *not* meet this measure, whereas the most recent panegyrists of Pushkin's poetry, adding to this salubrious, extensive and free-wheeling creative measurement the fractured yardstick of Nietzschean psychopathism, are so blind that they convince themselves and others of such a measurement's total success.

The point is not in the personal views of one or another critic. Both the Pisarevian and the Nietzschean points of view can have their relative legitimacy. The main point is, rather, that in the real historical Pushkin both these points of view do not have any actual application, and that is why judgments about the poet stipulated by them are simply senseless. We can bow down before the industriousness and craftsmanship of ants or admire the beauty of a peacock's tail, but it is not possible on this basis to scold the lark because he does not build an anthill, and still less permissible to exclaim with rapture: what a magnificent peacock's tail this lark has!

The old view about Pushkin's death as the fateful result of his clash with a hostile social milieu becomes appended (rather artificially and incoherently) to the false evaluation of him as a teacher of ancient wisdom and a prophet of a new or revived beauty. But the social milieu is usually at odds with those people who want to reform and regenerate it. Pushkin had no such desire; he resolutely rejected any reformist mission, which actually would not have become him at all. For all the difference in natures and characters, Pushkin more resembled Goethe than Socrates; and the attitude of the official and social Russian milieu toward him more resembled the attitude of Germany toward the Weimar Olympian than the attitude of Athenian democracy toward Socrates—indeed, even Socrates could live at liberty among this democracy to the age of seventy.

In general, the clash of a person with society must be too profound in principle in order to make a bloody denouement absolutely necessary and objectively inevitable. It seems that in all the history of humanity this has happened not more than once, and the dispute was strictly not between a person and society, but between God and "the prince of this world." However, as far as I know, even Pushkin's most fervent panegyrists did not recall Golgotha with respect to his duel; and the unfortunate poet was really least of all close to Christ when he fired at his adversary.

Pushkin was persecuted and was not acknowledged! But *what* exactly was it that was not acknowledged in him and was the subject of hostility and persecution? His artistic creativity? There is hardly to be found, however, another example of a great writer in world literature who became universally recognized and popular in his country as early as Pushkin. And one can speak of the persecutions to which our poet was ostensibly subjected only for the beauty of the syllables.

If several years of involuntary, but comfortable, life—in Kishinev, Odessa, and his own Mikhailovskii—is persecution and calamity, then what will we call the permanent exile of Dante from his homeland; the prison-cell of Camoens; the declared insanity of Tasso; the destitution of Schiller; Byron's ostracism; Dostoevsky's hard labor in exile, and so forth? The single calamity from which Pushkin seriously suffered was the censorship of that time; but first, this was the general fate of all Russian literature; and second, this "heavy hammer, breaking glass, forges Damascus steel." And consequently, censorship is less frightful for great writers than for others. Pushkin's external conditions were exclusively fortunate in spite of the censorship. In any event, one can rest assured that in the England of that day he would have gotten from society much more for his early "liberties" than in Russia from the government, as is clearly visible in the example of Byron. When they speak of the hostility of high society and the literary milieu toward Pushkin, they forget about his numerous and true friends in this very milieu. But why was "society" then more represented by Uvarov or Benkendorf than by Karamzin, by Vel'gurskii, Viazemsky, and so forth? And who were the representatives of Russian literature: Zhukovsky, Gogol, Baratinsky, Pletnev, or Bulgarin? There was hardly a time in Russia that a writer was surrounded by such a brilliant and dense circle of understanding and sympathetic people.

IX.

Pushkin could be completely satisfied with his social position as poet: he was famous through all of Russia during his lifetime. There were certainly also those among his contemporaries in Russia who denied his artistic significance or insufficiently understood him. But, in general, these were people who were immature aesthetically compared to him, which was just as inevitable as the fact that totally illiterate people did not read his works. To become offended and indignant would be just as strange in the one case as in the other. And Pushkin actually became offended and indignant at society not for this—not for the aesthetic obtuseness of people who were little educated—but for the coldness and dislike toward him of many people from the two circles to which he belonged: the literary circle and the circle of high society. But this dislike, reaching sometimes the point of direct hostility, related chiefly not to the poet, not to the priest of Apollo, but only to the one who at times, according to his own admission, was perhaps the vainest among the vain children of the world. Of course, there were spiteful fools and scoundrels in Pushkin's social milieu, just as there were in any other milieu: people for whom the superiority and gifts of the mind are intolerable in themselves. However, their enmity, which was awakened by the power of Pushkin, could be actively sustained only out of his weakness. He himself gave it sustenance and thrust his enemies and people who were not spiteful fools and scoundrels into one camp.

Pushkin's epigrams were his major misfortune. True, among them there are higher specimens of this rather inferior, technically speaking, form of literature; there are true golden flashes of good-natured playfulness and gay wit; but many others are of Pushkin's lower poetic dignity; and several are of inferior human dignity, in general, and as shameful for the author as they are abusive to his subjects. For example, when a respected scholar, having done nothing worse than leave an outstanding trail of his scholarship in history, is characterized thus:

> A slanderer without gift,
> He seeks staffs by instinct,
> And his daily sustenance
> By monthly lies,[14]

even Pushkin's most fervent admirer will hardly see here the "sacred sacrifice" that "Apollo requires of the poet." Here it is clear that only the personal merit of a man was being brought for sacrifice; that not Musaget, but a demon of rage demanded this sacrifice; and that, moreover, it was not possible to expect that the sacrifice feel reverence for its literary executioner.

Unfortunately, there were too many of such unworthy personal excesses even in his last years. Sometimes they appeared as in the cited example, absolutely alien to poetic inspiration, but sometimes they represented the abuse of poetry in Pushkin. One of them created a latent reason for hostile action and led the poet to his final catastrophe. This is the well-known verse "On the Recovery of Lucullus," very vivid and powerful in form but in meaning representing only a crude personal slander concerning then-minister of national education, Uvarov.

According to the testimony of a majority of Uvarov's contemporaries, his personal character could not evoke sympathy. But the exposure of somebody's personal shortcomings is not the task of poetry, even if satirical. And in his public activity, Uvarov had great merits: he was without doubt the most enlightened and gifted of all the Russian ministers of national education, and his activity the most fruitful. Uvarov did not give cause for serious satire inspired by society's interest; actually, Pushkin denounces only the private character of the minister, and his denunciation represents lampoon sooner than satire. But even correct satire that attacks common and public evil was not becoming to a poet who had earlier triumphantly declared that he had nothing to do with the public good and that a struggle with public evil was a matter for the police and not for poetry:

> From the noisy streets in your cities
> They sweep the rubbish—a useful labor!
> But, having forgotten their service,
> Altar and offering,
> Do pagan priests now take a broom from you?[15]

If writing the lines of "On the Recovery of Lucullus" and communicating them to close friends could be forgiven for the sake of their superficial beauty, then the promulgation of them through print in a journal has no justification.

Meanwhile, for one such as Uvarov, an influential and not very scrupulous man of means, it was easy to become the secret leader and inspirer of many other people who were insulted by the poet and to construct against him an active conspiracy of malicious talk, gossip, and intrigue. The goal was—to irritate and tease him continuously, and by this lead him to actions that would make his situation in Petersburg society impossible. But was it not in his power to hinder the achievement of this goal, which was calculated only on his moral weakness?

X.

The stupid matter of insult, for which Pushkin overindulged his talent and abused his genius, was so natural, and therefore so easy, for his enemies.

They were in their sphere; here they fulfilled their role, for them there was no fall—the fall was only for Pushkin. On the lower ground of personal spite and enmity, all the advantage was on *their* side; their victory here was necessary. But was it necessary for Pushkin to remain to the end on this agonizing, disadvantageous, and, for him, unfamiliar ground, on which every step he took was a fall? Pushkin's enemies do not have justification; but all the more his blame lies in the fact that he lowered himself to their level, became open for their base designs. A veiled struggle dragged on for two years; and how many moments were there during this time, when he could by resolution of will alone have torn apart the entire spider's web that had been erected on a summit *accessible to him*, where the invulnerability of a genius merged with the geniality of a Christian.

There is no life situation, even if arising according to our own fault, out of which it would not be possible to come out in a dignified way with good will. The luminous mind of Pushkin understood well what his higher calling and Christian convictions required from him; he knew what he should have done, but he gradually gave himself over more and more to the passion of insulted conceit with its false shame and spiteful vindictiveness.

Having lost inner self-control, he could have still been saved with outside help. After his first groundless duel with Heeckeren [D'Anthes], Emperor Nikolai Pavlovich took him at his word that in the event of a new clash he would notify the sovereign in advance. Pushkin gave his word, but did not keep it. Mistakenly convinced that an indecent anonymous letter was written by the very same Heeckeren, he sent him (through his father) a second challenge in a letter so exquisitely insulting that a bloody outcome was made inevitable. Meanwhile, for all that and with his temper in an extreme state, Pushkin did not reach the stage at which responsibility for acts ends and upon which his given word could simply be forgotten. After the duel, a letter to Count Benkendorf was found on him with a statement about his new clash; evidently it was to be passed on to the sovereign. He thought that someone's vulgar, dirty, and anonymous lampoon could discredit his honor, but his own consciously broken promise could not. If he was a "captive" here, then he was not a "captive of honor" as Lermontov called him, but only a captive of that passion of rage and revenge to which he had surrendered completely.

Even taking honor in a conditional sense, as corresponding to worldly understandings and habits, an anonymous lampoon can threaten no one's honor, apart from that of the one writing it—not to mention true honor, which requires only the observance of inner moral dignity, inaccessible to any external encroachment at all. If the erroneous supposition was true and the author of the letter was really Heeckeren, then by the same token he removed from himself the right to be called out to a duel, as a man having placed himself outside of the rules of honor by his action; and if it was not he that wrote the letter, then there was no basis for a second challenge. Consequently, this unhappy duel took place not on the strength of any outward necessity for Pushkin, but solely because he resolved to do away with a hated enemy.

But even here everything was not yet lost. At the time of the duel itself, when Pushkin had been very perilously but not mortally wounded by the adversary, he was still master of his fate. In any event, would-be honor was satisfied by the perilous wound. A continuation of the duel could be a matter only for savage passion. When the seconds approached the wounded one, he arose with angry words: "Attendez, je me sens assez de force pour tirer mon coup!"—and with a steady hand fired at his adversary, slightly wounding him.[16] This extreme spiritual strain, this desperate outburst of passion, finally broke the strength of Pushkin and actually resolved his earthly fate. *Pushkin was not killed by Heeckeren's bullet, but by his own shot at Heeckeren.*

XI.

The decisive burst of savage passion that finally undermined the poet's physical existence left him, however, the possibility and time for moral regeneration. The three-day mortal illness—breaking his connection with everyday spite and vanity, but not depriving him a clarity and vividness of conscience—liberated his moral forces and allowed him by an inner act of will to reconsider for himself the vital question of life conscientiously: the fact that a spiritual rebirth genuinely occurred in him prior to his death was noted immediately by the people close to him.

"Especially remarkable is the fact," writes Zhukovsky, "that in these final hours of life it was as if he became *different*; the storm, which for several hours had upset his soul *with insuperable* passion, disappeared, leaving in him not a trace; neither word nor recollection of what had occurred." And this was not a loss of memory, but an inner elevation and purification of moral conscience and his real liberation from the captivity of passion.

As Prince Viazemsky related, when his friend and second, Danzas, wishing to find out what were his sentiments for Heeckeren as he lay dying, asked him: Would he charge him with something regarding Heeckeren in the event of death?—"I require," he responded, "that you do not avenge my death; I forgive him and want to die as a Christian."

Describing the first minutes after death, Zhukovsky writes: "When everyone left, I sat alone in front of him and for a long while looked into his face. I never saw anything on this face like what was on it in this first minute of death . . . I am not able to express with words what was expressed on his face. It was for me so new and at the same time so familiar. This was neither dream nor peace; it was not an expression of the mind, formerly so characteristic of this face; neither was it a poetic expression. No! Some kind of important, surprising thought overflowed upon it, something resembling a vision, some kind of complete, profound, satisfying knowledge. All the while peering at him, I wanted to ask of him: What do you see, my friend? And what would he have answered, if he had been able to revive for a minute?"

Although it is not possible to guess which words the great poet, regenerated through death, would have spoken to his friend, it is possible to answer in all *probability* what he would *not* have said. He would not have said that which his foolish worshippers, making out of the great man their little idol, repeat over and over. He would not have said that he perished as the result of a wicked, hostile fate; he would not have said that his death was meaningless and aimless; he would not have started to complain about the world, the social milieu, his own enemies; there would have been no reproach, no grumbling, and no indignation in his words. And this indubitable certainty in what he would not have said—a certainty that has need of no proof whatever, because it is given directly by the simple factual description of his final hours—is a final blessing for which we should be grateful to the great man. The final triumph of the soul in him and his reconciliation with God and with the world reconcile us with his death: this death was *not* premature.

How is that?—they will say—and what of those wonderful artistic works he still carried in his soul and did not succeed in giving to us, and those treasures of thought and creations by which he could have enriched our literature in maturity and old age?

What a superficial, mechanical view! Pushkin could not have given us any new artistic creations, and he could not have enriched our literature with any new treasures whatever.

XII.

We know that Pushkin's duel was not superficial chance, not dependent upon him, but a direct result of the internal storm that enveloped him and to which he *consciously* gave himself over, in spite of any providential obstacles and cautions whatsoever. He consciously accepted his personal passion as the basis of his actions, consciously resolved to take his enmity to its conclusion, to drain his wrath to the dregs. In looking back to the history of the duel, one of his closest friends, Prince Viazemsky, in the same letter in which he describes his Christian end, notes: "He had to have a bloody outcome." We cannot speak about the undisclosed conditions of his soul; but two obvious facts sufficiently prove that his *personal* will irrevocably took shape in this respect and was not now accessible to any worldly influences—I mean: the broken word to the emperor and the last shot at the adversary.

Of the two factors about which we have a right to draw a conclusion regarding his interior condition, even his own wound or that of Heeckeren could not have subdued his psychical storm and changed his *resolve to bring the matter to an end*. The duel could have only two outcomes in the face of such resolve, which was unquestionable even for his friends: either the death of Pushkin himself or the death of his adversary. For other of the poet's worshippers, the *second* outcome would have been just and desirable. Why and how is a genius dead and a worthless man left among the living? Can it be that with this "successful'" duel on his soul, Pushkin could have created in peace new artistic works illuminated by the superior light of Christian conscience, which he had earlier already attained?

It is a childish game to make a supposition, forgetting about the actual nature and personal views of the man consitituting their subject. Let aesthetic idolatry place itself above the difference between good and evil; but what relation does this have to the real Pushkin, who never took this point of view and, near the end, came to positive Christian convictions that directly disallow such indifference? If Pushkin already in maturity started to feel the burden of contradiction between the requirements of poetry and the requirements of everyday vanity, then how could he have reconciled himself with the much more profound contradiction between service to supreme beauty, sacred and sublime, and the fact of murder out of personal malice?

We do not create Pushkin according to our image and semblance, but actually take Pushkin with his true character and with the convictions and views that really arose in him at that time. There is already in the sixth chapter of "Evgeny Onegin" a clear indication of how far the poet would have been from indifference, if he had happened to kill even a hated and contemptuous enemy in a duel:

> It is pleasant to enrage
> A blundering enemy with an impertinent epigram . . .
> *But it will hardly be pleasant for you*
> *To send him to his fathers.*[17]

Thus spoke the author of "Evgeny Onegin," not yet fully enkindled in all his youthful passion; what would the mature author of "The Prophet" and "Hermit Fathers and Chaste Wives" say?[18] Having voluntarily given himself over to a malevolent storm, which seduced him, Pushkin *wanted to* kill and *could* have killed the man; but with the actual death of the adversary this whole storm would have passed instantly, and only the consciousness of an irrevocably concluded evil and a mad act would have remained. Whoever joins the name of Pushkin to the actual spiritual image of the poet in his mature years will agree that the end of this duel—voluntary on his part and called forth by the poet himself—would in any event for Pushkin have been, with the death of the adversary, a living catastrophe. He could not have elevated himself as expansively as before to the summit of inspiration for "sweet sounds and prayers" with such a burden on his soul; he could not have carried a *sacred sacrifice* to the pure deity of poetry with the blood of an impure human sacrifice on his hands. For a destroyer of the moral law, it would not be possible now to feel himself a *tsar* over the mob; and for a captive of passion—to set the people's hearts ablaze with a liberated *prophetic word*. A facile and inexpensive accounting with conscience does not occur in the face of the spirit's eminence, which was accessible to him and which so obviously revealed itself in his last moments.

For reconciliation with himself Pushkin could have cut himself off from the world; he could have gone to a place like Athos, or he could have chosen the more difficult path of invisible humility in order to atone for his sin among the milieu in which he committed it and against which he was guilty by his moral feebleness, by his unworthy assimilation to the insignificant multitude.[19] But one way or another—whether in the guise of spiritual or worldly devotee—Pushkin would have in any event lived after the catastrophe only for the matter of personal salvation and not for previous service to pure poetry. Formerly, in the candid and exposed soul of the poet, a plenitude of life's impressions crystallized in a transparent "objective" prism, where a white ray of creative illumination that descended upon him in the moment of inspiration would become a living rainbow. But such a radiant, triumphant character of poetry inevitably had a foundation corresponding to it in the poet's psychical regime—that candid harmony with the universal good sense of existence, that cheerful and genial lucidity—all those attributes, by virtue of which Pushkin stood out until the catastrophe, and which he could not preserve after it. In the face of an outcome of the duel that other worshippers of Pushkin would desire, poetry would have won nothing and the poet would have lost very much: in place of three days of physical suffering he would have had to attain the same final goal—his spiritual rebirth—over many years of moral agony. Poetry in itself is neither good nor bad: it is a *flowering* and *radiance* of spiritual powers—good or evil. Hell has its own fleeting flower and its own deceptive radiance. Pushkin's poetry was not and could not be such a flower and radiance of hell; and he now could not have protected the good meaning of his poetry and elevated it to a new summit, since he would have had to put his entire soul into inward, moral reconciliation with the good that was lost in the bloody affair. Not that the business of a duel in and of itself was such a ghastly evil. It could have been pardonable for many; it could have been pardonable for Pushkin himself during his early youth. But for the Pushkin of 1837, for the author of "The Prophet," the killing of a personal enemy, even if in a duel, would have been a moral catastrophe, the consequences of which could not have been corrected "incidentally" during his free time, away from literary pursuits—his entire life would have been required for a restoration of spiritual balance.

The manifold paths by which people are called to spiritual rebirth and actually arrive at it are in essence reduced to two: either the path of inner crisis, of the inward resolution of a better will conquering lower enticements and leading a person to true composure; or the path of life's catastrophe, liberating the spirit from the excessive burdens of passions mastering him. Having unreservedly given himself over to his rage, Pushkin rejected the first path and by the same token selected the second—and should we really grieve about the fact that this path was not overburdened for him by the guilt of another's death and that a spiritual purification could be completed in three days?

Here is the entirety of Pushkin's fate. We should in conscience acknowledge this fate first *as good*, because it led a man to the best end—to spiritual rebirth, to his highest and only fitting good; and second, we should acknowledge it *as rational,* because it attained this best goal by the most direct and easiest, that is, by the best means in the given situation. Fate is not a tyrant over people. It cannot control human life without the participation of the will of a person; and in the given condition of the will of this man, what happened with him should have occurred and is the very best result of that which, in general, could have taken place with him, i.e., the *manifestly* possible.

The nature of fate in general (and, consequently, the fate of each human being) is not explained *fully* by that which we see in the fate of such a special man as Pushkin: it is not possible to take a chemical analysis of Narzan springwater absolutely for the analysis of all other water. Just as in Narzan there exists that which does not exist in any other water, so, on the other hand, for a full accounting of the constitution of our own water from the Neva River one must take into account such complexities as are not to be found either in Narzan or in any other curative source. But for all that, we probably will find in the river Neva, as well as in the Narzan and in all other water, the fundamental matter—hydrogen and oxygen—without which no kind of water can exist. With all its particularity, the fate of Pushkin shows us—only with greater vividness—those basic features we will search out, if we desire and are able to search, in any human fate, however complex or, on the other hand, however simplified it might be. Fate in general is not simply one element. It is broken down into two: supreme good and supreme reason; and a necessity peculiar to it is the subordinated power of the rational-moral order, independent of us at root, but embodied in our life only through our own will. And if it is so, then I think it would be better for us to replace the obscure word "fate" with a precise, fixed expression—*Divine Providence.*

7

✑

Mickiewicz

He was inspired from above
And gazed at life from on high
                    —Pushkin [1]

Looking at life *from on high* is absolutely not the same as looking at it
haughtily. For the latter it is necessary to have a predetermined high
opinion of one's personal significance in the actual absence of certain
moral qualities. But in order to look at life from on high it is necessary
first *to attain* this height, and for this it is insufficient to climb up onto
stilts or even up to one's parish belfry. This is why, amid such a multitude
of people looking upon everything haughtily over an entire century,
there can be found only one among the great about whom it is possible to
say, without betraying the truth, that he did not just take a glance at a
moment of poetic inspiration, but always *gazed* at life from on high. A
fraternal nation's glorious holiday has—that is, it can have and could
acquire—a special significance for us even independently of Russo-Polish
relations. It could have such a significance if the resurrected image of a

Source: "Rech' na obede v pamiat' Mitskevicha 27 Dekabria 1898," first appearing
in *Mir iskusstva* 2 (1899): 27–30. Reprinted in *Sobranie sochinenii* 9: 257–264.

great man who is still proximate to us, not yet having retreated into the darkness of the ages, could help restore explicitly to our consciousness a measure of human greatness that has been lost; could help restore this in order to remind us of those intrinsic conditions that make great not only a writer, poet, thinker, or politician, but make *a great man*—or a *superman* in a judicious sense of this abused word. Neither the highest pretentions to one's own superhumanness, nor the greatest capabilities in any particular concern, nor the greatest success in resolving any single historical task can essentially and actually elevate us above the common level and grant that which only wholeness of moral character and vital exploit in life can.

He "gazed at life from on high." When Pushkin gained such an impression after several conversations with him, Mickiewicz stood only on the first rung of these heights, had made his first spiritual ascent. How can a living person look at life from on high if these heights cannot in fact be attained by him as the truth of life itself? And how does one extract this higher truth, if one doesn't tear oneself away from the paltry, inadequate, unjustified phenomena of life? And if such heights of vital perspective must actually be conquered, and not just devised as invention, then a break with paltriness in fact must also be agonizingly endured and experienced. A child born into God's free world breaks the organic tie with the darkness and oppressiveness of uterine life once, but in order to stand on the heights from which the entire truth of life is visible, in order to be liberated from *every* fetal darkness and oppression, it is necessary to suffer not one, but a total of three momentous ruptures, three inner catastrophes.

And first of all, it is necessary to break with the fundamental and most powerful connection that pulls us toward personal happiness at its main locus—sexual love—when it seems that all truth and all the good of life has been incarnated for us in a woman, in this single woman, when we are ready to repeat with sincere conviction the words of the poet:

> Yes, only in the world—is that shady
> Tent of slumbering maples.
> Yes, only in the world—is that radiant
> Childish, pensive look.[2]

Within this concentrated sensation of love there is a great truth, a true presentiment of that which should be, of the absolute significance of fully human personality. But the great untruth here is in the fact that the presentiment is taken for the fulfillment, and a ready and gratuitous well-being is proposed in place of the vastness of a revealed mission. Meanwhile, in order that the exultation of sentiment not turn out to be empty fraud, it is necessary in any event to break with the darkness and oppressiveness of the all-absorbing elemental passion and to understand with heart and mind that the truth and goodness of life cannot depend on the chance luck of personal happiness. This first and most profound vital breach is, of course, also the most excruciating, and many excellent and noble souls cannot endure it. Mickiewicz, too, nearly ended up as Goethe's Werther. When he conquered blind passion while still a youth, a profoundly spiritual force elevated him so that he could gaze at life from these first heights achieved by moral struggle.

And this is the person that Pushkin became acquainted with, when he spoke his penetrating and prophetic word concerning him.* Prophetic, because soon Mickiewicz had to suffer a second, and then a third moral rupture, and entered onto new heights of vitally important perspective.

The same that was said about love for women should be said about love for the nation or toward the fatherland. Here, as well, in this most exclusive of feelings is the foreboding of a great truth—that nationality, as well as human personality, has an eternal and absolute purpose and should become one of the irreplaceable and intransient forms of intrinsic value for the fullness of life's content. But in order that the foreboding of a great truth not be converted into empty, false, and pernicious pretense, it is necessary that the indicative mood of a simple patriotic feeling— "I love my homeland"—cross over into the imperative mood of patriotic duty: "help the homeland in the consciousness and fulfillment of its higher mission." Of course, patriotism, just as every sentiment, grows not out of the head but is rooted deeper; it has its uterine roots, which persist and are also reinforced against the outward rupture:

> Lithuania! My fatherland, You are as health!
> Only he who has lost you will truly
> Find how much you should be valued,
> Today I see and describe your beauty
> In all its adornment, for I yearn for you.[3]

* It was said publicly only afterwards, but the impression was obtained upon first meeting.

Without these natural roots there is no real patriotism. Everyone knows, however, that in nature flowers and fruits never grow directly from the roots. Patriotism first needs to elevate itself above its uterine roots into the world of moral consciousness in order to flower and become fruitful. And this ascent does not occur without cost and is not obtained by abstract thought alone. Life requires a new rupture to be suffered through experience.

When Mickiewicz's spirit first lifted itself over the ruins of fantasized personal happiness, he gave himself over without reservation to other, more expansive dreams concerning national happiness. The Polish Werther, Gustav, was saved from suicide by his transformation into Konrad Wallenrod.[4] The idea here, in all the complexity of the subject, is essentially the idea of simple natural patriotism, which desires only to obtain for its country outward well-being in the form of political independence and triumph over the enemy, come what may. There is a formal falsehood here: *come what may*—and an untruth in content: *outward* well-being. For Mickiewicz this deceptive dream was destroyed by the catastrophe of 1830.[5] A second vital connection was severed, and a second spiritual ascent was completed.

I see this ascent in thoughts about the significance and calling of Poland that Mickiewicz expressed in a foreign land in the "Book of the Polish Nation and Pilgrimage" and in several lectures at the Collège de France. These thoughts received great distinction later under the influence of Towianski; however, they appeared in Mickiewicz earlier than his acquaintance with this mystic.[6] Our poet endured the rebirth of his patriotism on his own. I know that not only Russians but a majority of Poles as well cannot agree to find in Mickiewicz's advocacy abroad spiritual ascent or advancement of the national idea. I certainly will not begin to prove my point of view here, but will only say a couple of words in order to elucidate it.

What is important is not the fact that someone considers his nation as chosen—this is an attribute of almost everyone—but rather upon just what this chosen-ness rests. It is not important that Mickiewicz pronounced Poland as a Messiah-nation, but the fact that he bowed before it as before a Messiah who was not triumphant, but rather suffering; and he understood that triumph is not given for free and is not obtained by external force alone, but requires a difficult internal struggle and must be achieved through suffering. The error into which Mickiewicz fell was in fact harmless at that: he thought that the Polish nation, by its sufferings, atones for the sins of other nations. Of course, this is not so. Does not the Polish nation have its own national and historical sins? As far as the redemption of others by suffering goes, it has already been accomplished once and for all. And now every nation, just as every person, suffers only for itself, and of course not in some wild and fantastic sense of punishment and vengeance, but in the moral and actual sense upon the inescapable road from the worse toward the better—toward greater power and plenitude of one's intrinsic dignity. Given the facts of baser, more imperfect forms of life and a natural attachment of people and nations to these forms, it is logically necessary that a transition from them to a better and higher consciousness be perfected through painful ruptures, struggle, and suffering. No matter how disparate the historical fates of nations, it is clear that the road of inward ascent is the same for one and all; and what is important in Mickiewicz's new perspectives is precisely the fact that he acknowledged this moral road for *his* nation—a road leading to a higher, universal goal through self-renunciation, in place of the earlier Wallenrodian path. This unprecedented ascent of national consciousness into the realm of a higher moral order has been important since the time of the Jewish prophets. The fact that Mickiewicz had inaccurate or exaggerated notions about details of Polish history, and that he also subsequently even stumbled over the path indicated by them, disappears in the face of this.

But a third—and perhaps, the most difficult—experience still lay before him.

A young man concentrates the entire veracity and meaning of life onto the image of a chosen woman who will give him personal happiness. The young Mickiewicz derived from the ruin of this dream, together with the blossoming of his marvelous poetry and consciousness, the fact that veracity of personal happiness should not be a principle, but the conclusion of life's path, and that it is necessary to atone for the fulfillment of private life. Before whom? First of all before another chosen one, before the mother country. Having matured, Mickiewicz dedicated to her all of his strength and carried away a more elevated national idea out of her unhappiness and his separation from her, along with the captive image of his native land (in "Pan Tadeusz"). He carried away the idea that the outward well-being of the nation should be obtained by its moral exploit. Where did the strength for this come from? Mickiewicz had already anticipated the answer in his childhood:

Holy Lady who protects Jasno's Czestochowia!
You who illuminates the gate
And guards Nowogrodek's tower and faithful people.
When I lay ill in childhood,
You miraculously healed me.
There out of mother's tears, under Your wings,
You gave me strength to open my eyes,
And then I was able to come to Your shrine
To thank God for my life.
That is how you will return
Us miraculously to our fatherland.[7]

Just as Mickiewicz subordinated his personal happiness to the happiness of the fatherland, so he subordinated to religion the fate of the fatherland; this was both according to feeling and conscience—religion was the third suprapersonal and supranational chosen one. But here too, on the threshold of old age, a great internal struggle still awaited Mickiewicz. There was veracity in his youthful thirst for happiness and personal love; but he had to say to himself that truth cannot depend on whether Maryla Wereszak would prefer him, Adam, to Mister Puttkamer or not. He must have understood that the meaning of personal life cannot exist in itself, as mere chance, but should be connected with universal truth in order to be liberated in it from all chance. Let this truth then be embodied in a chosen one of another order—in the fatherland; but it is not the fatherland that is the source and measure of truth, but truth itself that is a norm even for the fatherland—this is how it must be. And, with all its pious recollection of the past, true patriotism could not notice the fact that it also required historical purgatory. Mickiewicz understood that the bearer of higher truth in the world could not be the Poland of the eighteenth century with its political falsehood of anarchy and with its social falsehood of cruel subjugation of the lower classes.[8]

And a whetted sword must continuously cut through the life of the nation, separating good and evil, truth and falsehood; and it should unceasingly reject the chance, the transient, the unbefitting. What will quench our thirst for full trust, selfless dedication, and final tranquility? Will it not be the third chosen one, the native and supranational, historical and suprahistorical, universal church? But is this good on our part to see it only as tranquility—to convey to this chosen one only a laziness of mind and will, a narcosis of the conscience, and to establish our union with her on the basis of such a poor gift? And will she in fact accept this gift from us? What does she need it for? Will not others who have an interest in the atrophy of our reason and in the muting of our conscience accept it in her name? No, there will never and should never be an anesthetizing of the human soul in this world. No, there cannot and should not be an authority that would take the place of our reason and conscience and would make a free and liberated quest unnecessary. The church, just as the fatherland, just as the biblical "woman of youth," should be an intrinsic force of tireless movement toward the eternal goal, not a pillow of tranquility for us. I do not reproach those who have become fatigued and have given up in this quest; but, in recalling a great man, it is necessary to remember as well the fact that spiritual fatigue is not a sign of great people.

We will not forget, moreover, that intellectual fatigue and resignation have two forms that go hand in hand: on the one hand, tranquility in blind dedication to some external authority; and on the other—tranquility in empty and facile denial. Some, in order not to trouble their mind and will, are satisfied with a domestic preparation of patented truth in pocket-format; and others, in similar patterns of spiritual comfort, deny in advance as ridiculous fantasy any task that, for them, is not at once understandable and easy. Both the one and the other—people of a lazy faith and people of a lazy lack of faith—have a common mortal enemy in what they call mysticism. Mickiewicz, too, was subjected to judgment as a mystic in both respects, especially with regard to the activity aroused amidst the Polish emigration by Andrzej Towianski. Regarding this activity, as far as I know, there were several first-degree truths—together with some second-degree errors (as, for example, the cult of Napoleon)—which had a right to exist in the Christian world; and first among them, the truth of the continuously inward growth of Christianity. If the world is still left standing so many centuries after Christ, this means that something is being done, something desirable is being prepared in it for our salvation; and if Christianity is really a God-man religion, then it is our duty to take part in this activity.[9]

For Mickiewicz, the religious crisis endured by him on the threshold of old age was not a rupture with the church itself, as his previous patriotic crisis was not a rupture with the fatherland itself, and as even earlier his ruination in love did not destroy his personal life and the heart within him. Mickiewicz parted ways not with the church, but only with the weak faith of certain ecclesiastic people who wanted to see in Christianity only the basic rule of everyday custom dedicated to the past. Mickiewicz did not place himself in opposition to the outward authority of the church, but he did place in opposition the obligatory principle of a common spiritual right even for the church: est Deus in nobis—God is in us. And it is not apparent that Mickiewicz retreated at any point from the religious temper expressed in a letter, where, rejecting the title of teacher, he speaks thus: "Believe no one among the people blindly, and judge my every word, because today I can speak the truth, and tomorrow a lie; today act well, and tomorrow—badly." He opposed every outward authority only with God's absolute truth, to which the conscience attests.

Truly, he was a great man and could gaze at life from on high because life itself elevated him. Onerous ordeals did not crush him, did not weaken and did not ravage his soul. He did not emerge a disillusioned misanthrope and pessimist out of the ruination of his personal happiness; the ruination of national happiness did not transform him into an indifferent cosmopolitan; and the struggle for inward religious conviction against outward authority did not make him an enemy of the church. He was great by the fact that, in ascending to new stages of moral heights, he carried onto those heights with him not proud and vain denial, but love for everything over which he was elevated.

Lermontov

The works of Lermontov—so closely connected with his personal fate—seem to me especially remarkable in one respect. I see in Lermontov the direct ancestor of that spiritual disposition and that current of sentiments and thoughts (and, in part, actions as well) which, for brevity's sake, can be called "Nietzscheanism"—after the name of the writer who more distinctly and shrilly than anyone else expressed this frame of mind and more vividly denoted this current.

Just as characteristics of an embryo are understood only thanks to the defined and developed appearance it receives from the adult organism, so too the definitive significance of all the chief impulses governing Lermontov's poetry—still partly combined with other styles—became for us fully apparent from the time that they took on an intelligibly distinct form in Nietzsche's mind.

Now, it seems everyone is in agreement that every error—at least every error about which it is worth speaking—contains in itself an indubitable truth, of which it is only more or less a profound distortion. An error is supported by means of a truth, it is attractive and dangerous by

Source: "Lermontov," Vestnik Europy 2 (1901): 441–459 (published posthumously). Reprinted in Sobranie sochinenii 9: 348–367.

virtue of it, and it can be exposed and refuted through it, as it indeed should be. Therefore, the first task of rational criticism relative to any error whatsoever is to find the truth that supports it and that it distorts.

A contempt for man, the conferral *in advance* upon the self of some kind of exceptional superhuman significance—upon the self, or upon the *I*, or upon the self and the other—and the requirement that this appropriated but as yet unjustified grandeur be acknowledged by others and become a valid norm—this is the substance of the current about which I speak. And it is certainly a great error.

What does the truth that holds it together and attracts minds consist in?

Man—the only earthly creature that can relate to itself critically—subjects to inner appraisal not just isolated situations and actions (which is also possible for animals), but also the very manner of his existence in toto. He judges himself, and through rational and unbiased judgment also condemns himself. Reason attests to man the fact of his imperfection in every respect, and conscience tells him that this fact is not *only* an extrinsic necessity for him, but is *also* dependent on himself.

Man naturally wants *to be more and better than he is* in reality. If he indeed *wants* to be, then he also *can* be; and if he can be, then he *must* be. But is this not nonsense—to be better, above, or more than reality? Yes, for an animal this is nonsense, since, for an animal, that which makes *it* is reality; but the reality of man, although he too is an already extant product of given reality, is at the same time, in one way or another, to one degree or another—that which *he himself makes* of it—makes more perceptible and evident in the capacity of a *collective* being, and less perceptible but just as indubitable in the capacity of an *individual* being.

One can argue about the metaphysical question of absolute freedom of choice, but the initiative of man, i.e., his capacity to act according to intrinsic motive—definitively according to perception of duty or conscience—is not a metaphysical question, but a fact of experience. All history consists in the fact that man makes of himself better and more, develops his present reality and *moves it aside* into the past, putting into the present that which still only recently was contrary to reality—a reverie, subjective idealism, a utopia.

Intrinsic, spiritual growth by initiative is the very same kind of inarguable fact as extrinsic, physical, passive growth, to which it is tied as if by intention.

And now the question is asked: Which direction, what aspect of life should be taken to perfect the change of the humanity given to us into a better humanity, an elevated humanity—a "superhumanity"?

If man is dissatisfied with himself and wants to be superman, then of course here it is not a matter of the extrinsic *form* (nor of the intrinsic form for that matter) of human existence, but only of the poor *functioning* of this existence in this form, an existence that does not depend on the form itself. We cannot, for example, be dissatisfied with the fact that we have two eyes, but only with the fact that we see poorly with them. But, in order to see better, there is no necessity for man to change the morphological type of optic organ—for example, to have a multitude of eyes in place of two—because he can have "pupils—as on a frightened eaglet."[1] With these two eyes it is possible to become a superman, but even with a hundred eyes it is only possible to remain but a fly.

In precisely the same way, every other human organ in any normal characteristic of its morphological structure does not prevent us from raising ourselves above our ugly reality and becoming supermen relative to it. Moreover, a concern for functionality exists not only in individual and particular *pathological* deviations, but also in phenomena that custom forces many to consider normal. Such is first and foremost the phenomenon of death and the decomposition of the organism. If we naturally feel some kind of burden, if we are fundamentally dissatisfied in our given reality, then, of course, this decisive phenomenon of our visible existence— its graphic result—amounts to nothing. A man who thinks only of himself cannot reconcile himself with the thought of his death; a man who thinks of others cannot reconcile himself with the death of others. In other words, this means that both the egoist and the altruist—and all people belong in various degrees of purity and mixture to one sort or the other— must identically feel death as an unbearable *contradiction*. That is to say, they identically cannot take this visible result of human existence for intrinsic finality. And this is the heading, according to logic, along which people who wish to raise themselves above given reality—those wishing to become supermen—should be followed with special attention. Because, what specifically differentiates the humanity that wants to elevate itself, if not precisely the fact that it is mortal? Man and mortal are synonyms. Already in Homer we find that the two chief categories of creatures—gods and people—continuously characterize themselves by the fact that the one is subject to death and the other is not—*theoi te Vrotoi te*.[2] And while

all other animals die as well, nobody will get it into their head to characterize them as mortal—this designation is not only taken as characteristic
of man, but in the expression "mortal," some kind of deplorable reproach
to himself is also felt. One feels that man, recognizing the inevitability of
death as the central characteristic of his actual condition, resolutely does
not want to reconcile himself with it, and does not become content with
himself in this recognition of its inevitability in the given conditions.
And in this he is certainly correct, because if death is completely inevitable in the present conditions, then who said that these conditions
are unalterable, inviolable? Now it is clear that if man is first of all and
in particular *mortal*, i. e., subject to death, vanquished and overcome by
it, then a superman should first of all be a conqueror of death, i.e, emancipated (has already freed himself?) from the essential conditions that
make death inevitable. He is consequently able to fulfill the conditions in
which it is possible either not to die at all, or, having died, to rise from the
dead. Let us suppose that such a victory over death cannot be achieved
immediately, which is not subject to doubt in the least. Let us suppose as
well—and this is already dubious, because it cannot be proved—that
such a victory, in man's current condition, cannot be achieved at all in
the boundaries of solitary existence—let it be so. But the road that leads
to this victory is possible and does exist, and so does a drawing closer to
it along this path. The fulfillment of these conditions is being accomplished on this path, even if it is currently far from the actual perfection
required for full realization of the goal, the final victory and the defeat of
death. The conditions under which death removes from us power and
overcomes us are sufficiently well known to us; so too should be the opposite conditions in which we take power from death and, in the final
analysis, are able to overcome it. Even if there were no actual superman
before us, *there is* a superhuman *path* by which man has gone, goes, and
will go, for the good of all; and certainly, the most important of our interests is that more people set out upon it, traverse it more directly, and
go farther along it.

And this is the authentic criterion for evaluating all concerns and
phenomena of human life. And it is necessary to apply this criterion fairly
and usefully, particularly to people who are gifted above the general level,
but who transform this general goal into personal and vain pretense. It is
necessary to apply it to those who are capable of sensing the true goal and
meaning of our existence, who are consequently also called—that is to
say, obligated—more than anyone else to draw near to it and bring oth-

ers near to it, but who repudiate in advance the necessary condition for achievement of the general goal.

Lermontov was undoubtedly such a genius: that is, a man who was already near to being a superman at birth, who acquired the rudiments for greatness of action, and who was capable, and consequently obligated, to accomplish it.

What did his special genius consist in? How did he view it? What did he do with it?—Here are the three basic questions with which we will now occupy ourselves.

We have an advantage with respect to Lermontov: the deepest significance and the character of his activity are illuminated from two facets—the figure of a remote ancestor as well as the writing of his immediate successor, Nietzsche.

In the thirteenth century, on the edge of the frontier between Scotland and England near the monastic city of Melrose, stood the castle Ercildoune, where lived Thomas Learmont, a knight who was famous in his own time and even more famous afterwards as a sage and seer. He had been found at an early age to have a certain cryptic relationship to a kingdom of fairies; later he collected inquisitive people together around a huge old tree on a hill of Ercildoune, where he prophesied—and, moreover, predicted—to the Scottish King Alfred III an unexpected and accidental death. The proprietor of Ercildoune was at the same time famous as a poet, and the nickname of versifier, or in the language of that day, rhymer—Thomas the Rhymer—stuck. His end was enigmatic: he vanished without a trace, following two white deer sent after him—as they say—from the fairy kingdom. Several centuries later, fate carried one of the direct descendents of this fantastic hero, bard, and seer—who vanished into a poetic fairy kingdom—into the prosaic Muscovite kingdom. Around 1620

> a native from the land of the Scots, the eminent man George Andreevich Lermont, came from Lithuania to the White city, and he entered the service of the great sovereign and by his request was baptised out of Calvinism and into pious faith. And the sovereign tsar Mikhail Fedorovich appointed eight villages and plots of wasteland of the Galician district, Zablotskoi region. And by *ukaz* of the great sovereign the boyar prince I. B. Cherkassky made arrangements with him, and he, George, became appointed to learn the mercenary cavalry order of newly baptised foreigners of old and new equipage, as Tatars.

Eight generations later, out of this cavalry captain of Lermont, our poet issues forth; and while he too is connected with a knightly order like his seventeenth-century ancestor, he is much closer in spirit to his ancient ancestor, the prophetic and demoniacal Thomas the Rhymer, with his affectionate songs, gloomy predictions, enigmatic existence, and fateful end.

The first and fundamental peculiarity of the Lermontov genius is a terrible tension and a concentration of thought upon oneself, upon one's *I*, the dreadful power of personal sensation. Do not search in Lermontov for a straightforward openness to all intimacy, so charming in the poetry of Pushkin. Even when Pushkin speaks of himself, it is as if of someone else; even when Lermontov speaks of others, there is a sense that his thought strives to return to itself from an infinite distance, turning toward the self occupied in its profundity. There is no need to introduce examples from the works of Lermontov, because so few of them could be found where this would not be the case. Not in a single *Russian* poet is there such a power of the personal sense of self as there is in Lermontov. Whereas this would not be a distinctive trait in the West, where more than a little power of subjectivity can be found in Byron as well as in Heine and Musset, this feature appears imitative when expressed particularly vividly in our poets.[3] Here, though, Lermontov is different in that he was not an imitator, but a younger brother of Byron; it was not out of books, but rather from his general heritage that he received this Western legacy, which was dear to him in an impersonal Russian milieu.[4] And the feelings expressed by him in an early and youthful poem—"Why am I not a bird, a crow of the Steppe"—were not posture alone or playful fantasy:

> To the West, to the West I would speedily fly,
> Where bloom the fields of my ancestors,
> Where in an empty castle on misty mountains
> Oblivious their ashes lie. . . .
> Between the hills of my fatherland and me
> Are spread the waves of the sea.
> The final offspring of valiant soldiers
> Fades amid foreign snows.[5]

A powerful development of the principle of individuality is a condition for greater consciousness of vital content; but the content of life itself is not provided by this, and the *powerful I* remains *vacant* in its absence. The collossal *I* of Lermontov could not remain *completely* vacant

because he was a poet of divine favor; and, consequently, everything endured by him was transformed into a creation of poetry, providing new
sustenance for his *I*. And without doubt, the most important thing in this
living material of Lermontov's poetry was his own love. But the motives
of love that predominated decisively in Lermontov's works, as is visible
from the works themselves, only partially occupied the poet's personal
sense of self, dulling the sharpness of his ego, softening his cruelty, but not
filling up his *I* entirely and not trumping it. In all Lermontov's love themes,
the main interest belongs not to love and the beloved other, but to the
beloved *I*. In all his works of love, the sediment of triumphant—even if
unconscious—egoism remains undissolved. I am not just speaking about
those works where the final triumph of egoism over an unsuccessful attempt
at love is the intended theme, as in "Demon" and "Hero of our Time." But
this triumph of egoism is also felt where it is not in mind directly—the real
importance belongs not to love and not to what it makes out of the poet,
but what *he* makes out of love, as *he* relates to it.

When a huge glacier is illuminated by the sun, it is said, a delightful
spectacle appears. This new beauty originates not so that the sun can make
something new out of the glacier—it surely cannot melt it—but only so
that the glacier, remaining unchangeable in itself, makes something out of
the solar rays, reflecting and refracting them on its surface in a different
manner. So it is with the special charm of Lermontovian love verses—it
is an optical charm, the charm of a mirage. Note that in these works, love
in reality, at the moment when it captures the soul and imbues a life, is almost never expressed. In Lermontov that moment has already passed, does
not govern the heart, and we see only a charming game of remembrance
and imagination.

> We have parted, but I keep
> Your *portait* on my breast;
> As a *pale phantom* of better years,
> It gladdens my soul.

Or another:

> No, it is not you that I love so ardently,
> The radiance of your beauty is not for me—
> I love in you only past suffering
> And my lost youth.

> Sometimes when I look at you,
> Penetrating your eyes in a long gaze,
> I am occupied with a secret discussion.
> But not with you—I speak with my heart.
> I speak with a girlfriend of younger days,
> In your features I search for other features
> In living lips, lips long silent,
> In eyes—the fire of looks expired.

And where the verb *love* appears in the present tense, it serves only as an occasion for melancholic reflection:

> I am sorrowful because I love you,
> And know your flowering youth. . . . [6]

In one marvelous poem the imagination of the poet, usually occupied with the memory of the past, plays with the possibility of future love:

> From under the mysterious, cold demi-mask
> Your comforting voice sounded, like a dream,
> Your captivating little eyes shone,
> And your wily lips smiled. . . .
> And I then created my beautiful woman according to the
> Slight features in my imagination,
> And since that time I carry, caress, and love
> A sterile vision in my soul.[7]

Love could not now be the source of worldly fulfillment for Lermontov, because he loved in the main only the personal condition of loving and, understandably, such a formal love can only be the *framework* and not the content of his *I*, which remained solitary and vacant. The first basic trait of Lermontov's poetry and life is this solitude and a desolation that was strained even for him, a concentrated personal energy not finding for itself enough satisfactory application.

A second trait—also inherited from his Western ancestors (perhaps a prismatic remnant of Scottish second sight)—was the ability to cross over the boundaries of the normal order of phenomena in sentiment and contemplation and to seize the uttermost part of life and worldly attachments.

This second peculiarity of Lermontov was intrinsically dependent on the first. The unusual concentration of Lermontov upon himself gave his scrutiny acuteness and power, in order at times to rip apart the net of extrinsic causality and to penetrate into another, yet deeper, connection of existence. This was a prophetic talent; and if Lermontov was neither prophet, in the actual meaning of this word, nor soothsayer like his forebear Thomas the Rhymer, then this was only because he did not give his talent any objective application. He was *occupied* neither by how his fatherland had come to this point in world history nor by the lot of his fellow creatures, but only by his own personal fate—and here he was certainly more of a prophet than any other poet. Later on I will introduce several examples of how plain Lermontov's fate was to him, but at present I will only indicate one amazing poem in which the peculiar capacity of Lermontov for second sight appears especially vividly: namely, the famous poem "The Dream." It is necessary, of course, to differentiate the actual fact that summoned the poet and that which was added by him in the transmission of this fact in structured poetic form. Lermontov usually exhibited superfluous compliance to the demands of rhyme; but the major point in this poem could not be contrived, since it turns out to be "faithful to the truth." Several months before his fateful duel, Lermontov saw himself lying with a deep wound from a bullet in his breast, motionless in the sand amidst cliffs in the mountains of the Caucasus; and he saw at the same time, in soporific visions, a woman close to his heart, but remote by thousands of miles, who was observing his corpse in a somnambulant condition in that valley. At least three dreams come out of the one here: (1) The dream of a Lermontov in good health, who saw himself mortally wounded—a comparatively ordinary matter. Although, in any event, this was a prophetic dream in its essential features, because several months after this poem was written in Lermontov's notebook, the poet was actually profoundly wounded by a bullet in the breast: he actually lay in the sand with an open wound, the ledges of cliffs crowding around him. (2) But, seeing a dying Lermontov, the Lermontov who was in good health saw at the same time that which is also being dreamt by the dying Lermontov:

> And I dreamed an evening feast illuminated by flames
> In my native country. . . .
> Among young women, crowned with flowers,
> A gay conversation passed about me.

Now this is worthy of wonder. It has probably happened to a few of you that seeing someone in a dream, you see at the same time also the dream that is seen by your dreaming vision. Yet the matter does not end with dream number two, but a dream number three also appears:

> But, there sat one pensive,
> Not entering into the gay conversation,
> And in a dreary dream her young soul
> Was immersed in God knows what.
> She dreamed of a valley in Dagestan,
> In that valley lay a body she knew,
> A smoking, blackening wound in its breast,
> And the blood ran out in a cooling stream.[8]

So Lermontov saw not only a dream of his dream, but also that dream which was dreamed by the dream of his dream—a vision in a cube.

In any case, the fact remains that Lermontov not only had a presentiment of his fateful death, but also directly saw it ahead of time. The astonishing phantasmagory by which this vision is immortalized in the poem "The Dream" has no analogy in world poetry and, I think, can be the creation only of the progeny of that prophetic magician and soothsayer who vanished into a fairy kingdom. This single poem is certainly sufficient to acknowledge innate genius transmitted to Lermontov through the progenitor of many generations. Now it remains for us to look at how Lermontov himself took this advance of a great fate and what he made out of it.

Lermontov's designation as a powerful being appointed to accomplish something great is either expressed directly in almost all his adolescent and early youthful works (of which many more survive than his mature works) or by a distinct consciousness of this that shines through. He could not yet even allude to *what* this great thing would consist *in* and *what* it would be related *to*. But it is without doubt that he is *called* to accomplish it. In his seventeenth year he says:

> I am born so that the entire world may be witness
> To my triumph or ruin.[9]

One can gather other declarations similar to this in the novice poet, but it would take much too long to cite them. We could just laugh at the

self-confident presumptuousness of the boy, if he had not actually revealed several years later unusual powers of mind, will, and creativity.
And since he did display them, then in these early pronouncements about
his future greatness we should acknowledge not empty pretense and not
the beginning of a mania, but only a certain state of health or an instinct of self-evaluation given to all chosen people. Lermontov's difference here is in the fact that the high self-appraisal while still in his early
years was, in him, connected with a much too intolerant appraisal of others, of the entire world—an appraisal of others composed in advance
and expressing a character trait, and not the result of any actual experience. In the same poem in which he acknowledges only the world in
its entirety to be a worthy observer of his great destiny, immediately
follows:

> What is the praise or haughty laughter of people?
> Their minds have not grasped the bard,
> Could not love his soul,
> Could not understand his sorrows,
> And share his raptures.[10]

And another poem (early as well) reports that life has taught the poet
to receive instinctively and everywhere ". . .'neath the haughty conceit of
a face—a foolish flatterer in a man and a Judas in every woman."[11] More
remarkable is another trait. In his early poems (and then in his later ones
too), Lermontov expresses the distinct presentiment of an inevitable and
premature death as often as the declaration of his greatness and of his
contempt for humanity. A certain stiltedness in the designation of this
death could also have—at least in the early poems—called forth a smile;
but both the desire and the right to laugh totally vanish in the presence
of the thought that the poet, in actual *fact*, perished prematurely. It is
clear that these two features of the Lermontovian general state of mind
flow directly from those peculiarities of his genius about which I spoke
earlier, i.e., his misanthropy—from the concentration and the intensity
of individual authority in him; and his invariable and correct premoni-
tion of ruin—from his second sight.

Having sensed in himself the power of genius beginning in his early
years, Lermontov received it only as a right and not as a responsibility,
as privilege and not as service. He thought that his genius authorized

him to demand from God and from people everything he wanted, not obligating him to anything regarding them. But then, God and people with magnanimity do not insist on responsibility from a man of genius. Indeed, God does not need anything, and the people should be thankful for the sparks that fly from the bonfire on which a man of genius burns. Let God in heaven and the people here on earth forgive him his gradual suicide. But does it make this easier for the third offended one — the genius himself? Is it easier for one who, to no purpose, burned and buried in dust and embers what was given to him, as to a powerful leader of the people for the great ascent on the road to superhumanhood? But how could he elevate anybody else, when he himself did not ascend? Yet a man ascends on his own only over the corpses of enemies killed by him: that is to say, his own evil passions. Is it possible to require this? This is not required of just anyone. Destiny or higher reason pose a dilemma: if you regard yourself as having received a superhuman vocation, fulfill the conditions necessary for it, lift up reality, overcome in yourself the base principle that pulls you down. And if you feel it is so much more powerful than you are that you even decline to grapple with it, then acknowledge your powerlessness, acknowledge yourself to be a simple mortal, even if gifted with genius. Here, it seems, is an absolutely rational and just dilemma: either actually stand above others or be modest. And he who does not want to accept this dilemma and insanely rebels against these a-b-c demands of reason as against some kind of insult — he who cannot ascend and does not want to be humble — will doom himself to inevitable ruin.

Realizing a genial nature in himself — the rudiments of a superman — Lermontov also acknowledged, beginning in his early years, the base principle with which he should have struggled. But instead of a struggle, this principle soon succeeded in calling forth the poet to its idealization.

The fourteen-year-old Lermontov still does not know how to idealize his demon — and this is as it should be — but he gives to it the following simple and precise description:

> He instills distrust
> He scorns pure love,
> He spurns all supplications
> He views blood indifferently,
> And he suppresses the sound of lofty feelings

With the voice of passions,
And the muse of gentle inspirations
Becomes terrified by unearthly eyes.

A year later, Lermontov speaks about the same thing:

Two lives exist in us till the grave.
There is a terrible spirit: he is alien to it;
Love, hope, grief, and revenge—
Everything, everything is subject to him.
He has founded a dwelling there,
Where we can keep memory safe,
And presages our ruin,
When it is already too late to escape.
He loves to torture and torment;
Often in his speeches is the lie . . .
He gnaws at life like a scorpion,
I believed in him. . . .

Another year later, Lermontov, now a young man, again returns to the characteristic of his demon:

He has gotten used to listening
To the vain, cold judgments of the world.
Words of greeting are absurd to him,
And every believer is ridiculous.
He is alien to love and regret,
He survives on earthly food,
Gobbles greedily the smoke of battle
And the steam from spilled blood. . . .
And while I live the proud demon
Will not leave me alone,
He will also come to illuminate my mind
With a ray of heavenly fire.
He will show an image of perfection
And suddenly will remove it forever,
And, having given a presentiment of bliss,
Will never give me happiness.[12]

All these descriptions of the Lermontovian demon could be received as the empty fantasies of a talented boy if it were not known from the poet's biography that, along with the most sympathetic manifestations of a sensitive and tender soul, acute traits of straightforward demonic spite had come to light in him already beginning in childhood. One of Lermontov's panegyrists—who it seems studies him more than anybody— relates that "an unusual penchant toward destruction developed in him. In the garden every now and then he broke shrubs and tore up the best flowers, scattering them along the paths. He crushed the unlucky fly with true satisfaction, and was glad when a thrown stone knocked a poor hen off her feet." It would, of course, be discomfiting to put a playful boy at fault for all this. I would not even mention this trait if we did not know from one particularly intimate letter of the poet himself that the adult Lermontov also comported himself relative to human beings—especially females—just as Lermontov the child did relative to flowers, flies, and hens. And here again the significance is not in the fact that Lermontov destroyed the peace and honor of society ladies—this can occur accidentally too—but that he found particular enjoyment and happiness in this absolutely nasty business, just as when he was a child, taking joy at knocking down a hen with a stone and crushing flies *with real satisfaction*.

Who among us, both great and small, does not do willy-nilly all kinds of evil to flowers, flies, hens, and even people? But everyone, I think, agrees that to enjoy the doing of evil is already an inhuman trait. This demoniacal delight did not abandon Lermontov even toward the bitter end; the worst tragedy occurred out of the fact that Lermontov's satisfaction in tormenting weak creatures met up with, in place of a lady, the courageous Major Martynov, as the fateful instrument of punishment for a man who should and could have been the salt of the earth, but became instead a pitifully and shamefully absorbent saline. Several true pearls of Lermontov's poetry remain that only actual animals could trample upon; unfortunately, there also remain in his works too many that are related to those very same animals. But the main point is that the absorbent saline of his genius remains. According to the word of the Gospel, this is given to people to trample.[13] And people can and should trample the saline of this demonism with hostility and contempt—of course, not for the ruined genius but for his ruinous principle of murderous falsehood. Soon this base principle took yet another turn in Lermontov's life. The demon of bloodthirstiness weakens over the years, giving away the greater part of its power to its brother—*the demon of vileness*. This second demon took control of the unhappy poet's soul without any impediments and much too early on left too many traces in his works.[14] And when he speaks about the "vices of delinquent youth" in one of his enlightened moments, this expression is—alas!—too close to reality. I will keep silent about the biographical facts—saying only several words about the poetic works infused by this demon of filth. First, there are too many of them, and second, they are too long: the most objectionable of them is a larger (though unfinished) poem written by the author in maturity. Third, and most important, the character of these writings creates a kind of depressing impression due to the complete absence of the light playfulness and grace by which, for example, Pushkin's more genuine works in this area are distinguished. Since I cannot at all buttress my judgment with citations here, I will elucidate it with a comparison. One gloomy day in a village I saw a swallow that was flying over a large marshy puddle. Something attracted it to this dark liquid, and it descended, seemingly just about to plunge into it or skim it with a wing. But this did not happen: not touching the surface, the swallow each time suddenly ascended upwards and chirped something innocently. Such is the impression made by these jests in Pushkin: you see a slimy puddle, you see a swallow and you see that there is no direct connection among them—whereas the pornographic muse of Lermontov is like a frog that has plunged and firmly settled there in the slime.

Or—in order to get nearer the point—in this instance, some kind of playful little imp, some kind of trickster, inspired Pushkin, whereas an actual demon of vileness commanded the pen of Lermontov.

Did Lermontov realize that the roads on which these demons were pushing him were false and pernicious? This consciousness was stated many times both in his verse and his correspondence. But the third and most powerful demon—the demon of pride—interfered with his making a real effort to free himself from the authority of the first two demons; he whispered: yes, this is bad, yes, this is lowly, but you are a genius, you are above simple mortals, everything is permitted to you, and you have from birth the privilege to remain elevated in baseness as well. . . .[15] Lermontov felt the weight of his fall and strove toward good and purity deeply and sincerely. But we will not find a single indication that he actually felt at any time the weight of his pride and turned to humility. And the demon of pride, as always the master of his interior dwelling, prevented him from really battling and evicting the two lower-ranking demons; and when he desired—he opened the door for them again and again. . . .

In speaking of pride and humility, I understand something entirely real and utilitarian. According to theological terminology, pride is the root evil or the major of the moral sins because it is a condition of the soul that makes any perfection or ascent impossible; pride consists in this very thing, to count oneself in need of nothing, excluding every thought of perfection and elevation. Humility is also for man the basic virtue because the acknowledgment of one's insufficiency directly gives cause for a need of and effort toward perfection. In other words, pride is for man a first condition for any creation of oneself as superman; thus, to say that *genius obligates one to humility* means only that genius obligates one to become a superman. It was all the easier for Lermontov to fulfill this obligation because, with all his demonism, he always believed in that which was loftier and better than himself alone, and in other lucid moments even felt this better thing over himself: "And in the heavens I see God. . . ."[16]

This religious feeling, often asleep in Lermontov, never died in him; and when it was awake—it struggled with his demonism. It did not disappear even when the base principle was victorious, but took on a strange form. In various of his works Lermontov already speaks of a Higher Will with some kind of personal offense. It is as if he considers it guilty against him, as having deeply insulted him.

In these early works, rivalry of the poet with God has, of course, a puerile character. Lermontov reproaches the Creator for the fact that he made him unsightly, for the fact that people—especially female cousins and other young ladies—do not understand and do not appreciate him, and so forth. But at a more mature age, after several attempts to change his life's path, after several fruitless impulses toward regeneration (fruitless because beginning in childhood the demoniacal master that was established in his soul could not be destroyed by subjective efforts, but required a complex and extended effort to which Lermontov did not agree), Lermontov stops struggling against the demonical forces and finds the ultimate answer to the question of life in *fatalism* ("Hero of Our Time" and "Valerik"). At the same time, he gives a new shifting form to his first childhood feeling of insult against Providence—namely, in the last reworking of the poem "Demon." The hero of this poem is the very same chief demon found in Lermontov himself—the demon of pride which we saw in his early verse. But in this poem he is terribly idealized (especially in its final draft); and if we are to judge impartially, even in spite of the idealization, the imagery of his actions sooner befits a youthful cornet-hussar than a person of such high rank and antiquity.[17] In spite of its magnificence of verse and gravity of design, for me to speak completely seriously about the content of the poem "Demon" is as impossible as returning to the fifth or sixth grade. But it is necessary to say something about it. Thus, the idealized demon is not at all any longer the spirit of evil described with such upright characteristics in the first verses of the genial boy. The demon of the poem is not only beautiful, but noble to the extreme and is, in essence, not really evil at all. Some kind of enigmatic misunderstanding at one time passed between him and the Most High, but he bears the weight of this quarrel and desires reconciliation. An occasion presents itself when the demon sees the beautiful Georgian princess Tamara dancing and singing on the roof of her parents' home. According to the Bible and sound logic—which is one and the same thing—the passion of the sons of God for the beauty of the daughters of men is a fall, but is a source of revival for demonism.[18] However, a revival does not occur. After the death of Tamara's fiancé and her withdrawal to a convent, the demon enters ready to do good; but seeing an angel guarding her innocence, he becomes inflamed with jealousy, seduces, and kills her. Unsuccessful in taking possession of her soul, he announces that he wanted to take another path, but that this was not permitted him and now with consciousness of his full right he becomes an actual demon.

Such a resolution of the problem finds itself in too much of an obvious contradiction with logic to make it worth refuting.

Such is the affected and contrived justification of demonism in theory, but the practice of the principle of fatalism is what Lermontov came to before his tragic end. Fatalism, in and of itself, is certainly not evil. If, for example, a man imagines that he should in a fateful manner be good, and does good, and unswervingly follows this destiny, then what could be better? Unfortunately, Lermontov's fatalism only covered his ugly tracks.

I will not begin to relate the manner of his actions during his latter days; I will say only that it was no better than his earlier days. Meanwhile, Lermontov did not possess complete conviction in the truth of fatalism, and he wanted, it seems, to be confirmed in it by experience. All the details of his behavior leading up to the final duel, as well as at the time of the duel itself, carry the features of a fatalistic experiment.

At the duel Lermontov conducted himself with nobility—he did not shoot at his opponent—but in actuality this was an insane challenge to higher powers, which could not in any case have a good outcome. In a terrifying storm, with flashes of lightning and peals of thunder, this turbulent soul passed over into another realm of existence.

Lermontov's end is called *ruination* both by him and by us. Expressed in this manner, we certainly do not in any way imagine this ruination either to be a theatrical failure in some kind of underworld where red devils dance, or to be a complete termination of existence. We have no reliable knowledge about the nature of existence beyond the grave, and therefore we will not speak of it. But there is a moral law as inviolable as a mathematical law, and it does not allow that a man experience after death arbitrary transformations not substantiated by his previous moral actions. If life's path continues beyond the grave as well, then he can evidently proceed only from the point at which he ended. And we know that as lofty as the degree of Lermontov's in-born genius was, his degree of moral refinement was base. Lermontov left with the burden of an unfulfilled duty—to develop the magnificent and divine gift that he had received gratis. He was called to impart to us, to his descendants, a more powerful impulse forward and upward toward true superhumanhood—but we did not receive it from him. We can grieve about this, but certainly that which Lermontov did not fulfill of his obligation to us does not remove from us our obligation to him. Before we can be obligated relative to our contemporaries—our brothers according to humanity and relative to progeny, and our children according to humankind—we have a responsibility to those who have passed on—to our fathers in humankind—and of course, for the current generation, Lermontov belongs among such fathers. So, is a responsibility of sons then required from us, such that we love, respect, and extol Lermontov for everything in him that is worthy of praise and remain silent about the rest? I do not understand a son's love and responsibility in this way. Imagine that we see a living father, having rendered all his merits and lofty gifts, but at present burdened by some kind of spiritual or physical (it makes no difference) weight. The responsibility of a son's love to such a father, of course, requires not that we praise his merits and gifts, but that we help him sleep in peace or, at least, ease his oppressive burden. And is this not so with regard to fathers departed as well? This is our responsibility—to ease the burden of their souls. And Lermontov had yet another heavy burden connected with the burden of his unfulfilled calling, which we can and must lighten. In expressing spurious forms of thought and sentiment in beauty, he at one time made them attractive for the inexperienced and continues to do so; and if even one of these little ones is drawn by him onto a false path, then the consciousness of what is now an unwilling and clear iniquity for him must lie as a heavy stone on his soul.[19] In unmasking the falsehood of the demonism praised by him, only blocking people on the path to their true superhuman goal, we in any case undermine this falsehood and lessen the burden that lies on this great soul, even if only slightly. Believe me, before speaking publicly about Lermontov I first considered: What does love for the departed require of me? What viewpoint should I express about his earthly fate? And I knew that here, as well as everywhere else, only one viewpoint based on eternal truth is in fact necessary, both for our contemporaries and for future generations, and in the first place—for the one who has passed on.

Appendix A

A Note in Defense of Dostoevsky against the Charge of a "New" Christianity ("Our New Christians," and so forth, K. Leontiev, Moscow: 1882)

"Every man is a falsehood."

"You seek to kill Me—*a man* who has told you the *truth*."

"Do you think that I came to bring peace to the earth? No, but division."

"And there will be one flock and one shepherd."

"*The fountain* of wisdom of ancient Masters."

"God is love. In love there is no fear; but *perfect* love will drive out fear."[1]

Source: Added to "Tri rechi v pamiat' Dostoevskago" in the 1884 edition. It first appeared as "Zametka v zashchitu Dostoevskago ot obvineniia v 'novom' khristianstve (Protiv K. Leontieva)" published in *Rus'* no. 9 (1883) under the title "Neskol'ko slov o broshiure g. Leontieva 'Nashi novye khristiane." Reprinted in *Sobranie sochinenii* 3: 219–223.

Is it possible to reduce all the essence of Christianity to humanism alone? Is the goal of Christianity a universal harmony and prosperity on earth, attained by humanity's natural progress?

Finally, is the *foundation* of Christian life and activity contained in love alone?

With the direct positing of these questions, an answer to them cannot be in doubt. If all truth is in humanism alone, why have a Christian *religion?* And why then speak about it at all in place of directly advocating a simple humanism? If the goal of life is attained by natural progress and consists in earthly prosperity, then why connect this to a religion established with mystery, miracle, and effort? Finally, if the entire point of religion is in the human sentiment of love alone, this means that in religion there is no point, and there is no need of it. For human love, with all its psychological complexity—is, in a moral sense, only a casual fact and in no way can constitute the basic content of religious advocacy. The apostle of love places at the foundation of his homiletics not a moral of love, but the mystical truth of the incarnation of Divine Logos:

> That which was from the beginning, which we have heard, which we have seen with our own eyes, which we have looked at and our hands have touched, concerning the Word of life. The life appeared; we have seen it . . . and proclaim to . . . you this eternal life, which was with the Father and has appeared to us. We proclaim to you that which we have seen and heard . . . so that you also may have . . . with us: and . . . with the Father and with the Son, Jesus Christ.
>
> (First Letter of John 1:1–3).

Now, love is mentioned for the reason that love can be fruitful only on the soil of a believing and reborn soul. But on purely human soil, it remains only a personal disposition, for it is neither possible to transfer love (as a simple sentiment) to others nor to require it from others; it is possible only to ascertain its presence or absence in a given case. Consequently, on its own, as a subjective condition, love cannot be the object of religious *duty* or a *mission* of religious activity. A blunt positing of the stated three questions and a resolute answer to them in the negative sense constitutes the main interest and virtue of the pamphlet "Our New Christians." That striving that the author attacks—to substitute a living plenitude of Christianity with a general abstract morality, concealed by the

Christian name but without Christian substance — is promulgated very much in our days, and it is worth noting. Unfortunately, in exposing the errors of pseudo-Christianity, the author of the pamphlet made them co-incident with the names of two Russian writers, one of whom, at least, was decidedly free from such errors.

The author of the pamphlet highly values — and justly so — the significance and merit of Dostoevsky. But the Christian idea that this remarkable man served was perverted in Dostoevsky's mind — according to the opinion of Mr. Leontiev — by a touch of sentimentality and abstract humanism. There may be a hint of sentimentality in the style of the author of "Poor Folk," but, in any event, the humanism of Dostoevsky was not the abstract morality that Mr. Leontiev points out; for Dostoevsky based his best hopes for man on actual faith in Christ and the church, and not in a faith in abstract reason or in that godless and possessed humanity, which in the novels of Dostoevsky himself more clearly than anywhere else reverberates in all its abomination. Dostoevsky's humanism was established on the mystical superhuman foundation of true Christianity, with the appreciation of an agent from a Christian point of view for whom this was the most important thing, something *upon which* he built and stood.

"Is it possible," asks Mr. Leontiev, "to build a new national culture solely on good feelings toward people, without, at the same time, specific definitions of the material and mystical objects of faith that are placed higher than this humanism . . . ?" And Dostoevsky would respond to this question just as negatively as the author of the pamphlet does. The ideal of true culture — both national and universal — was maintained by Dostoevsky not solely on the basis of good feelings toward people, but first of all on mystical subjects of faith standing elevated above this humanism — namely on Christ and on the church. And the very creation of true culture was to Dostoevsky first of all a religious "orthodox concern"; and "faith in the divinity of a crucified Nazarene carpenter at the time of Pontius Pilate" was the inspirational source of all that Dostoevsky said and wrote.

"Christianity believes neither in the best *autonomous* morality of a person nor in the reason of a collective humanity, intended to create sooner or later heaven on earth." And neither did Dostoevsky believe in anything of the kind. If he was a moralist, as Mr. Leontiev calls him, then his morality was not autonomous (self-legislated), but Christian — based on the religious conversion and rebirth of man. And the collective reason of humanity, with its attempts at a new Tower of Babel, was not only rejected by Dostoevsky, but also served for him as an object of witty gibes, and not just in the latter years of his life, but also earlier. Mr. Leontiev should at least reread "Notes from the Underground."

Dostoevsky believed in man and humanity only because he believed in the *God*-man and *God*-manhood—in Christ and the church.

"Christ will be known not other than through the church. Love first of all the church."

"Only through the church can you come together with the people—simply and freely—and enter into their trust."

"It is necessary to learn from the people to be humble intellectually, to understand that in their worldview there is more truth than in ours."

"Therefore humility before the people, for anyone aware of their feelings, is nothing other than humility before the church."

Without doubt, Dostoevsky would have subscribed to these excellent words. In "The Diary of a Writer," Mr. Leontiev could find many places that express these very thoughts. It is sufficient to remember what was spoken there against our populists, who wanted to unite with the people and be Benefactors to them *in place of the church.*[2]

Only in loving the church and serving it can one truly serve one's people and humanity. For it is not possible to serve two masters.[3] Service to one's neighbor must coincide with service to God, and it is not possible to serve God other than loving that which He himself loved—the single object of God's love, His Beloved and His Bride: that is the church.

The church is humanity deified through Christ and, with faith in the church, believing in humanity—this means only believing in its *capacity for deification*, believing according to the words of Saint Athanasius the Great, that in Christ God became man in order to make man god. And this faith is not heretical, but truly Christian, orthodox, and patriarchal.

And with this faith, any preaching or prophecy about universal reconciliation, universal harmony, and so forth, relates directly only to the final triumph of the church, when, according to the word of the Savior, there will be one flock and one shepherd and—in the word of the Apostle—God will be everything in everybody.[4]

Dostoevsky had to address people who had not read the Bible and had forgotten the catechesis. Therefore, in order to be understood, he had to utilize against his will such expressions as "universal harmony" when he wanted to speak about the triumphant, or orthodox church. And Mr. Leontiev points out in vain that triumph and glorification of the church must take place in the other world; but Dostoevsky believed in universal harmony here, on earth. For no such absolute boundary between "here" and "there" is supposed in the church.[5]

Even the earth itself, according to the Holy Scripture and the teaching of the church, is a term of *variable* meanings. One is the earth spoken about at the beginning of the Book of Genesis—it was invisible, formless, and darkness was over the face of the deep. Another "earth" is the one about which it is said: God appeared on earth and lived with man; and yet there will be another New Earth, in which truth lives.[6] The point is that the moral condition of humanity and all spiritual creatures is not, in general, completely dependent on whether they live here on earth or not; on the contrary, the condition of the earth itself and its relation to the unseen world is determined by the moral condition of the spiritual creatures. And the universal harmony about which Dostoevsky prophesied does not at all denote a utilitarian prosperity of people on the present earth, but precisely the beginning of a New Earth in which truth lives. The approach of this universal harmony, or the church triumphant, will take place not at all by the path of peaceful progress, but in the throes and pangs of a new birth, as described in Revelation—Dostoevsky's favorite book in his last years. "And a sign . . . appeared in the heavens, a woman arrayed in the sun and the moon beneath her feet, and on her head a crown of twelve stars. And in her womb ready . . . to give birth."[7]

And only afterward, after these throes and pangs, triumph, glory, and joy:

> And then I heard what sounded like a great multitude, like the sound of rushing waters and like loud thunder, shouting: allelujah, For our Lord God Almighty is enthroned. . . . Let us rejoice and be glad and give glory to Him, to the One who will come . . . and *His Bride* has made herself ready. And it is given to her to be arrayed in fine linen pure and clean; the fine linen of *the righteousness of the saints*. . . . Then I saw a new heaven and a new earth, for the first heaven and the first earth had passed away, and there was no longer any sea. . . . And . . . (John sees) the Holy City the new Jerusalem coming down out of heaven from God, prepared as a bride . . . for her husband. And I heard a voice from heaven saying: this is God's . . . from man, and he will live with them: and they will be his people and God himself will

be with them and be their God. And God will wipe away every tear from their eyes and death will be no more: neither crying, nor mourning, nor pain will be for . . . anyone, who passes here.[8]

Here is the kind of universal harmony and prosperity that Dostoevsky understood—only repeating with his own words the prophecies of New Testament revelation.

Appendix B
The Russian Symbolists

I. Review of Valerii Briusov and A. L. Miropol'skii, *The Russian Symbolists* (Moscow: 1894), 44 pp.

This little notebook of exercises has unquestionable virtues: it does not burden the reader with volume, and it entertains a bit with its substance.[1] The fun starts with the epigraph, which is taken by Mr. Valerii Briusov from the French decadent Stéphane Mallarmé:

> Une dentelle s'abolit
> Dans le doute du jeu supreme.*

And here is Mr. Briusov's Russian "prologue":

> The rose colorings die away
> In the pale reflection of the moon;

Source: "Russkie Symvolisti," *Vestnik Evropy* 8 (1894): 890–829; 1 (1895): 421–424; and 10 (1895): 847–851. Reprinted in *Sobranie sochinenii* 7: 159–170.
* In a literal translation this means: "lace is abolished in doubt of a royal game."

They freeze in icy stories
About the sufferings of spring.
From outcome to start
They have wrapped themselves in the mourning of sleep
And their garlands are interlaced
With the silence of color.
Under the rays of youthful reverie
The consonant roses do not flower
On flower-beds of void,
And through windows of incoherent sleep
Lulled daydreams
Will not see the blue stars.[2]

In the words "consonant roses on flower-beds of void" and "windows of incoherent sleep," one can see a rather faithful, though also symbolic, definition of this kind of poem. However, it is specifically Russian "symbolism" that is represented rather weakly in this little collection. Apart from the poems that are directly indicated as being translated verses, a good half of the rest are inspired vividly by other poets and, what's more, not even symbolists. For example, the one that begins with the lines

I met her accidentally,
And dreamed about her timidly, (a)

and ends with

Here is the old fairy tale, by which
Being different is always judged . . . (b)

undoubtedly descends from Heinrich Heine, although transplanted to "a flower-bed of void." The next one,

An indistinct dream enters on a stage,
It sets the door of an instant ajar . . . (c),

is an involuntary parody of Fet. Inspired by his verbless verse:

The starry dispassionate sky . . . (d),

only the lack of imitation's success can be taken for originality.

> The stars softly stirred . . . (e)

again a free translation of Heine.

> Bow your little head . . . (f),

idem.

And here is a poem I would have difficulty in calling either original or imitative:

> With tears the brilliant *little eyes*
> And the *little lips* that are mournfully pursed,
> And the *little cheek* that burns from caresses
> And the tangled-wrinkled curls . . . (g)[3]

and so forth. In any event, is enumerating in diminutive form the various parts of a human organism—which are well known to all even without this—really "symbolism"?

I have an objection of another sort against the following "finale" of Mr. Valerii Briusov:

> Golden fairies
> In Atlas's garden!
> When will I find
> The frosted avenues?
> The silvery splashes
> Of naiads in love,
> Where jealous planks
> Bar the path for you.
> Incomprehensible vases
> Illuminated by firelight.
> The dawn has cooled
> Over the flight of fantasy.
> Behind the dark of curtains
> Funeral urns,
> And the azure vault does not wait for
> Deceptive stars.[4]

In spite of the "frosty avenues in Atlas's garden," the subject of these lines is as clear as it is reprehensible. Carried away by a "flight of fantasy," the author peeps into a bathing place made out of planks where there are persons of the female sex bathing, whom he calls "fairies" and "naiads." But is it possible to make up for vile conduct with luxuriant words? And here is what symbolism brings us to in the *end!* We hope at least that the "jealous planks" turned out to be at the height of their calling. In the opposite case, it would remain for the "golden fairies" only to pour cold water over the indiscrete symbolist out of those "incomprehensible vases," which in common parlance are called tubs and are used in bathhouses for ablutions of the feet.

Without knowing Mr. Briusov's age, it is not possible to pronounce a sweeping judgment against him. If he is no more than fourteen years old, then a fair poet may yet come of him. If this person is an adult, then, of course, any literary hopes are out of the question. I have nothing to say about Mr. Miropol'skii. Of the ten little pages that belong to him, eight are occupied with prosaic excerpts. But reading decadent prose is a task that exceeds my power. "Flower-beds of void" can be tolerable only when "roses of consonance" grow on them.

II. 2ND ED. IZD. V.A. MASLOV (MOSCOW: 1894)

The breed of creatures that have named themselves Russian symbolists has as its major trait an unusual speed of reproduction. Just last summer there were only two, but now there are fully ten. Here are their names in order: A. Bronin, Valerii Briusov, V. Darov, Erl. Martov, A. L. Miropol'skii, N. Novich, K. Sozontov, Z. Fuchs and another two, one of whom hides himself under the letter "M." and the other under three asterisks. I am prepared to think that this breed reproduces by conception at will (*generatio aequivoca*), but such a hypothesis is hardly allowed by exact science. However, Russian symbolism is at present less enriched by sonorous works than by sonorous names.

There are in all eighteen original poems in the second edition; with ten authors this comes out to be one poem and a fraction (1.8 or 1 4/5) each. The reader will agree that up to this point my critical method is distinguished by a strictly scientific character and leads to completely inarguable results. I would like to hold to such a method as well in the evaluation of the qualitative virtue of the Russian symbolists, but this is now much more difficult: here you will not manage with arithmetic alone. It is necessary to establish general principles or norms of artistic activity and postulates flowing from them in order to grade a given work. Unfortunately, this singularly scientific means has one inconvenience: it would require many years of study on my part that would need to be set forth in a multi-volume work—but only a little review of a small notebook with verses of problematic worth is required of me. We must reject the scientific method; but on the other hand, I would not want to be subjected to a justified reproach of subjectivism and tendentiousness.

Is there, however, nothing in the middle between strict science and personal impression? Without a doubt, there is. Without backing away from absolute principles, it is possible as a norm of judgment to take not personal opinion, but the intention of the author or artist being criticized. So, for example, when a painter emphasizes on his picture with his own hand: *this is a lion!*—and at the same time anyone can see on it a badly drawn dog (while the intention of the painter to represent a lion in his essence did not go beyond the yellow color of the dog's fur alone), then any witness to this failure can acknowledge the picture as unsatisfactory without falling into subjectivism; for, independently of personal opinions, according to the nature of things it is clear that neither the yellow color nor the poor drawing is sufficient in itself to make a lion out of a dog. Such a means of judgment, which is based on the objective difference between two mammals, I call—the relative-scientific method. Applying it to the Russian symbolists is easier because they have concerned themselves with a most specific manner of expressing their intent. In the foreword, Mr. V. Briusov explains that the poetry that he serves along with his comrades is a *poetry* of allusion. Following our relative-scientific method, let us see how much, in actuality, the verses of the Russian symbolists represent the poetry of allusion:

> Strings rust
> 'Neath a wet hand
> Daydreams become numb
> And cover themselves with gloom.[5]

The little poem by Mr. Miropol'skii, who opens our collection, begins with this strophe and concludes with a repetition of it. Here a terrible fact—but one of little interest—is painted with an exaggerated *vividness:* the guitarist portrayed by the author suffers from a certain pathological phenomenon.

There is neither poetry nor allusion here. The first line—"strings rust"—
contains in itself yet another indication, but nevertheless a clear *indication*
and not an allusion—to the ignorance of Mr. Miropol'skii.

The second poem, "I Wait," consists almost entirely of the repetition
of two lines: "A ringing heart beats in the breast" and "Dear friend, come,
come!"[6] It is unclear as to what kind of allusions there are here. It is
sooner possible here to note an excessive striving toward clarity, for the
poet elucidates that the heart beats *in the breast*—in order that somebody
not think that it beats in the head or in the abdominal cavity.

Mr. Valerii Briusov, the one who, in the first edition of "The Russian
Symbolists," described his reprehensible peeping into a women's bath-place,
today portrays his own bath. This is certainly not a tragedy; but what is bad
is the fact that Mr. Briusov speaks about his bathing place with such words
that it is clear without any allusions; he demonstrates a not fully normal au-
thorial disposition. We warned him that pandering to base passions, even
under the guise of symbolism, would not lead to any good. Alas! Our fore-
bodings were realized earlier than our expectations! Judge for yourselves:

> In the silvery dust the midnight moistness
> Captivates tired dreams with rest
> And in *the vacillating silence of a sarcophagus stream*
> *A great man* does not listen to slander.[7]

To call a stream a sarcophagus and himself a great man is an absolutely
clear sign (and not just an allusion) of an unhealthy condition.

> A female corpse, rotting and foul-smelling,
> The great steppe, cast iron vault of heaven . . .
> And the long instant, revived as a joke,
> With reproachful laughter arises.
> A diamond dream . . . a drawing ignited overhead
> And the aroma, the tears, and the dew . . .
> Will abandon the rotting and foul-smelling corpse,
> And the raven pecked out its eyes.[8]

Here in this poem, signed by Z. Fuchs (let us hope that this Z. designates
Zahar and not Zinaida), it is possible to find an allusion—just not a poetic
one, but an allusion to the fact that the three municipal deputies of the

Tambovsk town council would have been perhaps not totally wrong in their opinion* if they had referred not to peasants who had only completed an elementary course of education, but to certain poets who call themselves symbolists. However—"In jene Sphären wag' ich nicht zu streben. . . ."[9]

I think that Mr. Z. Fuchs has sufficiently punished himself, having come out in print with such a work. Nevertheless, the impression created on me by this symbolist's poem is so strong that I do not have the necessary calmness of spirit for a relative-scientific analysis of other symbolist pearls. Moreover, on the last page our symbolists announce three new publications, one of which is titled "Les cshefs (!) d'oeuvre" [sic]. We will put off our final judgment until the appearance of these "cshefs d'oeuvre," and at present, for the sake of veracity, we will note that there is one poem examined in the notebook of exercises that recalls true poetry:

> Look child! there at the end of the street
> The bushes of night's beauty have spread . . .
> The fairies have taken the spring night's image . . .
>   My anguish you did not understand!
> There the rays of the sun from east until the night
> Pour passionate magical cups upon dream flowers . . .
> In vain he dashes if only once to look them in the eyes . . .
>   My anguish you do not understand!
> In the evening hour, hiding behind a mountain
> With the burning anguish of a deceptive dream,
> In impotence he sees their kiss with the moon . . .
>   My anguish you will likely understand![10]

III. More about Russia's Symbolists
The Russian Symbolists (Moscow: Summer 1895), 52 pp.

In the foreword to this new edition the young sportsmen who call themselves Russian symbolists "considered it necessary to explain their attitude"

---

* See the telegram in "New Times" of 16 December 1894 where it is recounted that three municipal deputies of the named meeting defended their opinion on the need to preserve corporal punishment.

toward criticism. In the opinion of Mr. Briusov and another, the majority of their critics were totally unprepared for this important assignment, and those who were prepared turned out to have criminal intent. This is precisely the case with the review in *Vestnik Evropy*. "In their time," write the gentlemen symbolists, "the reviews of Mr. Vl. S. could still have aroused some interest. There are really sensible observations in them (for example, on the imitativeness of many of the poems of Mr. Briusov in the 1st ed.); but Mr. Vl. S. became carried away with the desire to amuse the public a little, and this led him to a series of witticisms of doubtful value as well as to a deliberate perversion of the meaning of the poems. We say 'deliberate': Mr. V. S., of course, should easily grasp the most nuanced allusions of a poet, because he himself has written symbolist verse, as for example, 'Why Words' (*Vestn. Evr.* 10 [1892])."

Why, however, are the gentlemen symbolists so convinced that this poem—whether symbolist or not—belongs to the author of the review? The poem is signed: "Vladimir Soloviev," but the review is marked with the initials Vl. S., underneath which, perhaps, hides a Vladislav Syrokomlia or a Vlasii Semenov. I don't have to answer for Mr. Vladimir Soloviev regarding the accusation of printing a symbolist poem in *Vestnik Evropy*. But in answer to the accusation of me criminally distorting the meaning of the poems of Mr. Briusov and another, I, Vlasii Semenov, have to explain that even if I were inspired by the most infernal spite, then, for all that, it would be impossible to pervert the meaning of these poems—due to the complete absence in them of any meaning. With this new edition, the gentlemen symbolists have put the matter beyond any doubt. Just let someone try to pervert the meaning of a work such as this:

> A shadow of uncreated creations
> Flickers in a dream
> Like a worn fan
> On an enamel wall.
> Violet hands
> On an enamel wall
> In a demi-sleep draw sounds
> In a ringing-resounding silence
> And transparent kiosks
> In a ringing-resounding profundity
> Shoot off as if flashes

Before the lapis moon,
The naked body of luna rises
Before the lapis moon;
Sounds hover in a half-sleep
Sounds fawn upon me
Secrets of created creations
With caresses fawn upon me
And the patched shadow flickers
On an enamel wall.[11]

If I observe that it is not only unseemly but also completely impossible for a naked *luna* to rise before a lapis *moon*—since moon and luna are only two names for one and the same object—then is this indeed a "deliberate perversion of meaning"?

And how about this "cshef d'oeuvre":

The ray of a heart from the silver of agitation
Over the expanse of rime rises,
And, trembling, the crystal of prayer sounds
And swims, spattered with singing.
It swims with moaning modulation . . .
It beckons the starry ice from the abyss
Far off in haughty peace
A star sleeps . . . the star shines and sleeps.[12]

Or still another:

In the air, the pearls of collonade songs
And consonant crystal rings like a fountain
White masses have died off into azure
And in the rays of fog a dull granite
In the thoughts of foam the glow of languor beats
Gentle features are glimpsed fleetingly as lightning
To the heart from mansions of magic and dreams
Sound bridges have been bent like an arc
Vivid garlands wind around the facades,
An aromatic flash of Carrara marble
And serenades victoriously sound, then melt away
And an echo carries an inspired dance.[13]

Some symbolists relieve themselves of the work of composing meaningless verse with a rather successful trick. Having written one line, they then turn it inside out—and a different one appears:

> Over the dark plain,
> A plain dark,
> An indiscreet picture
> A picture indiscreet,
> Hanging fog
> Fog hanging,
> As if deceptions
> Deceptions without thought
> Without thought and connection
> In a story dispassionate
> In a dispassionate story,
> In a story unclear,
> Where the pale hues
> Of a sad denouement are
> Sad, like a fairy-tale
> About a distant native land.[14]

And here is a poem in which there is not only no meaning, but also no rhythm—it is as if written for an illustration of the expression—ni rime, ni raison:

> Corpses, illuminated by gas!
> Red ribbon on a sinful bride!
> Oh! We will go the window to kiss!
> You see, how pale the faces of the dead!
> This is—a hospital, where in mourning children . . .
> This is—on the icy oleander . . .
> This is—a dustcover of Romances without words . . .
> My dear, in the window the moon is not visible.
> Our souls are—a flower in your buttonhole.[15]

The gentlemen symbolists reproach me for being carried away by the desire to amuse the public a little; but they can see that this enthusiasm leads me only to a simple reproduction of their own pearls.

It should be noted that one poem in this collection has an unquestionable and clear meaning. It is very short—one little stitch in all: "O, cover your pale legs."

For full clarity it would be necessary, perhaps, to add: "or else you'll catch cold." But even without this, the advice of Mr. Briusov, apparently directed at a person who suffers with anemia, is the most sensible work of all symbolist literature, not just Russian, but also foreign. Of the examples of the latter translated in the present edition, the following masterpiece by the renowned Maeterlinck merits attention:

> My soul is in pain all the day,
> My soul is in pain with farewell,
> My soul struggles with silence
> My eyes meet a shadow.
> *And 'neath the lash of memory*
> I see spectres of inclinations.
> A half-forgotten trace leads
> *Dogs of secret desires*
> Into the thick of forgetful forests
> Of lilac reveries leashes are carried
> And yellow arrows—reproaches—
> Execute the deer of false dreams
> Alas! Alas! everywhere desires,
> Everywhere returning dreams,
> *And too much blue breath . . .*
> Upon the heart fades the face of the moon.[16]

Maybe in some other austere reader long ago "the dog of secret desire howled in the heart"—this was expressly the desire that authors and translators of such poems in future write not only "'neath the lash of memory," but also "under memory of the lash. . . ." But my personal critical leash is distinguished more by "playfulness" than by "spitefulness," and a "blue breath" called forth in me only an orange inclination for a violet work of yellow lines; while the pretentious peacock of vanity arouses me to share with the public three examples of my *gris-de-perles*, *vert-de-mer*, and *feuille-morte* inspiration.[17] Now at least Mr. V. Briusov and the others have a valid right to charge me with the publication of symbolist poetry:

I.

Vertical horizons
In chocolate skies
Like dreams half-mirrored
In laurel-cherry forests.
A spectre of fire-breathing ice-floe
In the vivid dusk was extinguished
And not listening stands
A Hyacinth Pegasus
Immanent mandragora
Began to rustle in the reeds,
And ears sickened by
The horny-decadent doggerel-verse.

II.

Above the green hill
Above the hill green
For us in love together
For us together in love
Shines at noon a star
At noon it shines
Though no one ever
Will notice that star.
But a wave-like fog,
But a fog wave-like
Out of radiant countries,
Out of a country radiant,
Slithers between the clouds,
Over dry waves,
Motionlessly flying
And with a double moon.

III.

Chandeliers burn in the heavens,
        And below—darkness
Did you go to him, or not?
        Tell us yourself!
But do not tease the hyena of suspicion,
        Mouse of anguish!

Take a look, how the leopards of vengeance
    Sharpen their fangs!
And do not call for the owl of reason
    On this night!
Asses of patience and elephants of meditation
    Have run off.
You yourself have given birth to the crocodile
    Of your own fate.
Let the chandeliers burn in the heavens
    In the grave is—darkness.[18]

Supplemental List of Soloviev's Relevant Writings

(Chronologically arranged)

The Mythological Process in Ancient Paganism (1873)

The Crisis of Western Philosophy [Against Positivism] (1874)

Metaphysics and Positive Science (1875)

The Experience of Synthetic Philosophy (1877)

Critique of Abstract Principles (1877–80)

Lectures on Godmanhood (1877–81)

The Spiritual Foundations of Life (1882–84)

Primitive Paganism, Its Surviving and Dead Remnants (1890)

On Lyrical Poetry. Concerning Recent Poems of Fet and Polonsky (1890)

The Illusion of Poetic Creativity (1890)

On Counterfeits (1891)

On the Collapse of the Medieval Worldview (1891)

A Buddhist Mood in Poetry (1894)

The Poetry of Tiutchev (1895)

The Poetry of A. K. Tolstoy (1895)

The Poetry of Ia. P. Polonsky. A Critical Essay (1896)

Justification of the Good. Moral Philosophy (1897)

Plato's Life-Drama (1898)

The Idea of a Superman (1899)

A Special Celebration of Pushkin (1899)

The Significance of Poetry in the Verse of Pushkin (1899)

Notes

INTRODUCTION

1. An Angelus message dated 30 July 2000 remembers Soloviev as "this Russian personality of extraordinary profundity who with great clarity also warned about the drama of the division among Christians and the urgent necessity of their unity. . . ." See ZENIT International News Agency, Castel Gandolfo, 1 August 2000.

2. Some of the most comprehensive sources on Vladimir Soloviev's life and thought are in Russian: Konstantin Mochul'skii, *Vladimir Soloviev: zhizn' i uchenie* (Paris: YMCA Press, 1951); Sergei M. Soloviev, *Zhizn' i tvorcheskaia evoliutsiia Vladimira Solovieva* (Moscow: Respublika, 1997); Evgenii N. Trubetskoi, *Mirosozertsanie Vl.S. Solovieva*, 2 vols. (Moscow: Put', 1913); and the collection of essays (including those by Nikolai Berdyaev, Vyacheslav Ivanov, and Aleksandr Blok) under the title *Sbornik Pervyi o Vladimire Solovieve* (Moscow: Put', 1911). Some of the more recent, relevant works on Soloviev's thought available in English are: Marina Kostalevsky, *Dostoevsky and Soloviev: The Art of Integral Vision* (New Haven and London: Yale University Press, 1997); Edith W. Clowes, "The Limits of Discourse: Solov'ev's Language of Syzygy and the Project of Thinking Total Unity," *Slavic Review* 55/3 (Fall 1996): 552–567; Caryl Emerson, "Solov'ev, the Late Tolstoy, and the Early Bakhtin on the Problem of Shame and Love" *Slavic Review* 50/3 (Fall 1991): 663–672; Jonathan Sutton, *The Religious Philosophy of Vladimir Solovyov: Towards a Reassessment* (New York: St. Martin's Press, 1988); and Paul Valliere, *Modern Russian Theology: Bukharev, Soloviev, Bulgakov: Orthodox Theology in a New Key* (Edinburgh: T & T Clark, 2000).

3. "O poddelkakh" (1891), in Sergei M. Soloviev and Ernst L. Radlov, eds., *Sobranie sochinenii Vladimira Sergeevicha Solovieva*, 2nd ed., 10 vols. (St. Petersburg:

"Prosveshchenie," 1911–14), 6: 339 [reprint with two additional volumes, Brussels: "Zhizn' s Bogom," 1966–70].

4. See Ernst Radlov, ed., *Pis'ma Vladimira Sergeevicha Solovieva*, 4 vols. (St. Petersburg: "Obshchestvennaia pol'za," 1908–23), 1: 33 [reprint, Brussels: "Zhizn's Bogom," 1970]. Emphasis added.

5. See Mochul'skii, *Vladimir Soloviev*, 22. Soloviev seemed to be quite familiar with Augustine's work. See, for example, "On So-Called Problems" (Sunday Letters), in Vladimir Wozniuk, ed. and trans., *Politics, Law and Morality: Essays by V.S. Soloviev* (New Haven and London: Yale University Press, 2000), 76–77; also see below, Appendix A, note 5. It would perhaps not be too much to suggest that Soloviev saw parallels between Augustine's apologia for Christianity against the attacks of its detractors, who saw in it the demise of pagan Rome's imperial greatness, and Soloviev's own justification of universal Christianity against what he understood to be the onset of neopaganism in Russia and the rest of Europe.

6. See for example, "Khristos voskres!" *Rus'*, 13 April 1897; "O dobrosovestnom neverii," *Rus'*, 20 April 1897; and "Znachenie dogmata," *Rus'*, 25 May 1897, all in S. Soloviev and E. Radlov, eds. *Sobranie sochinenii* 10: 34–57.

7. See Vladimir Wozniuk, "V. S. Soloviev and the Politics of Human Rights," *Journal of Church and State* 41/1 (Winter 1999): 33–50.

8. He once stated, "We all walk beneath the censorship's terror." For this and other comments regarding difficulties with the censors, see Radlov, ed., *Pis'ma* 1: 45, 67–68, 123; and 3: 13.

9. For Soloviev's use of the term, see, in this volume, "The Universal Meaning of Art" and "The Meaning of Love," Fifth Article, III, IV, V.

10. Lev N. Tolstoy, *What Is Art?* (New York: Crowell, 1899), especially chapters 3, 4, 20.

11. See, in this volume, "Three Addresses in Memory of Dostoevsky," Second Address.

12. See, for example, Umberto Eco, *The Aesthetics of Thomas Aquinas* (Cambridge: Harvard University Press, 1988), 22–24. For an early modern Christian theological interpretation of beauty as objective, see for example, Roland Andre Delattre, *Beauty and Sensibility in the Thought of Jonathan Edwards* (New Haven and London: Yale University Press, 1968), which introduces the "derivative" thought of another (albeit American) theologian; both excursions into aesthetics bear similarities to one another (or perhaps, more precisely, to medieval Christian writings), although there is no evidence that Soloviev even knew who Jonathan Edwards was.

13. See, in this volume, "Beauty in Nature," X.

14. See, for example, Nicholas Berdyaev, *The Russian Idea* (London: G. Bles, 1947), 166–168. The reference to his "theocratic Leviathan" appeared in 1885. See Radlov, ed., *Pis'ma* 1: 24. See also Wozniuk, "V. S. Soloviev and the Politics of Human Rights," 36–37.

15. Cited in Eco, *Aesthetics of Thomas Aquinas*, 28.

16. For a particularly coherent perspective on the centrality of proportionality to Thomism and the views of Augustine, Aquinas and other medievalists on symbol, allegory, and metaphor, see ibid., especially 56–57, 97–100, and 141–152. See also Plato, *Timaeus* 87c–d, and *Sophist* 228a–b.

17. For exceptions, see, for example, Gary Saul Morson and Caryl Emerson, *Mikhail Bakhtin: Creation of a Prosaics* (Palo Alto: Stanford University Press, 1990); and Caryl Emerson, "Keeping the Self Intact During the Culture Wars: A Centennial Essay for Mikhail Bakhtin," *New Literary History* 27/1 (1996): 107–126.

18. One of the principal purposes of my previous effort in rendering Soloviev into English was to address this problem of incoherence, with special attention to political themes.

19. See the prefatory comments to *Tvoreniia Platona* in S. Soloviev and E. Radlov, eds., *Sobranie sochinenii* 12: 360–366.

20. See Frederick de Wolfe Bolman, Jr.'s introductory comments regarding translation in Friedrich Schelling, *The Ages of the World* (New York: Columbia University Press, 1942), x.

1. Three Addresses in Memory of Dostoevsky

1. Godmanhood (*bogochelovechestvo*)—Soloviev's term for the incarnational imaging of Christ in humanity. The Christian basis for this term can be found in Psalm 82:6 ("You shall be like gods"). See also Romans 8:19, 23, 29.

2. Soloviev here addresses the ongoing debates about the purpose of art in the Russia of his day (as well as in the wider European context), aspects of which he returns to repeatedly in other essays in this volume; these debates could be traced back at least to the 1860s and the revolutionary movement in Russia. Nikolai Chernyshevsky's novel *What Is To Be Done?* (1863) waxed optimistic about a bright socialist future for humanity based on technical progress and symbolized by the 1851 London exhibition's "crystal palace," a symbol exploited by Dostoevksy in *Notes from the Underground* (1864). Lenin later used Chernyshevsky's title for one of his most famous treatises. The aesthetic question remained unresolved when Tolstoy later broached it with somewhat less urgency (and less satisfying results) in "What Is Art?"

3. Soloviev later wrote in similar fashion with reference to Plato's failure to follow through with the Socratic ideal late in his life. See "Plato's Life-Drama" in Wozniuk, ed., *Politics, Law, and Morality*, 253. My thanks to an anonymous reviewer for this insight.

4. See John 8:14–16 for Soloviev's adaptation of the theme of the "right" to judge.

5. Ibid. Here Soloviev implied Dostoevsky's years of incarceration, during which time he underwent a profound transformation, rejecting his former connections with the revolutionary movement in the so-called Petrashevsky Circle, which had been the reason for his sentence.

6. Dostoevsky's memoirs of his breakdown during this time are chronicled in his *Notes from the House of the Dead.*

7. Soloviev intermittently employed Dostoevsky's phrase "all is permitted" (*vse pozvoleno*) with reference to the moral universe if God does not exist. See *Brothers Karamazov*, bk. II, chap. 9. Dostoevsky himself may have derived this from the substance of 1 Corinthians 10:23, but an echo can also be found in Schiller's *Wallenstein's Camp* ("Whatever is not forbidden is permitted," Sc. vi).

8. Dostoevsky's term for George Sand. My thanks to an anonymous reviewer for this information.

9. Galatians 3:28; Colossians 3:11.

10. Anthills: republics. Dostoevsky apparently liked this metaphor, which can be found in *Notes from the Underground* (I, 9).

11. "Communists in North America": Soloviev's reference is to nineteenth-century quasi-socialist Christian utopian living experiments. See the commentary in A. Ia. Zis' et al., *V.S. Soloviev: Filosofiia, iskusstvo, literaturnaia kritika* (Moscow: Iskusstvo, 1991), 660. During a stay in London, Soloviev apparently read Charles Nordhoff's *The Communistic Societies of the United States* (New York: Harper, 1875). Perhaps most relevant among the American ideas and experiments at the time were those of John Humphrey Noyes (1811–1886), founder of the Oneida community, and Dr. Wilhelm Keil, a Prussian immigrant who established the Bethel (Missouri) and Aurora (Oregon) communities, which all reflected a lifestyle sometimes referred to as "Bible communism." It was condemned by many other Christians as heresy, but harked back to biblical teachings as found in the New Testament, particularly in the Acts of the Apostles.

12. Soloviev echoed the title of Nikolai Chernyshevsky's novel *What Is To Be Done?* See note 2 above.

13. John 3:3.

14. Raskolnikov, the main character in Dostoevsky's *Crime and Punishment*, seems to be implied here.

15. Dostoevsky's characters Svidrigailov (*Crime and Punishment*) and/or Ivan Karamazov seem to be suggested here.

16. "Islamic infidels and Roman Catholics": *basurmanstvom i latinstvom*.

17. The logic Soloviev used to arrive at this connection between Muslims and Jews remains somewhat obscure in context. Perhaps he drew from the biblical and genealogical connection between them: both religions are of "The Book," and both Arab and Jew trace their lines back to Abraham as father (Ishmael and Isaac).

18. The Apostle: St. Paul, whose excerpted words are from two chapters in the Letter to the Romans. See Romans 9:4–5, 11:1, 11:2, 11:25–26, 11:32.

19. Revelation 12:1–6.

20. A supplement to these three addresses can be found in Appendix A.

2. BEAUTY IN NATURE

1. *Republic* 410b–412a, and "Poetics" vi, 2–3.

2. In Soloviev's note—Leonid Egorovich Obolenskii: a contemporary of Soloviev; a philosopher, social and political writer, and critic, who believed ethics developed on a psychological foundation and that both pain and sympathy evolved from similar circumstances. He reasoned against materialism and positivism satisfying the requirements of ethics. Vl. Veliamovich, *Psikho-fiziologicheskaiia osnovaniia estetiki; sushchnost' iskusstva, ego sotsial'noe znachenie i otnoshenie k nauke i nravstvennosti: novyi opyt filosofii iskusstv* (St. Petersburg: Typ. L. V. Fomina, 1878).

3. Kant's notion of the "disinterested interest" of the observer is perhaps relevant here.

4. "One does not desire the stars; one is gladdened by their splendor." From Goethe's "Trost in Tränen," which was later set to music by J. Brahms, among others.

5. See especially Plato's *Phaedo* 74a−76e and 103e ff; and Arthur Schopenhauer, *The World as Will and Idea* (Garden City, N.Y.: Dolphin/Doubleday, 1961), third book, second aspect. Schopenhauer (1788−1860) was a disciple of Kant, with whom Soloviev indirectly waged a polemic in many of his essays. Both Kant and Schopenhauer also influenced Soloviev—most notably in his adaptation of the Platonic vision of cosmic will and ideas about the essential unity of all beings, which Soloviev later co-opted and adopted in somewhat revised form in his notion of "all-unity." See Plato, *Sophist* 244a−245d, and *Timaeus* 30c−d, 32c−33b.

6. Kant's concept of *Ding an Sich* (thing-in-itself), which is the *noumenon* behind the reality of any phenomenon, is echoed here.

7. Compare with Plato, *Gorgias* 494a, where the "life of a stone" is described as without pleasure or pain.

8. Eduard von Hartmann (1842−1906) was a philosopher who combined Schopenhauer's blind will idea with Hegel's rationalism. Among Hartmann's works is *The Unconscious from the Standpoint of Physiology and Heredity Theory* (1877).

9. *Svarog*: ancient slavic mythological deity of the heavens, father of the sun and fire, who may be related to the Sanskrit *svarga*, the place of habitation of lower divinities and the dead. *Varuna*: related to the Greek "uranos"; in Sanskrit texts, one of the heavenly gods appearing in the *Vedas* as creator and guardian of the world.

10. *Po vsei / Neizmerimosti ethirnoi / Nesetsia blagovest' vsemirnyi / Pobednykh solnechnikh luchei.*

11. *I kak mechty pochiushchei prirody / volnistya prokhodiat oblaka.*

12. *Kak neozhidanno i iarko / Po vlazhnoi neba sineve / Vozdushnaia vozdviglas' arka / V svoem minutnom torzhestve! / Odin konets v lesa vonzila, / Drugim za oblaka ushla; / Ona polneba obkhvatila / I v vysote iznemogla!*

13. From one of Soloviev's own poems, "L'onda dal Mar'divisa." *Volna v razluke s morem / Ne vedaet pokoiu, / Kliuchom li b'et kipuchim / il' katitsia rekoiu, / Vse ropshchet i vzdykhaet / V tsepiakh i na prostore, / Toskuia po bezbrezhnom, / Bezdonnom sinem more.*

14. *Kak khorosho ty, o more nochnoe, / Zdes' luchezarno,—tam sizo-cherno! / V lunnom siianii slovno zhivoe / Khodit, i dyshit, i pleshchet ono. / Na bezkonechnom, na vol'nom prostore / Blesk i dvizhenie, grokhot i grom . . . / Tusklym siyan'em oblitoe more, / Kak khorosho ty v bezliud'e nochnom! / Zyb' ty velikaia, zyb' ty morskaia! / Chei eto prazdnik tak prazdnuesh' ty? / volny nesutsia, gremia i sverkaia, / Chutkiia zvezdy gliadiat s vysoty.*

15. *Kogda vesennii pervyi grom, / Kak by rezviasia i igraia, / Grokhochet v nebe golubom. / Gremyat raskaty molodye . . . / Vot dozhdik bryznul, pyl' letit . . . / Povisli perly dozhdevye, / I solntse nivy zolotit . . . / S gory bezhit potok provornyi, / V lesu ne molknet ptichii gam, / I gam lesnoi, i shum nagornyi, / Vse vtorit veselo gromam . . . / Ty skazhesh', vetrenaia Geba, / Kormia Zevesova orla, / Gromokipiashchii kubok s neba / Smeias' na zemliu prolila.*

16. *Ne ostyvshaia ot znoiu / Noch' iul'skaia blistala, / I nad tuskloiu zemleiu / Nebo polnoe grozoiu / Ot zarnits vse trepetalo . . . / Slovno tiazhkiia resnitsy / Razverzalisia poroiu, / I skvoz' begliia zarnitsy / Ch'i-to groznia zenitsy / Zagoralis' nad zemleiu . . . [and]*

Odne zarnitsy ognevyia / Vosplameniaias' chereloi, / Kak demony glukhonemye / Vedut besedy mezh soboi. / Kak po uslovlennomu znaku, vdrug neba vspykhnet polosa, / I bystro vystupiat iz mraku / Polia i dal'nye lesa! / I vot opiat' vse potemnelo, / Vse stikhlo v chutkoi temnote, / Kak by tainstvennoe delo / Reshalos' tam, na vysote. . . .

17. Memnon: the Homeric hero (in Homer, son of Eos; in Hesiod, son of Eos, brother of Priam, King of the Ethiopians). The legend of the two statue guards (standing approximately sixty feet high) at Amenhotep III's temple at Luxor ringing/singing at dawn stems from the results of an earthquake in antiquity that brought down the collosi. This produced a crack in one of them, which reverberated with the heated air of the dawn, producing a moaning sound that the Greeks attributed to their legendary hero at Troy. Soloviev perhaps joined many famous persons in visiting the site, including the Emperor Hadrian in 130 A.D. However, long before Soloviev's time, the statue had been "repaired" (in 199 A.D.), never to "sing" again.

18. *Ty volna moia morskaia,/Svoenravnaia volna, / Kak, pokoias' il' igraia, / Chudnoi zhizni ty polna! / Ty na solntse li smeesh'sia, / Otrazhaia neba svod, / Il' miatesh'sia ty i b'esh'sia / V odichaloi bezdne vod.*

19. *O r'ianyi kon', o kon' morskoi, / S bledno-zelenoi grivoi, / To smirnyi, laskovo-ruchnoi, / To besheno-igrivyi. / Ty buinym vikhrem vskormlen byl / V shirokom Bozh'em pole, / Tebia on priadat' nauchil, / Igrat', skakat' po vole!*

20. *O chem ty voesh', vetr nochnoi, / O chem tak setuesh' bezumno? / Chto znachit strannyi golos tvoi, / To glukho zhalobnyi, to shumnyi? / Poniatnym serdtsu iazykom / Tverdish' o neponiatnoi muke, / I roesh', i vzryvaesh' v nem / Poroi neistovye zvuki! / O, strashnykh pesen sikh ne poi / Pro drevnii khaos, pro rodimyi! / Kak zhadno mir dushi nochnoi / Vnimaet povesti liubimoi! / Iz smertnoi rvetsia on grudi / I s bezpredel'nym zhazhdet slit'sia . . . / O, bur' usnu-vshikh ne budi: Pod nimi khaos shevelitsia! . . .*

21. Compare with Plato, *Timaeus* 30c–d, 32c–33b.

22. See also Romans 8:22 and Revelation 12:2.

23. The point does not come through in English. In Russian—*rastenie* (plant) and *rasti* (to grow).

24. *Kak budto chuia zhizn' dvoinuiu / I ei oveiany vdvoine— / I zemliu chuvstvuiut rodnuiu / I v nebo prosiatsia one.*

25. See Schopenhauer, *The World as Will and Idea*, second book, first aspect, 172–176.

26. Ibid.

27. Carl F. W. Claus (1835–1899): German zoologist, author of the widely translated standard reference text, *Grundzüge der Zoologie*, among many other scientific works.

28. Rudolf Leuckart (1823–1898): German zoologist, author of *Die menschlichen Parasiten und die von ihnen herrührenden Krankheiten*, among many other scientific works.

29. Carl Linnaeus (1707–1778), Swedish botanist who developed the standard system of classification.

30. Sven Ludwig Loven (1809–1895): Swedish biologist and author of *Echinologica*.

31. Soloviev engaged in wordplay here with the sound and meanings of the pair of words *cherv'* (worm) and *chrevo* (womb), which, curiously enough, have their analogy in English.

32. Jean Louis Rodolphe Agassiz (1807–1873), Swiss-born American naturalist. "Whoever has had the occasion to observe the love-making of snails, would not put in

doubt the seduction displayed in the movements and the looks which prepare and effect the double embrace of these hermaphrodites."

33. Xenarchus: Greek comedic poet, one of whose surviving fragments Darwin cites; Fritz Müller (1822–1897): naturalist and author of *Facts and Arguments for Darwin*.

34. Gustav Jaeger, M. D. (1832–1917), German naturalist and author of *Problems of Nature*.

3. THE UNIVERSAL MEANING OF ART

1. Compare with Plato, *Phaedo* 103e.

2. Hippolyte Adolphe Taine (1828–1893): French philosopher and critic.

3. In Soloviev's note: Jean-Marie Guyau (1854–1888) French philosopher who focused on ethical theory related to creativity. Viktor A. Gol'tsev (1850–1906), author of *Voprosy dnia i zhizni* (1892).

4. This echoes the final part of the Nicene Creed, to which Soloviev closely adhered: "We look for the resurrection of the dead, and the life of the world to come."

5. *An sich:* echoing Kantian idealism. The lines from Lermontov that Soloviev cited in his note are:

Est' zvuki - znachen'e / Temno, il' nichtozhno, / No im bez volnen'ia / Vnimat' nevozmozhno.

6. This appears to be a slightly revised version of Homer's *Iliad* 4: 164–165. *Budet nekogda den', i pogibnet sviashchennaia Troia. / S neiu pogibnet Priam i narod kop'enostsa Priama.*

7. From V. A. Zhukovsky's "*Torzhestvo pobeditelei*" (Schiller's "Das Siegesfest"): *Vse velikoe zemnoe / Razletaetsia kak dym: Nyne zhrebii vypal Troe, / Zavtra vypadet drugim. . . .* Soloviev found this poem useful enough to cite lines from it in several other places. See note 2 below in "The Fate of Pushkin."

8. *Otumanilasia Ida, / Omrachilsia Ilion, / Spit vo mrake stan Atrida, / Na ravnine bitvy son. . . —i. t. d.*

9. Aleksandr S. Griboedev (1795–1829): a diplomat by profession, but known principally for the work Soloviev refers to, *Gore ot uma*. He was killed in Teheran by an angry mob that stormed the Russian embassy.

10. "*Svad'ba Krechinskogo,*" part of a trilogy by Aleksandr Sukhovo-Kobylin (1817–1903).

11. Although lacking the benefit of modern critical approaches in biblical criticism to assist in appreciation of this aspect of the New Testament, Soloviev would later urge the adoption of biblical critical methods (largely pioneered by German theologians) in Russia. See "Forgotten Lessons" (Sunday Letters, 16 March 1897) in Wozniuk, ed., *Politics, Law and Morality*, 81–84.

12. "All that is transitory is only parable."

13. "The eternal feminine" is a theme that Soloviev adapted from Goethe and would develop more fully in "The Meaning of Love," leaving a deep imprint on the so-called second generation of Russian symbolist poets, especially A. Blok and V. Ivanov. See Goethe's *Faust*, 12110–12111 (Heaven, last line).

4. THE MEANING OF LOVE

1. Parthogenesis: literally, "virgin inception" and, according to standard dictionary definition (Webster's), "reproduction by development of an unfertilized gamete that occurs especially among lower plants and invertebrate animals." Thanks to Glen Ebisch, Charles Fish, and Burton Porter for their comments on an early draft of this section.

2. See Genesis 1:21.

3. More echoes of Kantian idealism appear here.

4. See notes 5 and 7 to "Beauty in Nature" above.

5. The reference is to Johann Wolfgang Goethe's tragic story of unrequited love, *Sorrows of Young Werther* [*Leiden des Jungen Werthers*]. This representative of Romanticism and the "Sturm und Drang" movement inspired real suicides, and Soloviev plays here and in the following paragraphs with the "reality" of the literary types.

6. Shakespeare is cited in English here without quotation marks.

7. Hellespontus is the Turkish strait that connects the Aegean to the Sea of Marmora.

8. A reference to mythical and literary characters in the work of the Roman poet Publius Ovidius Naso (ca. 47 B.C.–17 A.D.) and the Russian prosaist Nikolai V. Gogol (1809–1852), both innovators in their respective genres. In Ovid's *Metamorphoses*, Zeus and Hermes (Jupiter and Mercury), traveling incognito, find food and shelter in only one of the many Phrygian homes they visit, that of the poor elderly peasant couple Philemon and Baucis (Gk: Baukis), who are appointed to preside over a temple of Zeus in return for their hospitality. Gogol openly compares his elderly Ukrainian peasant couple, Pulkherina Ivanovna and Afanasii Ivanovich Tovstogub to Ovid's couple at the outset of his tale, "*Starosvetskie pomeshchiki*" (Old-fashioned Farmers).

9. This seems to be an indirect reference to Hegel's "objective spirit."

10. "God-sires"—*Bogootsy*. A difficult term to translate into English, it literally means "god-fathers," but in the specific and narrow sense of biological genealogy.

11. This term appears with reference to the origins of Christ; it seems to parallel "cosmogonical," which refers to the origins of the universe.

12. The reference is to Genesis 12:11–16, the story of Abram's "selling" of Sarai to Pharaoh.

13. See Genesis 38:6–26 for the complex account of Judah's unjust treatment of Tamar. To summarize briefly, Tamar's husbands (Judah's sons) keep dying, and under Mosaic law they consecutively inherit the obligation to care for the dead brother's wife and sire his children. In anger, Judah arbitrarily sequesters her, for which she then gains vengeance by posing as a shrine prostitute, whose services Judah employs. At the end of the account, Judah is forced to acknowledge that Tamar was more just than he in the course of these events.

14. "God-procreator"—*Bogoroditel'*.

15. Laban is the father of Rachel and Leah, and Jacob's kinsman, who "owns" his daughters and the fruits of the seven years of labor that Jacob paid for each. Although Jacob is outwitted by Laban in the course of betrothal and marriage, he later turns the table on his father-in-law by breeding livestock profitably at the latter's expense and escaping with the bounty and his wives. See Genesis 29:5–31:21.

16. Soloviev either missed or avoided some of the moral ambiguities implicit in the story of Judah and Tamar. See Genesis 38:11–26.

17. Also referred to as a "spy." For the story of Rahab the harlot, see Joshua 2:2–13. See also Hebrews 11:31 and James 2:25.

18. The reference, of course, is to David's sin with Bathsheba, wife of David's loyal servant, Uriah the Hittite. See 2 Samuel 11:1–26. For the story of Ruth and Boaz, see the Book of Ruth. Soloviev did not interpret these passages with much attention to detail, but extrapolated from the account according to ecclesiastical tradition, and with his very specific purpose in mind.

19. In Russian: *mirozdatel'nogo protsessa*.

20. See Genesis 2:4 and 5:1. Soloviev translated the Hebrew *haadam* here as "man" and not "Adam," as most later versions reflect. His transliterations of the Hebrew appear in cyrillic, which I have rendered into the Latin alphabet.

21. See Matthew 16:26 and Mark 8:36–37.

22. Soloviev had earlier severely criticized spiritualist activity—all the rage in his day—in his 1892 review of E. P. Blavatskaia, *The Key to Theosophy* (1889). See S. Soloviev and E. Radlov, eds., *Sobranie sochinenii* 6: 287–292.

23. While not entirely critical, Soloviev did not wholly approve of the transcendent character of these sacred ancient Hindu texts.

24. It is not clear exactly to what "schools" in history Soloviev was alluding, although he may have had in mind Plato's academy and later neoplatonist writings on love.

25. The passage seems to suggest that there is more here than can be discussed openly. Perhaps Soloviev was implying that he would have liked to have delved into Oedipal themes; he would almost certainly have been reluctant to do so out of concerns about the religious censor.

26. See Genesis 2:24 and Mark 10:7–9.

27. "Beginnings or rudiments"—Soloviev's penchant for wordplay appears intermittently, as here: "*zachatkakh ili zadatkakh.*"

28. There seem to be echoes here of at least some aspects of ancient Greek tradition and legend concerning the original male-female unity as a single creature, which was later split into two, doomed forever to yearn for a reunification into one entity.

29. "Minnesingers"—German lyrical love poets of the medieval period (12th–14th centuries).

30. The reference is to Koz'ma Prutkov's (pen name of A. K. Tolstoy and two cousins) "*Nemetskaia ballada,*" a nonsensical parody of Zhukovsky's translation of Schiller's poem "Ritter Toggenburg." See the commentary in Zis' et al., *V. S. Soloviev: Filosofiia. . .*, 652. Franz Schubert set the verse to music, and it became a popular German song.

31. A revised version of a stanza from Pushkin's poem, "*Zhil na svete rytsar' bednyi . . .*" *Lumen coeli! Sancta Rosa!* / *Vosklitsal on dik i r'ian,* / *I kak grom ego ugroza* / *Porazhala musul'man.* Pushkin had "*Lumen coelum, sancta Rosa! Vosklitsal vsekh gromche on, I gnala ego ugroza* / *Musul'man so vsekh storon.*" Considering the similarities of Pushkin's themes and images to Schiller's "Ritter Toggenburg," it seems clear that he was influenced by it. Mikhail Bulgakov once quoted lines one and three of Soloviev's citation in a personal remark. See Mikhail Bulgakov, *Sobranie sochinenii v piati tomakh* 1 (Moscow: Khudozhestvennaia literatura, 1989), 487.

32. A paraphrase of St. Paul. See Romans 8:22–23.

33. All these were, of course, "instant" classics of Tolstoy, with whom Soloviev carried on a long debate, sometimes cordial, sometimes not, concerning morality and faith. One gets the impression here that there is an underlying message aimed at Tolstoy about the futility of moralizing without a firm foundation in revealed religion.

34. An association attributed to Plato through Heraclitus, and which continues on to affirm wisdom as the ultimate goal of worship. See fragment 116 in Charles H. Kahn, *The Art and Thought of Heraclitus: An Edition of the Fragments with Translation and Commentary* (Cambridge: Cambridge University Press, 1979), 81. Heraclitus is also identified with the notions that the many are one, that the one is composed of many, and that the worship of idols is useless. While the complete fragment seems more relevant in context, Soloviev likely avoided a full citation out of both personal modesty and concern about the censor: "If it were not Dionysus for whom they march in procession and chant the hymn to phallus, their action would be most shameless. But Hades and Dionysus are the same, him for whom they rave and celebrate Lenaia [a festival]."

35. Latin script is used here.

36. Latin script is used here.

37. Lupanaria: Latin for brothels, derived from "she-wolf."

38. Living-but-dying lovers-of-deadness: *zazhivo umiraiushchie liubiteli mertvechiny.*

39. Alfred Binet (1857–1911) and Richard von Krafft-Ebing (1840–1902). Binet's work originally appeared under a cumbersome title, of which I offer only the relevant part, *Etudes de psychologie experimentale: Le fetichisme dans l'amour . . .* (Paris: 1888). Krafft-Ebing's was a medical forensic study which appeared the previous year, in 1887.

40. An older Slavonic version of Matthew 21:42 and Psalm 118:22–23 is cited. See also Isaiah 8:14 and 1 Peter 2:7–8.

41. "Believe in no love or relegate it to poetry." The line is perhaps from Goethe or Schopenhauer, both of whom Soloviev quoted regularly. Thanks to Sarah Leonard for advice on rendering the fragment from German.

42. Genesis 1:27 and Ephesians 5:32. Soloviev cited the Ephesians verse in an older Slavonic form.

43. Soloviev seems to have been encapsulating the logic of Ephesians 5:22–30.

44. Alter ego—Latin script is used here.

45. This is a paraphrase of Hebrews 11:1.

46. This echoes the notion of a world of forms that is central to Platonic philosophy. See, for example, Plato, *Sophist* 253d–e.

47. Heavenly Aphrodite and Public Aphrodite, or Aphrodite from the Heavens and Aphrodite of the People.

48. Latin: pleasure for man and god. This forms part of the opening of Lucretius's *De Rerum Natura* ("Aeneadum genetrix, hominom divomque voluptas alma Venus. . . .")

49. Two lines from the third stanza of A. A. Fet's "Alter Ego" (1879): *I ia znaiu, vzglianuvshi na zvezdy poroi, / chto vzirali na nikh my, kak bogi, s toboi.* See note 50 below.

50. From the second stanza of Fet's "*Izmuchen zhizn'iu, kovarstvom nadezhdy. . .*" (1883): *Eshche temnee mrak zhizni vsednevnoi, / kak posle iarkoi osennoi zarnitsy.* Interestingly, the epigraph to this verse is from Schopenhauer: "Die Gleichmässigkeit des Laufes der Zeit in allen Köpfen beweist mehr, als irgend etwas, dass wir Alle in denselben Traum versenkt sind, ja dass es Ein Wesen ist, welches ihn träumt." See A. A. Fet,

Liricheskie stikhotvoreniia v dvukh chastiakh 1 (St. Petersburg: 1894), 57. Since Soloviev's citation from "Alter Ego" (see previous note) appears on p. 53 in the same volume, it is not unreasonable to speculate that Soloviev might have used this edition of Fet as a reference text while he wrote.

51. These images are drawn from Hebrews 6:8 and 11:13–16.

52. "Dead faith"—See James 2:17.

53. See James 5:7–11.

54. This appears to be an imprecise citation from Fet's "*Naprasno . . .*": *Razbei etot kubok, v nem zlaia otrava taitsia.* In Fet: *. . . v nem kaplia nadezhdy taitsia.*

55. Soloviev engages in wordplay: ***pritiazhenie*** *. . .* ***protiazhenie*** (emphasis in the original).

56. Latin: contradiction in what is added; a logical fallacy between a noun and adjective.

57. Newton conceived the universe as God's sensorium.

58. Although the term comes from the Greek and means "yoked together" "combination," or "conjunction," Soloviev must have been aware that it also describes astronomically the rectilinear configuration of three celestial bodies in a gravitational system (see *The Oxford English Dictionary*, 2nd ed., 1989).

59. The third and fourth stanzas from Fet's "*Poetam*" (1890): *Tol'ko u vas mimoletnye grezy / starymi v dushu gliadiatsia druz'iami / Tol'ko u vas blagovonnye rozy /* **Vechno** *vostorga blistaiut slezami. / S torzhishch zhiteiskikh, beztsvetnykh i dushnykh, / Videt kak radostno tonkie kraski, / V radugakh vashikh prozrachno-vozdushnykh / Neba rodnogo mne chudiatsia laski.*

5. A First Step Toward a Positive Aesthetic

1. The Russian literary critic Dmitri I. Pisarev referred to Pushkin in his article "Pushkin and Belinsky" as "the greatest representative of the Philistine perspective on life." See the commentary in Zis' et al., *V. S. Soloviev, Filosofiia*, 651.

2. *I dolgo budu tem liubezen ia narodu, / Chto chuvstva dobryia ia liroi probuzhdal. / Chto v sei zhestokii vek ia proslavlial svobodu / I milost' k padshim prizyval. . . .*

3. While the overall reference is to Nietzsche's work, particularly *Beyond Good and Evil*, Dostoevsky's phrase "all is permitted" (*vse pozvoleno*) appears once again to describe the moral universe if God does not exist. See note 7 above in "Three Addresses in Memory of Dostoevsky."

4. Dahomey: former French possession in West Africa (Benin); Matabeland: region of Southeast Rhodesia (Zimbabwe). Lobengula (1833–1894) was Zulu king of the Matabele.

5. See *Beyond Good and Evil* (part 9, "What is Noble?") and *The Genealogy of Morals* (second essay, 24); the reference to Antichrist also more generally calls to mind 1 John 2:18 and 4:3 and 2 Thessalonians 2:3–12 in the New Testament.

6. While Soloviev's perspectives anticipate the school of thought of political idealism in international relations, in that they acknowledge signs of progress in human affairs as visible in positive law, they also could be considered prescient in a world that had not yet developed nuclear weapons or other means of mass destruction.

7. Another title, *Kriticheskiia stat'i: Pushkin, Gogol', Turgenev, Ostrovskii, Lev Tolstoi, Shchedrin, i dr,* appeared under the same name in 1895.

8. *Komu venets: bogine l' krasoty, / Il' v zerkale eia izobrazhen'iu? / Poet smushchen, kogda divish'sia ty / Bogatomu ego voobrazhen'iu. / Ne Ia, moi drug, a Bozhii mir bogat: V pylinke on leleet zhizn' i mnozhit, / I chto odin tvoi vyrazhaet vzgliad, / Togo poet pereskazat' ne mozhet.*

6. The Fate of Pushkin

1. Pushkin's lines from "*Brozhu li ia v dol'. . .*" (1829): *I pust' u grobovogo vkhoda / Mladaia budet zhizn' igrat', / I **ravnodushnaia** priroda / Krasoiu vechnoiu siiat'.* See the commentary in V. M. Markovich and G. E. Potopova, eds., *A. S. Pushkin: Pro et contra* 1 (St. Petersburg: Izdatel'stvo Russkogo Khristianskogo gumanitarnogo instituta, 2000), 662.

2. A slightly revised version of V. A. Zhukovsky's lines from "*Torzhestvo pobe-ditelei*" (1829), Schiller's "Das Siegesfest": *Zhizn' ego* [originally: '*tvoiu*'] *ne vrag ot'ial, — / On **svoeiu** siloi pal, / Zhertva gibel'nago gneva. . . .* Soloviev found this poem and its theme of the fall of Troy relevant enough that he cited lines from it in several other places. See, for example, note 7 above in "The Universal Meaning of Art."

3. Soloviev again echoes Dostoevsky's phrase "all is permitted" (*vse pozvoleno*).

4. *Schein der Idee*—the semblance of an idea; in context, this carries with it the suggestion of deception or hypocrisy, a theme that Soloviev proceeded to develop. The letter to which Soloviev referred is addressed to Aleksei Nikolaevich Vulf and dated 7 May 1826. See Thomas Shaw, trans., *The Letters of Alexander Pushkin* (Madison: University of Wisconsin Press, 1967), 309.

5. See Nikolai Gogol, *Dead Souls,* chapter 9. See also *A.S. Pushkin, pro et contra,* 62.

6. *Kogda tvoi mladyia leta / Pozorit shumnaia molva, / I ty, po prigovory sveta, / Na chest' utratila prava; / Odin sredi tolpy kholodnoi, / Tvoi stradan'ia ia deliu / I za tebia mol'boi bezplodnoi / Kumir bezchuvstvennyi moliu. / No svet . . . Zhestokikh osuzhdenii / Ne izme-niaet on svoikh: / On ne karaet zabluzhdenii, / No tainy trebuet dlia nikh. / Dostoiny ravnago prezren'ia / Ego tshcheslavnaia liubov' / I litsemernyia gonen'ia— / K zabven'iu serdtse prigo-tov; / Ne pei muchitel'noi otravy; / Ostav' blestiushchii dushnyi krug, / Ostav' bezumnyia zabavy; / Tebe odin ostalsia drug.*

7. See Aristotle, "Poetics" xxiv, 13–18.

8. Several lines from various of Pushkin's poems appear in this paragraph. In order of citation, they are: "*V chasy zabav il' prazdnoi skuki . . .*" (1830); "*Kogda b ne smutnoe vlechen'e . . .*" (1833); "Evgenii Onegin," (chapter 6, line 40—a slightly revised rendering); "19 Oktiabria" (1825). See *A.S. Pushkin, pro et contra,* 662.

9. Monotheletism: a seventh-century doctrine, condemned as heretical by the Council of Constantinople 680, concerning the nature of Christ's human and divine wills.

10. *Khvalu i klevetu priemli ravnodushno—.*

11. *Byl dolzhen okazat' sebia / Ne miachikom predrazsuzhdenii, / Ne pylkim mal'chikom, boitsom, / No muzhem s chest'iu i s umom.*

12. *Ty—tsar', zhivi odin!*

13. Byron is quoted on solitude in English. The second verse is cited in Russian: *Monblan—monarkh sosednikh gor: / One ego venchali.*

14. An epigram directed at Mikhail T. Kachenovskii (1775–1849), editor of the journal *Vestnik Evropy*, historian and author of *Dva razsuzhdeniia o kozhanykh den'gakh i o russkoi pravde* (1849, published posthumously). *Klevetnik bez darovan'ia, / Palok ischet on chut'em / I dnevnogo propitan'ia / Ezhemesiachnym vran'em.*

15. *V gradakh vashikh s ulits shumnykh / Smetaiut sor,—poleznyi trud! / No, pozabyv svoe sluzhen'e, / Altar' i zhertvoprinoshen'e, / Zhretsy l' u vas metlu berut?*

16. "Wait, I have enough strength to take my turn!"

17. *Priiatno derzkoi epigrammoi / Vbesit' oploshnago vraga . . .—i. t. d. / **No otoslat' ego k otsam / Edva l' priiatno budet vam.***

18. "Prorok" and "Otsy pustynniki i zheny neporochny."

19. The monastic reference to Mount Athos stands in sharp contrast to the earlier Byronic reference to Montblanc.

7. MICKIEWICZ

1. Epigraph: *On vdokhnoven byl svyshe, I s vysoty vziral na zhizn'.*

2. From the second stanza of an 1883 verse by Fet: *Tol'ko v mire i est', chto tenistyi / Dremliushchikh klenov shater, / Tol'ko v mire i est', chto luchistyi / Detski zadumchivyi vzor.*

3. The opening lines of "Pan Tadeusz" (1834)—Soloviev provided Russian translations (by Berg) in his footnotes, but quoted the Polish directly throughout the text: *Litwo! Ojczyzno moja, ty jestes jak zdrowie! / Ile cie trzeba cenic, ten tylko sie dowie, / Kto cie stracil. Dzis pieknosc twa w calei ozdobie / Widze i opisuje, bo tesknie po tobie!* My thanks to Karolina Kabala and Isabella Wolanski for advice on my translation of these lines and the verse in note 7 below.

4. Both references to Romantic poems glorifying the nation: Gustaw, a hero of Mickiewicz's complex play-in-verse "Dziady" ("Forefathers") (1823); and "Konrad Wallenrod," Mickiewicz's "historical poem" about the fourteenth-century origins of the Polish-Lithuanian state, published in Petersburg during Mickiewicz's several years in Russia (1828). After the failed Polish revolt of 1830 against Russian rule, Mickiewicz added a new part to "Dziady" in Germany, and introduced a new hero, also named Konrad, who replaces Gustaw (1832).

5. Another reference to the Polish revolution of 1830, brutally suppressed by Russian forces.

6. Andrzej Towianski: a Polish mystic with a messianic message who wielded influence over Mickiewicz. Mickiewicz's "Ksiegi narodu pielgrzymstw polskiego" (1832), written in exile, and his lectures as a professor of Slavonic literature in Paris, 1840–1844.

7. Also from "Pan Tadeusz": *Panno Swieta, co Jasnej bronisz Czestochowy / I w Ostrej swiecisz Bramie! Ty co grod zamkowy / Nowogrodzki ochraniasz z jego wiernym ludem' / Jak mnie dziecko do zdrowia powrocilas cudem / Gdy od placzacej matki pod Twoja opieke / Ofiarowany martwa podnioslem powieke, / I zaraz moglem pieszo do Twych swiatyn progu / Isc za wrocone zycie podziekowac Bogu,— / Tak nas powrocisz cudem na ojczyzny lono.*

8. "Political falsehood of anarchy"—a reference to the infamous liberum veto, which created constant instability in the weak parliamentary system maintained by the

Polish nobility. The liberum veto is often blamed as the cause of Poland's subsequent collapse and subjugation by Russia.

9. God-man: *bogochelovecheskaia*, the adjectival form of Godmanhood, referred to earlier as the incarnational imaging of Christ in humanity. See note 1 above in "Three Addresses in Memory of Dostoevsky."

8. LERMONTOV

1. *Veshchie zenitsy kak u ispugannoi orlitsy*: from Pushkin's poem "The Prophet." Parts of the introduction to this essay also appeared at about the same time in one of Soloviev's lengthy book review essays, which he titled "The Idea of a Superman" (1899).

2. Greek: To gods and men.

3. Alfred de Musset (1810–1857), French playwright.

4. "Not an imitator," likely refers to Lermontov's own assertion about himself in verse: *Net, ia ne Bairon, ia drugoi.* (No, I am not Byron, I am somebody else.)

5. *Na zapad, na zapad pomchalsia by ia / Gde tsvetut moikh predkov polia, / Gde v zamke pustom na tumannykh gorakh / Ikh zabvennyi pokoitsia prakh.*

Mezh mnoi i kholmami otchizny moei / Razstilaiutsia volny morei. / Poslednyi potomok otvazhnykh boitsov / Uviadaet sred chuzhdykh snegov.

6. *Razstalis' my, no tvoi portret / Ia na grudi moei khraniu; / Kak blednyi prizrak luchshikh let, / On dushu raduet moiu. . . .*

Net, ne tebia tak pylko ia liubliu, / Ne dlia menia krasy tvoei blistan'e, — / Liubliu v tebe lish' proshloe stradan'e / I molodost' pogibshuiu moiu. / Kogda poroi ia na tebia smotriu, / V tvoi glaza vnikaia dolgim vzorom, / Tainstvennym ia zaniat razgovorom, / No ne s toboi — ia s serdtsem govoriu. / Ia govoriu s podrugoi iunykh dnei, / V tvoikh chertakh ishchu cherty drugiia / V ustakh zhivykh usta davno nemiia, / V glazakh — ogon' ugasnuvshikh ochei. . . .

Mne grustno potomu, chto ia tebia liubliu, / I znaiu molodost' tsvetushchuiu tvoiu. . . .

7. *Iz-pod tainstvennoi, kholodnoi polumaski / Zvuchal mne golos tvoi otradnyi, kak mechta, / Svetili mne tvoi plenitel'nye glazki, / I ulybalisia lukavyia usta./*

I sozdal ia togda v moem voobrazhen'i / Po legkim priznakam krasavitsu moiu, / I s toi pory bezplodnoe viden'e / Noshu v dushe moei, laskaiu i liubliu.

8. *I snilsia mne siiaiushchii ogniami / Vechernii pir v rodimoi storone . . . / Mezh iun- ykh zhen, uvenchannykh tsvetami, / Shel razgovor veselii obo mne.*

No, v razgovor veselyi ne vstupaia, / Sidela tam zadumchiva odna, / I v grustnyi son dusha eia mladaia / Bog znaet chem byla pogruzhena. / I snilas' ei dolina Dagestana, / Znako- myi trup lezhal v doline toi, / V ego grudi, dymias', chernela rana, / I krov' lilas' khladeiush- chei struiei.

9. *Ya rozhden, chtob tselyi mir byl zritel' / Torzhestva il' gibeli moei.*

10. *Chto khvala il' gordii smekh liudei? / Dushi ikh pevtsa ne postigali, / Ne mogli dushi ego liubit', / Ne mogli poniat' ego pechali / I ego vostorgov razdelit'.*

11. *Pod gordoi vazhnostiu litsa — v muzhchine glupago l'stetsa i v kazhdoi zhensh- chine Iudu.*

12. *On nedoverchivost' vseliaet / On prezrel chistuiu liubov', / On vse molen'ia otver- gaet, / On ravnodushno vidit krov'. / I zvuk vysokikh oshchushchenii / On davit golosom strastei, / I muza krotkikh vdokhnovenii / Strashitsia nezemnykh ochei.*

*Dve zhizni v nac do groba est'. / Est' groznyi dukh: on chuzhd emu; / Liubov',
nadezhda, skorb' i mest' — / Vse, vse podverzheno emu. / On osnoval zhilishche tam, / Gde
mozhem pamiat' sokhraniat', / I predveshchaet gibel' nam, / Kogda uzh pozdno izbezhat'. /
Terzat' i muchit' liubit on; / V ego rechakh neredko lozh'. . . . / On tochit zhizn', kak skorpion. /
Emu poveril ia. . . .*

*K nichtozhnym, khladnym tolkam sveta / Privyk prislushivat'sia on, / Emu smeshny
slova priveta, / I vsiakii veriashchii smeshon. / On chuzhd liubvi i sozhalen'ia, / Zhivet on
pishcheiu zemnoi, / Glotaet zhadno dym srazhen'ia / I par ot krovi prolitoi. /*

*I gordyi demon ne otstanet, / Poka zhivu ia, ot menia, / I um moi ozariat' on stanet /
Luchom nebesnago ognia. / Pokazhet obraz sovershenstva / I vdrug otnimet navsegda, / I,
dav predchuvstvie blazhenstva, / Ne dast mne schast'ia nikogda.*

13. See Matthew 5:13, 7:6; Mark 9:50; Luke 14:34.

14. A flash of Soloviev's prose style appears in compact form in the sonority and
cadence of this sentence, nearly poetic in quality: *Slishkom rano i slishkom bezprepiat-
stvenno ovladel etot vtoroi demon dushoiu neschastnago poeta, i slishkom mnogo sledov ostavil
v ego proizvedeniakh.*

15. Another echo of the Dostoevskian phrase "all is permitted."

16. *I v nebesakh ia vizhu Boga.* . . .

17. "A person of such high rank and antiquity"—this appears to be a reference to
the angel Lucifer. See Isaiah 14:12.

18. See Genesis 6:4.

19. See Matthew 18:6; Mark 9:42; Luke 17:2.

APPENDIX A: A NOTE IN DEFENSE OF DOSTOEVSKY . . .

1. See, for example, Romans 3:4; Psalm 62:9; John 8:40; Luke 12:51; John 10:16;
Proverbs 13:14; 1 John 4:16–18.

2. "Populists": *narodniki*

3. See Matthew 6:24 and Luke 16:13.

4. See 1 Corinthians 15:28.

5. This is also one of Augustine's major points in *City of God*, a work with
which Soloviev seemed to be quite familiar. See also above, Introduction, note 5.

6. Parts of the citations from Revelation appear in an older Russian form.

7. Revelation 12:1–6.

8. Revelation 19:6–8 and 21:1–4.

APPENDIX B: THE RUSSIAN SYMBOLISTS

1. *Svoimi razmerami:* perhaps wordplay, referring to poetic meter as well as size or
volume. Briusov and the first generation of symbolists could only be disappointed with
Soloviev's lack of approval of their "school." Yet Soloviev himself did not live to see
the talent and subsequent influence of Briusov grow or the rise of the so-called second
generation of symbolists—including Vyacheslav Ivanov and Aleksandr Blok—who
claimed Soloviev as an important inspiration for their brilliant poetry.

2. *Gasnut rozovyia kraski / V blednom otbleske luny; / zamerzaiut v l'dinakh skazki / O stradaniiakh vesny. / Ot iskhoda do zaviazki / Zavernulis' v traur sny, / I bezmolviem okraski / Ikh girliandy spleteny. / Pod luchami iunoi grezy / Ne tsvetut sozvuchii rozy / Na kurtinkah pustoty, / A skvoz' okna snov bezsviaznykh / Ne uvidiat zvezd almaznykh / Usyplennyia mechty.*

  3. a. *My vstretilis' s neiu sluchaino, / I robko mechtal ia o nei,*

   b. *Vot staraia skazka, kotoroi / Byt' inoi vsegda suzhdeno —*

   c. *Nevniatnyi son vstupaet na stupeni, / Mgnoven'ia dver' priotvoriaet on —*

   d. *Zvezdnoe nebo bezstrastnoe, —*

   e. *Zvezdy tikhon'ko sheptalis' —*

   f. *Sklonisia golovkoi tvoieiu —*

   g. *Slezami blestiashchie **glazki** / I **gubki**, chto zhalobno smiaty, / A **shchechki** pylaiut ot laski / I kudri zaputanno-smiaty,* — i.t.d.

  4. *Zolotistyia fei / V atlasnom sadu! / Kogda ia naidu / Ledianyia allei? / Vliublennykh naiad / Serebristye vspleski, / Gde revnivyia doski / Vam put' zagradiat. / Neponiatnyia vazy / Ognem ozaria, / Zastyla zaria / nad poletom fantazii. / Za mrakom zaves / Pogrebal'nyia urny, / I ne zhdet svod lazurnyi / obmanchivykh zvezd.*

  5. *Struny rzhaveiut / Pod mokroi rukoi, / Grezy nemeiut / I kroiutsia mgloi.*

  6. *Serdtse zvonkoe b'etsia v grudi . . . Milyi drug, prikhodi, prikhodi!*

  7. *V serebrianoi pyli polunochnaia vlaga / Pleniaet otdykhom ustalyia mechty, / I v **zybkoi tishine rechnogo sarkofaga** / **Velikii chelovek** ne slyshit klevety.*

  8. *Trup zhenshchiny, gniushchii i zlovonnyi, / Bol'shaia step', chugunnyi nebosvod . . . I dolgii mig, nasmeshkoi voskreshennyi, / S ukornym khokhotom vstaet. / Almaznyi son . . . Chertezh vverkhu zazhzhennyi . . . / I aromat, i slezy, i rosa . . . / Pokinut trup gniushchii i zlovonnyi, / I voron vykleval glaza.*

  9. "In that harmony and balance I do not want to endeavor." This is a slight variation on a line in Goethe's *Faust* ("Zu jenen Sphären wag' ich nicht zu streben," 767).

  10. *Ditia, smotri! tam pri kontse allei / Nochnoi krasavitsy raskinulis' kusty . . . / Ikh obraz prinyali vesennei nochi fei . . . / Moei toski ne ponimala ty! / Tam solntsa luch s voskhoda i do nochi / L'et chary strastnyia na sonnye tsvety . . . / Naprasno rvetsia on khot' raz vzglianut' im v ochi . . . / Moei toski ne ponimaesh' ty! / V vechernii chas, skryvaias' za goroiu / S toskoiu zhgucheiu obmanutoi mechty, / V bezsil'i vidit on lobzan'ia ikh s lunoiu . . . / Moiu tosku poimesh', naverno, ty!*

  11. *Ten' nesozdannykh sozdanii / Kolykhaetsia vo sne / Slovno lopasti latanii / Na emalevoi stene. / Fioletovyia ruki / Na emalevoi stene / Polusonno chertiat zvuki / V zvonko-zvuchnoi tishine. / I prozrachnye kioski / V zvonko-zvuchnoi glubine / Vyrostaiut tochno blestki / Pri lazorevoi lune, / **Vskhodit mesiats obnazhennyi** / **Pri lazorevoi lune**; / Zvuki reiut polusonno, / Zvuki lastiatsia ko mne, / Tainy sozdannykh sozdanii / S laskoi lastiatsia ko mne, / I trepeshchet ten' latanii / Na emalevoi stene.*

  12. *Sertsa luch iz serebra volnenii / Nad prostorom ineia vstaet, / I, drozha, zvuchit khrustal' molenii / I obryzgan penoiu plyvet. / On plyvet . . . steniashchim perelivom / Led zvezdy iz bezdny on manit . . . / Daleka v pokoe gordelivom / Spit zvezda . . . zvezda blestit i spit.*

  13. *V vozdukhe povisli pesen kolonnady, / I kristall sozvuchii kak fontan zvenit, / Zamerli v lazuri belyia gromady / I v luchakh tumana matovyi granit. / V mysliakh penoi b'etsia zarevo tomlenii, / Molniei mel'kaiut milyia cherty, / K sertsu ot chertogov char i snovidenii /*

Peregnulis' arkoi zvonkie mosty, / *Iarkiia girliandy obvili fasady,* / *Mramora Karrary aromat-*
nyi blesk . . . / *I zvuchat pobedno, taiut serenady,* / *I rasnosit ekho vdokhnovenyi plesk.*

14. *Nad temnoiu ravninoi,* / *Ravninoi temnoi,* / *Neskromnoi kartinoi,* / *Kartinoi*
neskromnoi, / *Povisli tumany,* / *Tumany povisli,* / *Kak budto obmany,* / *Obmany bez mysli,* /
Bez mysli i sviazi / *V razskaze bezstrastnom.* / *V bezstrastnom razskaze,* / *V razskaze neias-*
nom, / *Gde blednyia kraski* / *Razviazki pechal'noi* / *Pechalny, kak skazki* / *O rodine dal'noi.*

15. *Mertvetsy, osveshchennye gazom!* / *Alaia lenta na greshnoi neveste!* / *O! my poi-*
dem tselovat'sia k oknu! / *Vidish', kak bledny litsa umershikh?* / *Eto — bol'nitsa, gde v traure*
deti . . . / *Eto — na l'du oleandry . . .* / *Eto — oblozhka Romansov bez slov . . .* / *Milaia, v*
okna ne vidno luny. / *Nashi dushi — tsvetok u tebia v buton'orke.*

16. Briusov: "*O, zakroi svoi blednyia nogi.*" Maeterlinck: *Moia dusha bol'na ves'*
den', / *Moia dusha bol'na proshchan'em,* / *Moia dusha v bor'be s molchan'em* / *Glaza moi*
vstrechaiut ten'. / **I pod knutom vospominan'ia** / *Ia vizhu prizraki okhot.* / *Poluzabytyi sled*
vedet **Sobak sekretnago zhelan'ia.** / *Vo glub zabyvchivykh lesov* / *Lilovykh grez nesutsia*
svory, / *I strely zheltyia — ukory —* / *Kazniat olenei lzhivykh snov.* / *Uvy, uvy! vezde zhelan'ia,* /
Vezde vernuvshiesia sny, / **I slishkom sinee dykhan'e** . . . / *Na serdtse merknet lik luny.*

17. "Share with the public": *podelit'sia s publikoiu.* Soloviev engages in wordplay;
the verb is close to *podelat'sia,* which means to put on or imitate; and *poddelka* is a coun-
terfeit or forgery.

18. I: *Gorizonty vertikal'nye* / *V shokoladnykh nebesakh,* / *Kak mechty polu-zerkal'nyia* /
V lavro-vishnevykh lesakh. / *Prizrak l'diny ognedyshashchei* / *V iarkom sumrake pogas,* / *I stoit*
menia ne slyshashchii / *Giatsintovyi Pegas.* / *Mandragory immanentnyia* / *Zashurshali v kamy-*
shakh, / *A shershavo-dekadentnyia* / *Virshi v vianushchikh ushakh.*

II: *Nad zelenym kholmom,* / *Nad kholmom zelenym,* / *Nam vliublennym vdvoem,* /
Nam vdvoem vliublennym, / *Svetit v polden' zvezda,* / *Ona v polden' svetit,* / *Khot' nikto*
nikogda / *Toi zvezdy ne zametit.* / *No volnistyi tuman,* / *No tuman volnistyi,* / *Iz luchistykh*
on stran, / *Iz strany luchistoi,* / *On skol'zit mezhdu tuch,* / *Nad sukhoiu volnoiu,* / *Nepod-*
vizhno letuch / *I s dvoinoiu lunoiu.*

III: *Na nebesakh goriat panikadila,* / *A snizu — t'ma.* / *Khodila ty k nemu, il' ne khodila?* /
Skazhi sama! / *No ne drazni gienu podozren'ia,* / *Myshei toski!* / *Ne to smotri, kak leopardy*
mshchen'ia / *Ostriat klyki!* / *I ne zovi sovu blagorazum'ia* / *Ty v etu noch'!* / *Osly terpen'ia*
i slony razdym'ia / *Bezhali proch'.* / *Svoei sud'by rodila krokodila* / *Ty zdes' sama.* / *Pust' v*
nebesakh goriat panikadila / *V mogile — t'ma.*

General Index

Index of Biblical References

VLADIMIR WOZNIUK is professor of government at Western New England College in Springfield, Massachusetts.